The
Real Value
of
Training

Measuring and Analyzing
Business Outcomes and
the Quality of ROI

RON DREW STONE

New York   Chicago   San Francisco   Lisbon
London   Madrid   Mexico City   Milan   New Delhi
San Juan   Seoul   Singapore   Sydney   Toronto

1 2 3 4 5 6 7 8 9 0   DOC/DOC   1 6 5 4 3 2 1

ISBN: 978-0-07-175997-7
MHID: 0-07-175997-2

e-ISBN: 978-0-07-176124-6
e-MHID: 0-07-176124-1

This publication is designed to provide accurate and authoritative information in regard to the subject matter covered. It is sold with the understanding that neither the author nor the publisher is engaged in rendering legal, accounting, securities trading, or other professional service. If legal advice or other expert assistance is required, the services of a competent professional person should be sought.

—From a Declaration of Principles Jointly Adopted by a Committee of the American Bar Association and a Committee of Publishers and Associations

Library of Congress Cataloging-in-Publication Data

Stone, Ron.
  Real value of training : measuring and analyzing business outcomes and the quality of ROI / by Ron Stone.—1st ed.
      p. cm.
  Includes bibliographical references and index.
  ISBN 978-0-07-175997-7 (alk. paper)
  1. Performance standards.   2. Rate of return.   3. Personnel managment.   I. Title.
  HF5549.5.P35S75 2011
  658.3'124—dc22

                                                                              2011008990

McGraw-Hill books are available at special quantity discounts to use as premiums and sales promotions or for use in corporate training programs. To contact a representative, please e-mail us at bulksales@ mcgraw-hill.com.

This book is printed on acid-free paper.

♦ ♦ ♦

Contents

Acknowledgments

To my former colleagues at Teledyne-Brown Engineering, Lockheed, McDonnell-Douglas, Alabama Industrial Development Training, Southern Company, and FranklinCovey, thank you for your encouragement and contribution to my professional growth.

To those around the world who have participated in my workshops and ROI certification and to my clients, for whom I have provided consultation and coaching through the years, thank you for your thought-provoking and relentless tough questions. You have kept me challenged and made me and my work significantly better.

To Donald Kirkpatrick, who blazed the path to evaluation for our profession, thank you for aiming us in the right direction.

To Jack Phillips, who had a vision about ROI and stuck with it even when others were not interested, thank you for your support through our many years of friendship.

♦ ♦ ♦

Introduction

THE GLOBAL ECONOMIC AND BUSINESS LANDSCAPE

Because of the financial crisis that had been lurking for years and ultimately surfaced in 2008, the business and economic landscape is undergoing transformation on a global scale. Executives will no longer support funding for training that does not make a visible contribution to the goals and strategic direction of the business. Agency directors in government organizations and educational institutions are also feeling the squeeze as they scramble for funding and look for ways to cut costs. Economic order has been replaced by economic disorder. No organization can escape the damage and the rubble as the new landscape continues to take shape. Nobody knows for certain what the landscape will look like in five or ten years, or even next month. One thing is certain: it has changed, and it is not likely to go back to business economics as usual.

Executives are demanding a training partner that knows how to address performance issues with solutions that make a measurable difference. They are demanding a versatile training organization that is resourceful and will shift priorities on short notice—a partner that aligns solutions with the business and sustains results. They demand focused solutions that aim for the end in mind and actually achieve it.

Bringing Measurement and Evaluation into the Conversation

The increased need for information and accountability brings measurement into the conversation. Measurement has always been important in organizations, but the changing landscape is placing a renewed emphasis on targeting and measuring results. Executives want to know up front what results programs and solutions will achieve. From time to time, they want to see follow-up evidence that business solutions—including training—are contributing to solving problems, serving customers, and improving the business. They want assurance that the organization is learning from its mistakes and making wise use of funds to create improvement initiatives.

This book provides a methodology, Stone's Measurement and ROI Process™, that is devoted to demonstrating how training and HR solutions make a contribution to the organization. The methodology takes training ROI to a new level of credibility by analyzing and reporting the quality of the ROI. While most of the book addresses how to measure results and ROI, the final chapter addresses how to forecast the results and ROI from a training solution. As an added benefit, the principles in this book are an excellent guide to designing training solutions that will achieve results.

Lessons Learned from Crawling out of the Economic Rubble

Like all of us, executives have learned many lessons from the fallout from the financial crisis. One of the most significant lessons has been the realization that relying only on quantitative data, or relying only on a number such as ROI, can lead to a train wreck. That is, we may be witnessing a runaway train, but we don't even know it unless we look under the numbers to see what is driving the train. While ROI continues to be an important measure, it must be viewed in a different way within the new landscape. This book is dedicated to that undertaking as well as to analyzing and reporting other important training success measures, such as business outcomes and execution in the work setting.

THE ROI ADVOCATE MEETS THE ROI CRITIC

ROI has been an evaluation tool for training since the 1980s, when Jack Phillips brought it to the forefront. Since that time, hundreds of vendors and training professionals have created measurement processes and implemented ROI calculations to show the contribution of training. As ROI has been applied through the years, three camps have formed, and they still exist today. Each camp has differing viewpoints regarding the use of ROI as an evaluation tool for training. In one camp stand the ROI advocates. In another camp stand the ROI critics. Somewhere near the middle stand two uncommitted groups. These are the "curious" and the "wait-and-see" crowd. The curious will eventually become more educated about ROI and will develop into either advocates or critics. Those in the wait-and-see crowd will probably continue their idle stance until some external force moves them to consider joining one of the extreme camps.

Who Are the ROI Advocates, and What Is Their Creed?

The advocates may be executives who are looking for evidence that workplace learning programs make a contribution to the business, or they may be training, HR, or performance professionals who have been trained in ROI and often apply its principles to show the contribution of training. Many advocates subscribe to ROI as the ultimate measure of success and will argue this point endlessly. They believe it is the "end to all ends" and nothing else quite compares to it. Hopefully, they have not been blinded by drinking too much ROI Kool-Aid. To their credit, many advocates are enthusiastic believers with a mission, and they are working hard to improve the practice and benefits of measurement and ROI.

Who Are the ROI Critics, and What Is Their Creed?

The ROI critics are a different breed. Some are executives who want projects to achieve an ROI but are not sold on the process of calculating ROI for training solutions. Other critics are training, HR, or performance professionals who are not sold on the merits of ROI processes and will stand their ground while daring anyone to try to move them. They will cite chapter and verse as to why ROI processes are a road to nowhere, a magician's concoction, snake oil at its finest. To their credit, they will provide measurement alternatives that they believe are superior to ROI.

How This Book Addresses the Disparity between ROI Advocates and Critics

What road does this book take with regard to the advocates and the critics? Stone's Measurement and ROI Process was created and has been continuously improved by listening to both critics and advocates. More than 15 years of conducting and directing hundreds of measurement and ROI studies and teaching, certifying, and coaching thousands of practitioners have taught me many lessons. In the past, I have been responsible for measurement practices that would violate my current standards. Some of these past practices were called into question by both ROI critics and ROI advocates.

When executives, clients, and constituents give constructive feedback, it is best to listen and act on it. The processes and tools in this book address the criticism and advice of the ROI critics as well as possible by accounting for their concerns with the principles and guidelines created for this measurement and ROI process. The conviction and passion of ROI advocates has also influenced this measurement and ROI process. Their willingness to stay the course and apply ROI has been of tremendous value to the profession, and I have learned from them. I have incorporated many of the advocates' ideas and addressed their concerns about ROI and measurement as they chose to wear the critic's hat. After all, even an advocate must be a critic.

THE MANY FACES OF ROI: WHAT IT IS AND WHAT IT IS NOT

ROI is a single metric that expresses the financial relationship between an expenditure to create and deliver a solution (training, a change initiative, or something else) and the business benefits that result from that expenditure. ROI answers the question: did the expenditure pay for itself? Standing alone, the ROI calculation informs us of nothing except the relationship of the monetary benefits to the expenditure. ROI is

- Only one way to show business value
- Feedback about what the value is in relation to the cost
- An important metric that should never be allowed to stand alone when communicating results
- An evaluation alternative that should be applied strategically to a small sample of learning programs or solutions

ROI is not "the results." The results are the business outcomes that are influenced by the solution through the performers as they execute in the work setting. Business outcomes are positive changes in strategic measures and key performance indicators, such as improvements in quality measures, increases in revenue, higher profit margins, increased market share, increased customer or employee satisfaction, reduction in turnover, shorter cycle times, reduced complaints, cost reductions, improved turnaround time to customers, and countless other business and customer service measures. These results are often assigned a monetary value in order to arrive at the business benefits and calculate the ROI. Some results are intangible in nature. ROI does not replace intangible results. However, the measurement and ROI process does capture and interpret the business contribution of intangibles.

The real truth about the performance results is often concealed and even inflated by ROI calculations. This is strikingly similar to the *Titanic* hitting the iceberg and continuing on its course as though things were okay. For an extended period of time, the crew and passengers were unaware of what was lurking underneath and the dangers it posed. As with the *Titanic*, what appears to be a good ROI (even one that is quite high) may in fact be concealing results that, could we see them, would be unacceptable.

Perhaps no measure is as misunderstood or as inappropriately used and communicated as ROI. Many practitioners, consultants, and even executives are misusing or misapplying the ROI of training and performance solutions. Throughout the upcoming chapters, this book illustrates how this is happening and demonstrates the correct way to calculate, utilize, and communicate the value and ROI of training. Specific chapters address collecting and analyzing credible data to establish a chain of evidence from learning readiness, to execution, to the influence on business outcomes. The process shows how to connect the dots that link learning solutions to execution in the work setting and business outcomes.

QUESTIONING THE QUALITY OF ROI— THE RIGHT THING TO DO

The new business landscape means that ROI as a metric is more important than ever. But it also means that the ROI calculation must be understood and not taken literally as a metric. The quality of any ROI should be questioned to determine whether the calculation is credible or whether the ROI is deceiving. The factors underneath that are driving the ROI metric must be discovered, analyzed, reported, and discussed. A process and tools are needed that reveal the truth about any ROI calculation. Stone's Measurement and ROI Process answers this call.

PUTTING MEASUREMENT AND ROI TO WORK FOR TRAINING—THE NEW VIEW OF ROI

Every process has its faults. Even with its faults, ROI is a necessary and powerful tool to demonstrate accountability for training expenditures. Stone's ROI quality analysis (RQA) uncovers the flaws in any ROI calculation and reports the true performance results. This new view of ROI is a practical and credible way to address the truth with ROI calculations. As addressed in Chapter 9, RQA is an inherent part of Stone's measurement process.

THE UNIQUE CHALLENGES FOR TRAINING PROFESSIONALS

Training professionals have two unique challenges. One challenge exists on the front side of training solutions, and the other resides on the back side. To tackle the first challenge, training professionals must allocate and expend resources to research and design effective solutions rapidly. In today's environment, there is not enough time for extended needs assessments. Performance situations must be assessed quickly, alternative solution designs created, forecasting applied to assess transfer risk, and delivery expedited.

To tackle the second challenge, from time to time resources must be allocated to analyzing and reporting the performance results that are influenced by training solutions. This is necessary for three reasons. (1) The results from training and performance solutions are not always evident. There are many factors in the work environment that can influence a change in business metrics. (2) The results that come about because of training solutions must rely on someone else (the trainee and others). Changes in performance do not happen simply because people learn. (3) There must be a basis for continuous improvement actions. Measurement and evaluation is a key contributor to continuous improvement decisions and actions.

To ensure that they meet these challenges successfully, training professionals must partner with clients and sponsors and use every avenue available when applying training and performance processes in order to achieve two goals. The first goal is to use credible processes to rapidly design solutions that have a greater opportunity to make a contribution to the business. Prior to the implementation of each training project, partners should have a high level of confidence that the solution is correctly aimed at the end in mind and that it will meet the objectives and make the appropriate business contribution.

The second goal is to apply credible processes to measure and evaluate performance readiness (including learning), execution in the work setting, business outcomes, and, when appropriate, ROI. Evaluation data should be used to cultivate continuous improvement throughout the training and performance process by learning what does and does not work.

A SNAPSHOT OF WHAT'S INSIDE

It is difficult to address measurement and evaluation without first setting the table regarding performance. Chapter 1, "Talking about Performance Results," establishes a frame of reference for addressing performance issues. It establishes why it is important to begin measurement up front and provides a performance-centered framework as a context for performance discussions and measurement. A nontraditional view of training design is presented that is applicable to designing and measuring training solutions in the twenty-first century.

Chapter 2, "Stone's Measurement and ROI Process: A View from Above," provides an overview of the complete measurement and ROI process and an evaluation framework to help in dealing with different types of performance data. The 12 guiding principles of the process and the ROI formula are presented.

Chapters 3 through 11 provide a detailed breakdown of each step in the measurement process, with examples, case scenarios, tools, and templates. These chapters provide in-depth coverage on planning the postprogram impact study, collecting and analyzing data, and reporting results and ROI. A progressive multipart case study is used in these chapters to show the application of the methodology all the way through to reporting results.

- Chapter 3, "Begin on the Right Foot: Partner to Create a Measurement Strategy," is about the initial meeting with the client and how to partner with the client to understand the objectives of the solution that is being evaluated and identify the stakeholders' expectations. It focuses on defining the purpose of the evaluation project, gaining agreement as to how the evaluation study should be carried out, identifying resource and support requirements, clarifying roles, and dealing with key data collection and reporting issues. The collection of baseline data and the creation of a data collection strategy and plan are covered.

- Chapter 4, "Collect Relevant Performance Data," addresses the eight methods and 10 typical sources of data collection. Proven tools and templates with examples are provided. The 12 key focus areas recommended for follow-up evaluation are covered in detail.

- Chapter 5, "Analyze Results and Adjust for Causal Influence," is the first step in analyzing follow-up performance data. The key influences on performance are addressed, along with three credible methods to determine whether the solution being evaluated actually caused any performance change. Tools and templates are provided, including a decision-making tool to help in deciding which method to apply in a given situation.

- Chapter 6, "Analyze Results and Adjust for Sustained Impact," addresses three important considerations when developing conclusions about whether the performance will be sustained. Performing this analysis is significant to avoiding overstating the results and developing a credible ROI.

- Chapter 7, "Go/No-Go: Assign a Monetary Value to Business Outcome Data," is about developing monetary values for business outcomes in order to calculate ROI. Three credible methods and variations of each method are presented. Tools and ideas are provided to assist in assigning monetary values to soft data.

- Chapter 8, "Calculate the Fully Loaded Cost of the Solution Design," emphasizes the importance of using fully loaded costs when calculating ROI and discusses the consequences when you don't. Guidelines for a credible approach to determining the costs are presented.
- Chapter 9, "Calculating the Return on Investment and Assessing the Quality of ROI," addresses the actual calculation of ROI and how to ensure its credibility by focusing on the quality of the calculation. The ROI quality analysis tool, a one-of-a-kind tool, is covered in detail, and templates are provided.
- Chapter 10, "Measuring the Contribution of Solutions: Alternatives to ROI," addresses the intangible results that are present when results are analyzed. Making the most of capturing and reporting intangibles is discussed.
- Chapter 11, "Communicate the Results," covers the presentation of results and how to tell the complete story. A framework for reporting results is suggested, along with tips that optimize efficient communication and educate stakeholders.

While Chapters 3 through 11 are about postprogram evaluation, Chapter 12, "Opportunity Forecasting: Predicting Performance Improvement and ROI," presents guidelines and a tool for forecasting performance improvement and ROI. It includes the acid test to determine whether a solution is likely to achieve results and analyzes the risk of transfer to the work setting.

To download many of the tools and templates illustrated in this book, visit my Web site at www.performanceandroi.com.

The reader will learn how to apply a measurement and ROI process that is not perfect, but is very practical for professionals who must believe in it and use it, and is credible to executives in the C-Suite who must depend on it. This process has been tested and improved again and again as hundreds have participated in my workshops and ROI certification, and as I have provided consulting and coaching to hundreds of professionals worldwide to develop and present ROI studies to their executive team. I wish you a successful journey as you learn, enjoy, and put it into practice!

1

Talking about Performance Results

Yes, this book is about measurement and evaluation. The process of measurement and evaluation actually begins up front, when a training professional partners with a client or sponsor to address the performance issues and expectations involved in a specific training solution. Prior to negotiating and designing a learning engagement, the professional and the client or sponsor must agree about the end in mind. When there is a failure to identify the end in mind for a training solution up front, the alignment of the solution with the business is left to chance. It is also difficult to successfully measure and evaluate a training solution whose expected outcome has not been defined.

VIEWING RESULTS THROUGH A PERFORMANCE-CENTERED LENS

When they are addressing the needs of workplace performers, training professionals often focus too much of their attention on learning and not enough on performance. Perhaps we should emphasize that the focus on learning is taking place at the wrong time. The time to identify a solution for operating deficiencies or strategic issues is after the performance factors and root cause have been properly identified, not before. Sometimes the client has done this prior to calling the training department, but sometimes she has not.

Training as a Single Solution Is Gone Forever

There was a time when a training solution consisted of a few learning strategies aimed at facilitating the knowledge and skills required to deal with a specific performance need or deficiency. These isolated "training-only" solutions were designed and implemented in the belief and hope that training alone was enough to bring about the desired results. Often, only a limited effort was made to seek reinforcement from management, and only rarely was attention given to such things as companion strategies. Because this procedure was rarely challenged and because evidence of results was rarely required or presented, this became the routine way in which training was delivered in many organizations.

Today, some managers, clients, and others still believe that training can be successfully delivered in this isolated way—no management reinforcement, no companion actions and strategies, no bundled solutions, just a training course by itself, doing its performance thing. Send people to the training room or the desktop, and when they return to the work setting, things will improve. Training professionals today have experienced enough frustration to know that this is not the case. The unfortunate truth is, training as a single solution is gone forever. The performance-centered framework challenges those involved in identifying solutions to think about and analyze all the relevant performance readiness factors beyond learning.

The framework that many training professionals have historically used in evaluating the need for and fit of a training solution is too narrow. Many of them have relied on Kirkpatrick's four levels of evaluation as a performance framework. This limited view places a narrow focus on learning (Kirkpatrick's level 2) as the solution to a performance issue. Many potential performance factors are overlooked when the training is focused only on "knowledge and skills."

When a client or sponsor requests a training or development program, it is natural to launch into a conversation about the learning because that is why the training department has received the call. But training professionals must resist closing the deal on a learning solution before sufficient conversation (and perhaps even a little rapid research) to identify the deficient performance issues and the root cause of those issues has taken place. Only then can expectations be clarified and a proper solution (nonlearning as well as learning) be identified, designed, and delivered.

A Twenty-First-Century Performance-Centered View

The training professional should partner with the client and use a simple performance framework to enable discussion about how a requested training solution will address specific performance needs. A performance framework provides a context that helps to

- Frame the right questions to identify the desired performance, analyze performance deficiencies, and identify the root cause of the problems.
- Identify performance objectives and measures for projects and performance solutions.
- Communicate with clients, team members, training suppliers, and others to negotiate expectations and determine readiness solutions and strategies (learning and nonlearning) aimed at closing the performance gap.

Figure 1.1 illustrates a performance-centered framework that can be used as a tool to facilitate a performance discussion, while at the same time assuring the client that his needs will be met.

The three components of the performance-centered framework (business outcome, execution, and readiness) are linked within a relationship—

Figure 1.1   Performance-Centered Framework

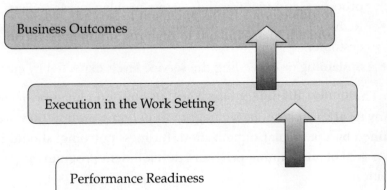

that is, performance readiness should influence the desired execution, and execution, in turn, should influence the desired business outcome. Without going into how to conduct a needs analysis, which is beyond the scope of this book, let's elaborate on the relationship among these three components. This should help in understanding how to reframe a discussion about learning into a focused discussion about performance. The performance discussion should focus on business outcome and execution and eventually lead back to decisions on designing, delivering, and supporting an appropriate solution. The idea is to move up and down the framework until all relevant questions are answered.

Business Outcome   This component refers to how a business or government agency will benefit when the performers involved execute as expected. Business outcomes include improvements in key performance indicators and other business measures that represent the end in mind, such as

- Reducing the cost of doing business
- Improving the profitability of the business (for nonprofits, diversity and sustainability of funding)
- Improving the quality (effectiveness) of the organization's business products, processes, and services
- Increasing the output (quantity) of products and services (sales, products manufactured, products delivered, services provided, orders filled, and so on)
- Reducing the time it takes to complete tasks, complete business processes, and identify and correct problem areas (efficiency)
- Reducing cycle time to close sales or to improve service to the customer
- Sustaining or exceeding the service levels expected by customers

There are additional categories of business outcome measures and many measures within each category, depending on how they are uniquely defined by a particular organization. Business outcomes should be the ultimate goal of any training program, development program, or performance solution.

In a perfect world, when a client requests training, she will identify a specific deficiency in business outcomes as the driving force for the request. However, the world is not perfect. Sometimes the focus is only on the training as an event. This is the worst possible scenario because the training professional must have the skill to move the conversation toward performance, sometimes having to overcome client resistance. Other times, the client may focus on his team's lack of execution in the work setting. This is a good thing because it is often easy to address execution and then move the conversation toward business outcomes and then back to readiness or learning.

Execution in the Work Setting   Execution is the performance of the work itself, the work processes, and how performers go about getting the work done. It identifies what a specific population should be doing or not doing (behavior), and how individual or team execution may influence the status of one or more desired business outcomes. For example, the problem may involve the sales associate implementing the six steps of the sales process when engaging a customer, or the supervisor coaching her team and providing feedback and recognition, or the customer call center representative handling a customer call and resolving service issues. Execution is arguably the most important component of the performance framework because it is the link between the readiness solution and the business outcome. A significant amount of time, effort, and money can be packaged as a training solution, but unless people execute the process that they have been taught when they are in the work setting, the business outcome (end in mind) will not be achieved. If we could mix a secret sauce to achieve results, we would aim it squarely at execution.

When training professionals are discussing training needs with a client, execution is where they should focus much of their attention. When prompted with the right questions, it is quite natural for a client to engage in a discussion about what people are doing now and what they should be doing differently. A relevant solution cannot be identified until the execution deficiency and its root cause are known. When the root cause is associated with knowledge, skills, or confidence, then a training solution may be an appropriate part of a bundled solution package. This is where performance readiness comes into the picture. Now the right questions can be asked to determine how to design or customize the best solution.

Performance Readiness: Applying the 80/20 Rule   If execution is to happen as expected, people must be performance-ready. Performance readiness is not just about learning. It answers the question, "What will it take to get the performers to be 'ready to perform,' and how can the surrounding work environment be optimized to put them in the best possible position to execute and achieve the expected results?" When a team is not performing as expected, or when new requirements are introduced, the relevant readiness factors must be identified. More than one readiness factor may be a key contributor to the root cause. The dimensions of performance readiness are as follows:

- *Individual or team compatibility.* Is the job the proper fit; do employees have the mental and physical capacity to do the job?
- *Individual or team competence for specific job requirements.* Given that the job is a proper fit, do the employees have the knowledge, skill, and confidence required to perform in the job setting?
- *Ineffective habits.* Even though the employees may know how to perform, are their current habits contributing to ineffective behavior?
- *Active management reinforcement (AMR).* AMR is actually about management carrying out its responsibility to facilitate performance by influencing employees' motivation, confidence, and capability to execute in the work setting. It's about the responsibility of management to create and sustain a work environment that puts employees in the best possible position to execute and achieve the expected results. We should ask, is the immediate manager *actively* reinforcing and supporting the desired behavior by personally doing the following?

  1. Providing advance and ongoing communication of goals and expectations regarding work roles, workload distribution, responsibilities, and development
  2. Providing performance incentives and consequences
  3. Providing timely coaching, feedback, recognition, and support

4. Providing adequate tools, equipment, technology, and resources
5. Providing proper design of work space, job tasks, policies, procedures, and processes

Certainly not every training request requires detailed scrutiny of each of these key readiness factors. It doesn't take long to pare these factors down when the right people are asked the right questions. It may be obvious that some of the factors are functioning properly, while others may require further analysis. In any case, in today's business world, time is usually of the essence, and a smart assessment must be done quickly. Therefore, the 80/20 rule is applied. That is, you need to identify the 20 percent of readiness needs that, when resolved, are likely to provide an 80 percent realistic opportunity to influence the desired execution in the work setting. A packaged performance readiness solution that includes learning as well as one or more additional readiness actions as determined by the analysis may be created.

CREATING A PERFORMANCE DESIGN THAT CLIENTS WILL SUPPORT

By analyzing needs beyond learning, an 80/20 bundled solution can be designed that is performance-driven and has an enhanced opportunity to influence execution and drive the desired business outcome. This provides a true performance design, as opposed to a single-solution learning design that has serious performance limitations. Table 1.1 (see page 8) shows an example of a performance design for a high-potential leadership program implemented by a multinational company. The program spans nine months with two facilitator-led, one-week learning engagements. The program for high-potential employees is driven by the need to develop bench strength for anticipated leadership replacements resulting from the company's rapid growth. It has the business benefit of developing the best and the brightest and keeping them in the company instead of allowing them to become a turnover statistic.

In the twenty-first-century workplace, isolated solutions rarely get results. We are not just talking about training here. Single solutions such as changing a work process, putting in new technology, communicating a new expectation, setting a goal, or sending someone to training does not necessarily

Table 1.1 Performance Design—Example of a High-Potential Program

BEFORE LEARNING ENGAGEMENT	DURING FIRST ONE-WEEK FACILITATOR-LED LEARNING ENGAGEMENT	DURING SIX MONTHS BETWEEN LEARNING ENGAGEMENTS	DURING SECOND ONE-WEEK FACILITATOR-LED LEARNING ENGAGEMENT	AFTER THE LEARNING ENGAGEMENT
Orientation Webinar and introductory packet	Leadership expectations and success measures, conducted by CEO	Action learning by sponsor/coach	Developing others to their potential	Coach follow-up with high-potential employees on action plan dealing with ineffective leadership habits
CEO conducts Webinar for manager of high-potential employees	Engaging people and leading diverse teams	Cross-functional team project work	Action plan to identify and overcome ineffective leadership habits	Continuing coaching sessions for three months
360-degree assessment, feedback, and coaching agreement	Strategic thinking	Individual coaching sessions per individual plan	Minding the shop—managing the business	Within one year, attend approved high-profile external executive leadership program
Pre-reading • Personal • Assigned	Critical thinking and problem solving	Continued work on individual plan from 360-degree assessment	Goal setting and achieving the end in mind	
Dialogue between high-potential employee and manager	Decision making our way	Cross-boundary three-month leadership job assignment	Case study—building value into our business	
	Case study—building value into our business	Personal dinner with CEO, unstructured	Team presentations on cross-functional project	

drive the desired performance change. It takes a bundled solution. A bundled solution is a performance solution that includes one or more companion strategies.

Companion strategies are aligned solutions that focus on more than one readiness factor. Each strategy is well understood and executed by those who are assigned an execution, support, and reinforcement role. The example in Table 1.1 includes multiple companion strategies to influence performance results, and complement the two one-week traditional learning engagements. Examples are the Webinar conducted by the CEO to gain commitment from the managers of the high potential employees, the 360-degree assessment and coaching, the cross-functional three-month job assignment, the action plan to identify and overcome ineffective leadership habits, and the personal dinner with the CEO. Each of these could be considered a companion strategy to support and reinforce the goals of the high-potential program. Of course, a performance design does not have to be as comprehensive as this one. Each design is crafted to fit the needs of the situation and the objectives of the specific solution.

A training solution should focus on a design for performance, with learning being a central key, but not the only contributor. There are several key benefits of a proper performance design:

- It encourages partnering with the sponsor to clarify expectations and conduct any necessary front-end performance analysis to identify relevant performance factors and recommend companion strategies.
- It focuses on application and links the key performance factors together. It answers the following questions: (1) what is the business outcome that needs attention, (2) how will execution of specific processes by a specific population influence the desired business outcome, and (3) how will this performance readiness solution influence the desired execution?
- The bundled solution with companion strategies builds in active management reinforcement (from client expectations and front-end analysis) that the stakeholders agree can best influence performance in the work setting.
- It encourages client involvement by reinforcing the message that "training alone" has limited potential to influence performance results in the work setting.
- It pinpoints the factors that should be addressed when conducting a follow-up evaluation.

- It educates stakeholders by ultimately demonstrating the various performance designs that work best to achieve the desired performance results.

The central issue in creating an effective training solution is, what design will work best to enable learning and influence performance in the work setting? The answer is always situational because of the many variables involved in a given scenario. A set of guidelines is helpful here. After conducting hundreds of ROI evaluation studies with clients on all types of training solutions, I have identified seven ingredients (the Secret Sauce) to create a performance design that gives the best opportunity to achieve expected results. Table 1.2 includes the ingredients of the Secret Sauce.

Here are a few comments about each of the seven ingredients. These could be considered as criteria for a successful solution design.

1. *Partner with the client up front to identify deficiencies and their root causes, target the desired business outcome, and agree on expectations and success measures.* Apply the 80/20 rule to identify the key factors that, when corrected, will contribute most to achieving the desired business outcome. For example, if ten performance issues are contributing to the business deficiency, which two (20 percent) can be corrected quickly by implementing a solution that will influence at least 80 percent of the desired result? Negotiate the client's role in the solution's success.

Table 1.2 Performance Design: Seven Secret Sauce Ingredients

1.	Partner with the client up front to identify deficiencies and their root causes, target the desired business outcome, and agree on expectations and success measures.
2.	Create linked performance objectives and communicate them to everyone involved.
3.	Create a complete performance solution design that addresses readiness needs beyond learning (the 80/20 rule applies).
4.	Communicate the practical limitations of the typical learning solution and negotiate companion strategies to engage management and drive performance results.
5.	Facilitate collaborative problem solving and deep thinking during the learning engagement. Build in diverse learning approaches, application assignments, and individual accountability.
6.	Identify ineffective performance habits and set goals to implement corrective action.
7.	Implement at least one situation-specific companion strategy or convey a compelling reason why none are needed.

2. *Create linked performance objectives and communicate them to everyone involved.* The objectives and measures should set the expectation for transfer of the desired performance to the work setting. Learning objectives (and nonlearning strategies) should be linked to execution objectives. That is, each readiness objective or companion strategy should drive one or more execution objectives aimed at application in the work setting. Each execution objective should drive the achievement of one or more business outcome objectives.

3. *Create a complete performance solution design that addresses readiness needs beyond learning (the 80/20 rule applies).* The solution design addresses relevant readiness needs beyond learning by (a) including solution strategies for key nonlearning factors linked to the root cause that present a significant barrier to performance, and (b) building a practical plan and gaining client agreement to support both learning and nonlearning strategies that are part of the solution design and span the entire experience (before, during, and after the learning engagement).

4. *Communicate the practical limitations of the typical learning solution and negotiate companion strategies to engage management and drive performance results.* Educate the client on any budget, time, or situational restrictions that may inhibit the depth and scope of learning and skill practice provided by the learning solution. Clarify the sustaining role of managers and partner on companion strategies that enlist their active management reinforcement (AMR) to build participants' confidence and speed time to competency.

5. *Facilitate collaborative problem solving and deep thinking during the learning engagement. Build in diverse learning approaches, application assignments, and individual accountability.* Encourage deep thinking to bring to the surface alternative viewpoints, ideas, and practical solutions that will work in the job setting. Questioning techniques, learning strategies, and team problem-solving exercises should focus on "why" and "how." Diversify the learning experience by using social media or networking platforms, coaching, job application assignments, and other blended learning modalities to enable a successful learning experience. Use action planning or contracting to build in individual accountability.

6. *Identify ineffective performance habits and set goals to implement corrective action.* Implementing new knowledge and skills may not be enough to overcome ineffective performance habits. Depending on which is practical, implement either (a) or (b) as follows: (a) Before or during the learning engagement, facilitate activities that allow participants to identify ineffective performance habits. Use action planning to set goals for and gain personal commitment to follow-up corrective action. Engage managers to become involved in follow-up action to eliminate the ineffective habits. (b) Create a tool for managers and coach them to implement the activities and follow-up action described in (a).

7. *Implement at least one situation-specific companion strategy or convey a compelling reason why none are needed.* Include one or more companion strategies (transfer strategies) in the solution design to build confidence and influence sustained application in the work setting. When a follow-up companion strategy is not part of the solution design, convey a compelling reason why no such strategy is needed. When the other six ingredients of the Secret Sauce are properly addressed, additional companion strategies may not be needed.

Training solutions that include these seven ingredients demonstrate the greatest success in transferring learning to the work setting and influencing the targeted business measures. What matters most is that the performance design is created to influence execution and move the business metrics. Changing the design is likely to change the result.

BUSINESS METRICS FROM A TO Z

Many types of business outcome measures exist in business organizations and government agencies. They are often referred to as key performance indicators (KPIs), key performance measures (KPMs), or strategic business measures of some type. Every business unit and team contributes to these measures in one way or another. Some contribute directly, others indirectly. Some contribute by providing revenues and profits. Others contribute by operating in cost-effective ways while sustaining customer service and quality, and consistently finding ways to take cost and inefficiencies out of the business.

Of course, the opposite is also true. Sometimes revenue suffers, market share shrinks, and costs creep upward. These inefficiencies may be the result of people and processes that are working less efficiently or the never-ending wave of change that keeps moving the performance targets. Enter corrective strategies and performance interventions. This is where training professionals and performance consultants make their money and their contribution.

Enabling Performance—What Training Professionals Do

When a developmental program needs to be designed, or when a client that is in need of a performance solution approaches, training professionals offer their expertise. They begin the task of identifying the need and its root cause, and designing or matching a custom solution to fit the situation. While many training professionals see their job as designing and facilitating learning, this is only a small part of their contribution. In the bigger picture, they are actually enabling performance.

By partnering with clients and stakeholders to identify business and performance needs and to design and deliver solutions, training professionals make an indirect but significant contribution. Their contribution is indirect because it is an enabling process. That is, a learning engagement relies on two types of transfer. First, the learner must indeed learn from the engagement. Second, the learner must decide to execute and apply the learning in the work setting. So at a minimum, achieving performance results is dependent on a two-phase transfer process, and that's assuming that the needs have been identified correctly and that the solution is aligned with the business.

Moving the Needle

Success relies on a multitude of things going right in a dynamic environment in order to achieve the end in mind. The end in mind is improving or sustaining one or more business metrics (business outcome), even though these metrics may not always be identified and specifically targeted. When solutions are designed and delivered, there is a better opportunity for success when everyone involved knows what the end in mind is and what he must do to move the needle.

Depending on the context in which you view each of items A to Z in the following list, they may represent measures of execution (what people do to influence business measures), or they may represent business outcomes that contribute to the overall success of the organization. Each needs to have an identified measure of success. Whether they are associated with revenue, profit, or the cost of doing business, some of these measures can be assigned a monetary value more readily than others.

A. Achieve the organization's goals and strategic objectives as indicated by key performance measures or indicators (KPMs or KPIs).

B. Achieve and sustain the competitive position of the organization.

C. Sustain and improve the organization's customer and partner relationships.

D. Achieve, sustain, or improve the organization's sales and profit.

E. Control and contain the organization's costs.

F. Achieve, sustain, or improve the quality of the organization's products and services.

G. Achieve, sustain, or improve the quality of supervision and management so that they can engage, enable, and lead the workforce to achieve the organization's goals.

H. Achieve, sustain, and grow the market position of the organization.

I. Research and create new products or services that are marketable by the organization or useful to society.

J. Sustain, improve, or reengineer the organization's processes and procedures.

K. Protect the safety and health of employees, customers, and the public.

L. Leverage the organization's human capital to achieve its goals and results.

M. Maintain a versatile, responsive, efficient, and effective workforce.

N. Contribute to licensing, accreditation, or other organization compliance requirements.

O. Contribute to the organization's positive image, reputation, ranking, status, or brand recognition.

P. Achieve, sustain, or improve the organization's shareholder value.

Q. Leverage the organization's facilities, equipment, property, and financial resources to benefit the organization.

R. Eliminate, reduce, or minimize the organization's liability or losses.

S. Eliminate, reduce, or restructure the organization's debt.

T. Contribute to the efficiency and reliability of the organization's supply chain.

U. Contribute to the organization's ability to receive and sustain funding.

V. Contribute to benefiting the community, charitable organization, or society.

W. Contribute to achieving, sustaining, or improving the organization's political persuasion.

X. Eliminate or minimize bad debt and/or unprofitable customer segments or accounts.

Y. Maintain or improve the security of the organization's assets and resources.

Z. Contribute to achieving the organization's mission (if there is anything that was not covered by points A through Y, then this point covers it).

Training solutions can have a positive impact on many of these metrics when there is a need relating to knowledge, skills, and behavior change. That impact has the best opportunity to occur when the performance relationship between the deficiency and the solution is in alignment and when the Secret Sauce ingredients in Table 1.2 (see page 10) are applied to the solution design.

WHAT MANAGERS AND C-SUITE EXECUTIVES WANT TO KNOW

Managers and C-Suite executives want pretty much the same things, but from a different perspective. Operational managers are focused on getting the job done and achieving the objectives at their team or unit level. They are expected to align the performance of their unit with the mission, goals, and strategies of the larger organization. It follows that each time they initiate a request for a training engagement (or there is a mandatory corporate program), they have four key concerns:

1. How will this engagement contribute to helping my team execute in the work setting and achieve our day-to-day operational objectives?
2. Will this engagement align with and make a positive contribution to the key business measures that I am held accountable for?
3. How do we get this accomplished successfully in a short time frame and with the least amount of disruption to the work?
4. Will I look good when this engagement is over?

Depending on the circumstances and what is driving the need for the learning engagement, the concerns, needs, priorities, and key issues of the operational managers will vary. The key focus is on getting the team to execute—that is, to meet a new performance requirement, to behave in a new way with customers, to ramp up quickly on changes in the work processes, or something similar. Of course, business outcomes are also a key concern, but getting the team to perform is a prerequisite to moving and sustaining the business metrics.

C-Suite executives make funding decisions. They decide why, if, and when a department is chartered. They can withdraw support for a charter at any time. Executives are always concerned about whether they are making good decisions when they commit scarce funds to a department, program, or project. Executives have four key concerns:

1. Are the larger organization's business needs, goals, and strategies being supported in some way by the funding decisions?
2. Are staff functions serving the broad range of needs of managers and employees to help them to achieve organizational performance and their own career goals?
3. Are the specific (expected) contributions of programs and projects being identified and targeted on the front end, before funds are allocated and expended?
4. What are people doing (execution) to achieve the organization's goals and make the organization tick? Executives want to know what continuous improvements are being initiated based on lessons learned when programs and projects are implemented. They know

that things never work perfectly, and they know that performance is a moving target.

Executives do not have the time to continuously hold court and determine whether and how these things are happening. However, they want to see success indicators, and from time to time, they want to see evidence that the train is being driven for the right reasons by the right people, and is progressing in the right direction. Of course, that's where measurement and evaluation enter the picture.

2

Stone's Measurement and ROI Process: A View from Above

Evaluation is a necessary activity if an organization is to learn how training solutions make the expected contribution to the organization and to assess the need for improving the training and performance process. The scope of evaluation can range from determining what participants learned and what they think about a specific training solution, to how performance actually changed and why, to how the business benefited and whether a true ROI was achieved. The need for evaluation resources and support can vary considerably, depending on the scope and type of evaluation that is being conducted.

Most of this book is dedicated to the process of follow-up evaluation to determine how training and performance solutions enable employee performance and make a contribution to the business. *Employee performance* is defined as "execution, or what people do in the work setting to meet the expectations of the organization." *Contribution to the business* means having a positive influence on business outcomes (the success of the business) as indicated by specific key performance measures of the organization, including a return on investment when required. The final chapter is dedicated to forecasting training results and ROI.

COMPONENTS OF A SUCCESSFUL EVALUATION METHODOLOGY

When an evaluation is being carried out, a systematic and credible process must be used to collect and analyze data and report findings, conclusions, and recommendations. Among other things, the process must include a systematic and comprehensive approach, a framework to define types of data, tools and templates to make the process efficient, and a set of standards or guiding principles to promote uniformity and credibility in the collection, analysis, and reporting of quantitative and qualitative data.

Like any other activity, evaluation requires resources and support. Follow-up evaluation (execution in the work setting, business outcome, and ROI) naturally requires more resources, time, and support than evaluation that takes place during a learning engagement (initial reaction and learning). While follow-up evaluation is not necessary after the delivery of every training solution, an overall evaluation strategy that covers the scope and breadth of a training organization's products and services must be in place. Using sampling, sufficient follow-up evaluation activities must be pursued on an ongoing basis to ensure that three things are evident: (1) expenditures are prudent, (2) training and development solutions are aligned with and contributing to the strategic and operational needs of the organization, and (3) continuous improvement requirements are identified and implemented. Figure 2.1 illustrates the key components necessary for a successful evaluation methodology.

The central component necessary for measurement and ROI evaluation is a systematic and comprehensive measurement process, illustrated by the center circle in Figure 2.1. The components represented by the four outer circles are necessary to enhance the credibility of the process and to help drive the success of any evaluation project.

Sponsorship

The inner workings of today's organizations are characterized by changing priorities, ambiguity, and the need for speed and results. Sometimes it is difficult to know who wants what, and the expectations are subject to change as a result of the dynamics of a changing environment. Even in a stable

Figure 2.1   Key Components of a Successful Evaluation Methodology

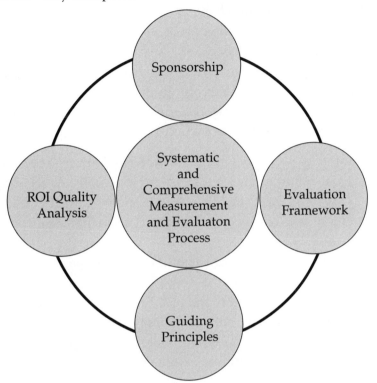

environment, a follow-up evaluation project should never be undertaken without sponsorship and an agreement on what is expected. Of the factors required in order to complete an evaluation project successfully, the need for sponsorship is at the top of the list. There are four significant issues that make sponsorship a necessity for measurement and follow-up evaluation. These issues exist for any follow-up evaluation project, not just ROI measurement. The issues are

- People view data collection as a disruption.
- People who are asked to provide data are often reluctant to cooperate because of a concern about how the data may be used or misused.
- People often feel threatened because of a concern that the evaluation may develop into an assessment of their own performance, instead of an evaluation of the training and performance process.

- Since a follow-up evaluation is time-spaced, often over several months, to allow sufficient elements of the performance cycle to occur, sustaining the evaluation project and completing the process can be difficult on two fronts: (1) sustaining cooperation from those providing the data, given that they may be experiencing a redirection of priorities and multiple distractions and demands, and (2) overcoming the impatience of stakeholders, who may seek to shortcut the process because they want to know the results quickly.

Any of these four issues can be a significant barrier to successfully implementing any follow-up measurement or evaluation project. Together, they can make for a difficult journey indeed. A sponsor, usually a client or another member of the management team, can help significantly in overcoming these barriers. For example, a sponsor can reduce the perceived threat of measurement through personal assurances and positive communication and reinforcement. Sponsors can also encourage cooperation in data collection efforts by appealing to the team's ownership of improvement initiatives. Sponsors are a vital ally in initiating and sustaining the evaluation project. The training professional should carefully plan the sponsor's role and provide coaching in the execution of that role.

Systematic and Comprehensive Measurement and Evaluation Process

The measurement and evaluation process shown in the inner circle in Figure 2.1 is the central component of the methodology. The purpose of this process is to systematically develop a business impact study that will establish the connection between the training solution (or other intervention), the participants' performance in the work setting, and the impact on key business results.

When properly implemented along with the four supporting components shown in Figure 2.1, the measurement methodology provides the evaluation practitioner with a reasonable representation of the contribution that an intervention is making to the business. In addition, it provides sufficient data to allow corrective action to be taken to improve the training and performance process. An impact study will provide the executive suite and other stakeholders with information in their language that provides a snapshot of how a training investment is paying off.

There are many measurement and evaluation methodologies in use today. Some are more credible than others, and some are more practical. The best measurement methodologies inherently include the features shown in Table 2.1.

Table 2.1   Inherent Features of a Good Measurement Methodology

FEATURE	WHY THE FEATURE IS IMPORTANT
• Is systematic, comprehensive, and flexible	It can be applied to all types of programs and solutions in any type of organizational setting.
• Is practical, employing tools, templates, and sampling techniques	This simplifies the measurement process by employing the least costly and most effective approaches, allowing for relative ease and speed of application.
• Establishes specific measures to track, analyze, and report a chain of evidence	Each measurement project is different. The end in mind of the solution being measured must be identified, along with the client's expectations for the measurement project (what evidence will be of value and what must be measured).
• Accounts for all relevant variables and how they act to change the metrics that are being measured	Metrics and key business measures are often influenced by many factors, not just the intervention that is being measured. Evaluation must determine, within reason, what causes key business results and performance improvement.
• Accounts for the extent to which results are likely to be sustained beyond the data collection time frame	Data are often collected during an abbreviated time frame several months following the delivery of a solution. It is important to determine how performance is likely to play out months later, after the data collection, instead of assuming that it will continue.
• Is capable of analyzing both tangible and intangible data to report benefits and assign monetary values to calculate ROI	Most solutions should provide both tangible and intangible benefits. Both must be analyzed and reported in ways that demonstrate their contribution to the business. Calculating ROI should be available but optional, depending on stakeholders' interest and requirements.
• Accounts for the quality of an ROI calculation when ROI is part of the impact study	ROI is a single metric that can be misleading and can even be manipulated to make an unacceptable result appear to be acceptable. An ROI quality analysis reveals the truth about the calculation.

These features help to provide a consistent, reliable, and credible process that practitioners can master and apply to demonstrate contribution and value.

Evaluation Framework

An evaluation framework is necessary to support the measurement process. It is integrated into the measurement methodology. The idea is to use the framework as a context or reference point to identify the different types of measures that will be or are influenced by a solution and the type of evaluation data that stakeholders require. The training professional should partner with the client or program sponsor and use the framework to clarify expectations for the evaluation project. This discussion focuses on several issues, such as (1) reviewing the training objectives and clarifying the performance results that should be influenced by the solution, (2) identifying the type of data that should be collected to determine whether the objectives have been met and to satisfy the information needs of the client and other stakeholders, and (3) identifying credible sources that can provide the data. This discussion ultimately develops the stated purpose and scope of the evaluation project. The evaluation framework in Figure 2.2 has four components. Three of these components have the same characteristics and are based on the same principles and performance relationships as the performance-centered framework covered in Chapter 1 (performance readiness, execution, and business outcome).

When a training solution is delivered, the expectation is that the dedication and hard work that go into the solution set off a chain reaction of performance. When a decision is made to conduct a follow-up evaluation, after clarifying the purpose of the evaluation, a chain of evidence is sought to demonstrate what happened. As shown in Figure 2.2, two types of readiness data are collected to determine the success of performance preparation: First, did the participants view the training solution as relevant and successful (initial reaction)? Second, did the participants learn and gain the confidence to apply their new knowledge and skills in the work setting (performance readiness)?

Two types of performance data are collected to determine follow-up performance success. Did the participants actually apply what they learned

Figure 2.2   Evaluation Framework

Evaluation of Follow-up Performance	
Business Outcome*	Verifies changes in targeted business outcome measures from the organization's records or other credible sources.
Execution in the Work Setting	Evaluates the successes and disappointments of the performance solution to verify the execution of key targeted objectives, tasks, and behavior in the work setting. Includes evaluation of active management reinforcement, companion transfer strategies, and corrective action to eliminate ineffective habits.
Evaluation of Performance Preparation	
Performance Readiness	Measures participants' readiness to execute targeted objectives and tasks in the work setting (awareness, knowledge, skills, confidence, habits, and other readiness factors identified in the specific solution design).
Initial Reaction	Measures initial reaction and satisfaction with delivery of the training and performance solution.

*After the performance solution's influence on the business outcome is determined, the resulting improvement data may be assigned a monetary value to calculate the return on investment. The net benefit is compared to the fully loaded cost of the performance solution to determine the ROL.

in the work setting (execution)? Did the execution by participants influence one or more business measures (business outcome)? When desired, evaluation of business outcome measures can be broadened to determine whether the solution paid for itself (ROI). The framework in Figure 2.2 is used during the evaluation planning stage to identify and clarify the different types of measures that should be influenced by the solution being evaluated and to make decisions on the types of data to collect, analyze, and report.

The purpose of a specific evaluation study determines which types of data are collected, analyzed, and reported. For example, an evaluation whose purpose is to determine the participants' satisfaction with a training solution will collect and analyze initial reaction data. This type of data is typically collected through a questionnaire, affectionately referred to as a smile sheet. Initial reaction data is of most benefit to the training organization and is of limited value to other stakeholders. An evaluation that has the purpose of determining whether employees are actually applying what they learned in the work setting will collect and analyze execution data. There are numerous possibilities for collecting execution data, such as interviews, observation, focus groups, and questionnaires. Data collection methods and sources are determined during the planning phase of an evaluation project, preferably before the solution is delivered.

Interest level in a type of evaluation and the value of the data will vary depending on the situation. A client or stakeholder who provides funding for a training solution will have a greater interest in knowing the ROI than one who does not provide funding. While management is usually interested in achieving an ROI, it is not always interested in allocating resources to determine whether this actually occurred.

Guiding Principles

Guiding principles, or standards, are necessary for any methodology to help ensure that it provides credible approaches and systematic application. They help guide the user to apply conservative decision making when collecting, analyzing, and reporting data. Even when guiding principles exist, they rely on the competence and motives of the analyst to apply them objectively and in a uniform way. As shown in Table 2.2, Stone's methodology includes 12 guiding principles that are integrated into the measurement process.

There will always be debate about refining a measurement methodology to make it more objective and more credible to researchers and other interested parties. However, the resources available to apply the methodology are often limited. I have asked managers and senior executives many times why they do not require more objective data when they make decisions. Their answer is always the same. It goes something like this: "I would like more objective data, but I do not have the luxury of unlimited time or an unlimited checkbook, and scarce resources need to be reallocated to other initiatives." Converted into plain English, this means, give me evaluation data, but make it quick, fix what is broken, apply the lessons learned, and then go to work on other priorities. In the end, urgency, practicality, and simplicity will win out over cost and wait time.

The application of these principles should be discussed with clients and other management stakeholders when planning an impact study and communicating the results of the study. Each of these 12 principles and the appropriate applications are discussed in detail throughout the upcoming chapters.

Table 2.2   Twelve Guiding Principles

1.	Partner with the sponsor on the evaluation project up front, and reach agreement on the purpose, scope, and expectations for the project, as well as the resources and support required.
2.	When collecting data, apply the five Cs and collect sufficient data to establish linkages among performance readiness, execution, and business outcome.
3.	Conduct success and disappointment analyses and report both types of data.
4.	Choose the most conservative alternative when analyzing data and reporting results.
5.	When sources estimate results, make an adjustment for the potential error of the estimate.
6.	Identify the key factors that influence business outcome measures and apply the appropriate method to adjust for causal influence.
7.	In determining the sustainable impact of improvements, use only credible sources and make adjustments accordingly.
8.	Calculate ROI only when it satisfies the purpose of the evaluation project and has utility for one or more interested stakeholders.
9.	When they are available, use organization records as a first source to report outcome improvement data and to determine monetary values, then resort to other credible sources.
10.	When comparing net benefits to solution costs to calculate ROI, use fully loaded costs.
11.	Always accompany ROI calculations with an ROI quality analysis.
12.	When reporting tangible and intangible results, communicate the linkage of these results and their contribution to the organization's key business strategies or measures.

ROI Quality Analysis: Finding and Reporting the Truth about ROI

As mentioned in the introduction, an ROI calculation can be deceiving. A training solution that does not achieve an acceptable performance result can actually yield a positive ROI, even a very high ROI. As Chapter 9 addresses, this is possible because of the many input variables that contribute to the development of an ROI calculation. A measurement methodology that includes ROI must account for this inherent flaw. This is why Stone's measurement and ROI process includes Guiding Principle 11, which states, "Always accompany ROI calculations with an ROI quality analysis." The ROI quality analysis (RQA) reveals and reports the flaws in the calculation so that it is not relied upon as the only indicator of performance success. Thus, the true value of the performance results can be demonstrated, regardless of what the ROI calculation implies.

OVERVIEW OF STONE'S MEASUREMENT AND ROI PROCESS

Stone's process meets the criteria for a successful methodology shown previously in Table 2.1. The process inherently includes all of the components previously addressed in this chapter that are necessary to conduct a thorough impact study. An impact study is a systematic, thorough, valid analysis that takes all relevant parameters into account to measure key business results and performance improvements that are influenced by training and performance initiatives. It includes an ROI calculation when one or more stakeholders are interested in a cost-benefit-type analysis. If the purpose of a specific evaluation study is to calculate the ROI, the entire process (11 steps) is implemented. If the purpose is only to determine whether learning occurred, or to determine whether execution in the work setting took place, then the evaluation will stop short of collecting business outcome data and calculating the ROI. The process is applied to address only the data that are needed to satisfy the stated purpose.

As any evaluation process is applied, it is important to remember that the data that are collected, analyzed, and reported as business outcome results must be linked back to the solution through a chain of evidence. Even though methods to determine the causal influence of the business outcome will be applied later in the evaluation process, there must be a chain of evidence for all three stages. As illustrated in Figure 2.3, there must be evidence that learning (readiness) did occur in Stage 1, and there must be evidence that the solution was applied in the work setting in Stage 2 (execution). When evidence is lacking in any part of the path of this chain, it is not plausible to establish a causal relationship.

Each type of result in the performance chain should influence the next result. In Figure 2.3, when a training solution from Stage 1 achieves its learning objectives, the performers (participants) should be "performance ready." Thus, the learning and any companion strategies enable execution in the work setting in Stage 2. When performers execute as expected, business outcomes in Stage 3 are influenced. It is a simple-looking process, but there are many complexities that can cause breakdowns in the path to performance. The most frequent breakdowns occur between the end of Stage

Figure 2.3 Chain of Performance

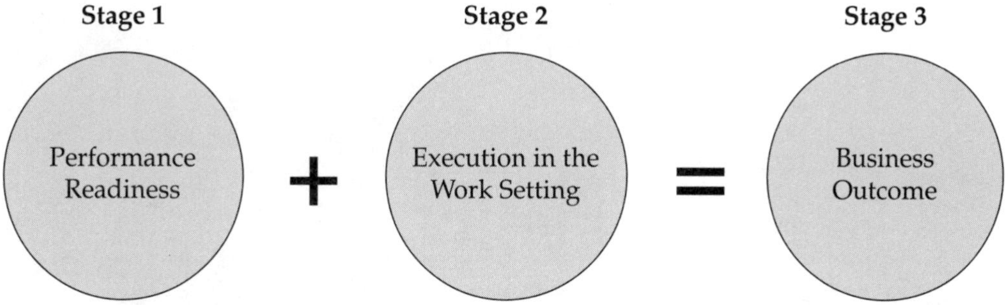

Stage 1   **Stage 2**   **Stage 3**

Performance Readiness **+** Execution in the Work Setting **=** Business Outcome

1 and the beginning of Stage 2. Hundreds of business impact studies that I have completed reveal a compelling conclusion. The key weakness in the training and performance process is a solution design that focuses only on learning. That is, transfer to the work setting is frequently left to chance.

When the solution design ignores other elements of readiness, such as the need for active management reinforcement or other types of needs, the opportunity for success is diminished. A good evaluation strategy must examine the possibilities and report any weaknesses in the solution design. The evaluation methodology covered in this book and shown in Figure 2.4 (see page 30) enables practitioners to plan and execute evaluation strategies to complete this task and more.

The measurement and ROI process includes five phases with eleven steps to plan, implement, analyze data, report results, and follow up on the recommendations. When the entire process is utilized, business outcomes are identified and the ROI is calculated.

Phase One: Partner and Plan the Evaluation Project

An evaluation study begins in Phase One of the process when a client or sponsor designates or agrees to a program to be measured. This decision should occur before the training solution is implemented to allow for effective planning. A planning meeting is held with the client to discuss issues, make decisions about the specific purpose of the evaluation, and identify support requirements.

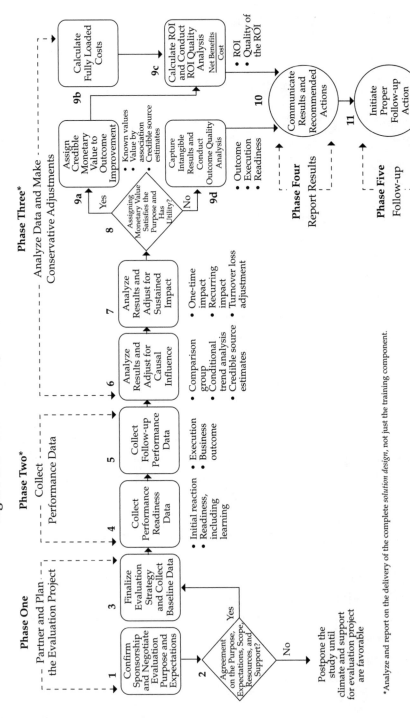

Figure 2.4 Stone's Measurement and ROI Process

*Analyze and report on the delivery of the complete *solution design*, not just the training component.

Copyright © 2008, Ron Drew Stone. All rights reserved.

30

The result of the client meeting is a partnership supporting an evaluation plan and strategy that will be implemented during Phases Two through Five. The necessary answers may not all be available during the initial meeting, and additional discussion and discovery may be required. As indicated by Step 2, when a satisfactory agreement on key issues cannot be reached, the study should be postponed until a more favorable time, or, depending on the reasons for the lack of agreement, perhaps a different program may be selected for evaluation. When the impact study is completed, the key deliverable is a written report and presentation that includes findings, conclusions, and recommendations. The data reported should be comprehensive enough to satisfy the purpose of the study that was identified during the planning phase.

Phase Two: Collect Performance Data

Step 4 begins the implementation of the data collection plan and strategy that was developed in Step 3. In Step 4, someone has usually already been designated to collect performance readiness data during the delivery of the solution (initial reaction and learning readiness). These data are reported later, along with follow-up data from Step 5 (execution and business outcome). Throughout Steps 4 and 5, data are collected to show a chain of impact up to the highest level that satisfies the purpose of the study.

Step 5 follows the evaluation strategy and plan to collect data in the work setting from the business performance records and other credible sources. Data collection instruments and methods are carefully planned to collect the most credible data from the most reliable sources to determine the contribution.

Phase Three: Analyze Data and Make Conservative Adjustments

The data analysis phase begins with Step 6 to determine the performance results. The potential causal influences that drive the targeted business outcome measures are identified, and a method and strategy are applied to differentiate between the effects of the solution design and any other influencing factors. An adjustment is made to the performance results to account for the influence of the solution.

Step 7 addresses the sustainability of the results that are influenced by the solution and makes the necessary adjustment to account for either a one-time impact or a recurring impact. When a decision is made to annualize the performance results, an adjustment must be made to account for the turnover experienced by the population being sampled.

Step 8 is a key decision point to determine whether specific business outcome results will be assigned a monetary value or whether they will be reported as intangible results. Intangible results are any business outcomes that are not assigned a monetary value. The decision to assign monetary values is initially made at Step 3, during the planning process, as are all other key decisions. However, the planning step takes place months before the data are actually collected and analyzed. The situation may have changed when it is actually time to perform the analysis. For example, determining monetary values for a specific measure may be much more difficult than anticipated, and it may not be wise to expend the resources necessary to proceed. The client is consulted when it is deemed necessary to change the original plan. The decision could still be made to allocate the resources, take more time, and assign a value.

Data that are assigned monetary values (some values are known; others may need to be developed) are used to determine the monetary benefits (Step 9a) and to calculate the ROI (Step 9c of the process). To calculate the ROI, net monetary benefits that are influenced by the solution design are compared to the fully loaded costs, which are calculated in Step 9b. Data that are not assigned a monetary value are processed in Step 9d as intangible data. These data are considered intangible because they have no known monetary value, and therefore they cannot be used to calculate ROI.

Concurrent with or following the ROI calculation, the ROI quality analysis (part of Step 9c) is performed. This is a thorough examination and analysis of all the inputs into the ROI calculation to determine whether the calculated ROI is really representative of the performance results achieved and to identify the deficiencies and strengths of the evaluation.

Sometimes an evaluation does not include an ROI calculation because the key stakeholders are not interested in allocating the resources required to determine ROI. In this case, Steps 9a, 9b, and 9c are not included in the process. In this instance, only the intangible results from Step 9d are reported and an outcome quality analysis is performed.

Phase Four: Report Results

Impact studies that include an ROI calculation usually yield both tangible and intangible results from a training solution. The data from Step 9a through 9d are analyzed, and the findings, conclusions, and recommendations are reported in Step 10. The interests and preferences of key stakeholders are taken into account when the data are collected and analyzed and the report is drafted. During the presentation to key stakeholders, the results, recommendations, and issues are discussed, and follow-up actions are communicated.

Phase Five: Follow-Up

Step 11 focuses on finishing the job by implementing the approved recommendations. Some recommendations may be course- or solution-specific and therefore are likely to be narrow in scope. Others may involve the entire training and performance process and how it is managed by the training function, utilized by stakeholders, or aligned with the business.

THE MISUNDERSTANDING ABOUT ROI AND THE BENEFIT-COST RATIO

Some practitioners confuse return on investment (ROI) with another common measure of payback called the benefit-cost ratio (BCR). As a result, both formulas are sometimes applied or communicated incorrectly. The two are similar in that they are both expressing a relationship between benefits and costs. But the equation is calculated differently, and the answers they yield have a different meaning and are expressed in a different way.

Benefit-Cost Ratio (BCR)

To determine the benefit-cost ratio, the total monetary benefits influenced by a solution design are compared to the costs by dividing total benefits by the costs, as shown here. A benefit-cost ratio of 1 means that the benefits equal the costs. This is known as breaking even.

$$BCR = \frac{\text{Solution Benefits}}{\text{Fully Loaded Solution Costs}}$$

Example: There are $300,000 in total benefits from the solution, and the fully loaded cost of the solution is $200,000.

$$BCR = \frac{\$300,000}{\$200,000} = 1.5 \text{ (usually written as 1.5:1)}$$

The answer communicates a ratio of benefits to costs of 1.5 to 1. That is, the benefits exceed the costs by 0.5. It is expressed as a ratio of 1.5:1. The 1 to the right of the colon always represents one dollar spent. Compared to $1.50 returned in the example, the gain is only 50 cents (1/2 dollar). So the answer as expressed in this example (1.5) does not factor out the investment. While there is a result of 1.5 ($1.50), the gain is only 0.5 ($0.50) because the dollar spent is included in the $1.50.

Return on Investment

As shown in the following formula, in calculating ROI, net monetary benefits influenced by the solution design are compared to the fully loaded costs. The ROI formula differs from the BCR formula in two ways: net benefits are used in the numerator, and the answer is expressed as a percentage returned on the investment.

$$ROI = \frac{\text{Net Solution Benefits}}{\text{Fully Loaded Solution Costs}} \times 100$$

Using the same example of $300,000 benefits and $200,000 fully loaded costs, here is the ROI:

$$ROI = \frac{\$100,000 \ [\$300,000 - \$200,000]}{\$200,000} = 0.5 \times 100 = 50\%$$

Net benefits are defined as total benefits minus cost (300,000 minus 200,000 in the example); thus, the figure in the numerator is $100,000. ROI is a comparison of net benefits to the costs, and it is expressed as a percentage. Therefore, following the calculation, the answer (0.5 in the example) must be multiplied by 100 to convert the decimal to a percentage. So in the example, 50 percent ROI is the gain. It is a net number. This is why it is called a "return" on the investment. The BCR is not a return; it is a ratio. It is incorrect to say, "The BCR is a return of 1.5." Think of it this way: it is impossible to get an ROI without first recovering the costs. Unlike the BCR, the answer from the ROI calculation is a gain, a return on the investment.

Breakeven for ROI is zero. Another way to remember the difference between BCR and ROI is that the BCR will always be greater than the ROI by a factor of 1. For example, a BCR of 2.65 is the same as an ROI of 165 percent (1.65 x 100). Calculating ROI for training puts training investments on a level playing field with other types of investments by using a formula that is similar to other concepts and investment calculations used to determine payback. Executives understand and respect this language, since they use it to make decisions about other types of business investments. The ROI quality analysis is used to deal with any concerns executives may have that the process used to develop training ROI might communicate the value improperly.

HURDLE RATE FOR ROI

Hurdle rate is the term that is used to establish a minimum acceptable ROI for investments. Generally, there is no acceptable standard for hurdle rate. Most organizations establish a minimum acceptable ROI or a minimum acceptable range in order to have some flexibility in comparing investment options. Generally the minimum expected return ranges from 10 to 20 percent, based on numerous issues such as alternative investment opportunities available, the cost of financing and the availability of money, the nature of the investment, the strength of the linkage of the investment to the strategies of the organization, how the investment contributes to the competitive position of the organization, and so on.

A reasonable hurdle rate for training and HR solutions can be established at the higher end of the range noted here, or 20 percent. Each situation should be considered on its own merit as determined by the key stakeholder (client or sponsor). Several choices are available for consideration, as follows:

- The client may accept a range of 10 to 20 percent, or the same as that for other investments.
- The client may suggest a different number that matches its own expectations, either higher or lower than that for other investments.
- The client may suggest a breakeven ROI (0 percent).
- The client may state that he has no interest in allocating resources to determine ROI.

When a client asks the training professional to suggest a target hurdle rate for a specific program, it may be best to set it at the high end of the range for other investments, or 20 percent.

CRITERIA FOR BUSINESS OUTCOME AND ROI EVALUATION DECISIONS

Since most of a training organization's funding is dedicated to assessing needs and designing and delivering solutions, evaluation dollars are usually scarce. Therefore, follow-up evaluation decisions must be planned carefully and the dollars spent wisely. Evaluation of business outcomes and ROI should be reserved for those programs that meet specific criteria. While general criteria are provided here, each training organization should refine the criteria to meet its own requirements. Table 2.3 provides a good starter for the criteria.

Applying the criteria in Table 2.3, decisions to evaluate programs are based on the resources and evaluation expertise available. Sampling is also used to conserve scarce evaluation resources. For example, suppose that a decision to evaluate a key leadership program is made based on the criteria in Table 2.3. The program is offered six times this year from February to September, with 30 people participating in each offering. To sample the contribution of the program, two offerings (60 participants), one in February and one in March, are selected for evaluation. Another option is to sample a percentage of participants from all six offerings. However, this option is not advisable because of the lengthy time span involved and the existence of a multitude of variables that would significantly complicate data collection and analysis.

Some follow-up evaluation projects have the single purpose of focusing on execution in the work setting. These evaluations often target programs

Table 2.3   Evaluation Criteria for Business Outcome and ROI

CRITERION	COMMENT
• Linkage of the solution to the organization's goals, KPIs, or strategic objectives.	Many programs may fit this criterion, so prioritize them based on the expected benefits of the evaluation.
• Client or management interest in the demonstrated results of a specific solution.	This usually comes down to a key stakeholder's own criteria, such as high interest in a specific measure or business problem that the solution should affect.
• High percentage of budget allocated to the solution.	A rule of thumb is, if 20 percent or more of the training budget is allocated to a solution, that solution is high cost.
• The solution has high visibility in the organization.	Some solutions have higher visibility because they are controversial or because of perceptions of their relative value.
• A high percentage of the workforce is to be involved in the solution.	For example, a solution may be offered to all engineers, all employees of one department, all company employees, or some other such group.

involving new employees who are being brought on board or programs involving customer relationships and customer transactions. These programs could also become candidates for business outcome and ROI evaluation. Compliance programs whose purpose is aimed at employees following regulatory requirements, safety requirements, job procedures, and the like are often targeted for evaluation of execution in the work setting.

3

Begin on the Right Foot: Partner to Create a Measurement Strategy

Follow-up evaluation activities require varying amounts of resources and will span different calendar timelines, depending on the scope of the solution that is being evaluated and the scope and expectations of the evaluation itself. Hence, an evaluation initiative should be treated like a project, meaning that the expectations, success measures, resources, support, and analysis and reporting requirements must be identified and negotiated with the partner up front. Projects of any type rarely succeed unless they are carefully planned and executed with the end in mind and with stakeholder buy-in. As illustrated in Figure 3.1 (see page 40), Steps 1, 2, and 3 are the beginning of the measurement and ROI process. During these steps, key decisions are made about planning and executing the evaluation project. The entire project is planned from the beginning of data collection to the final step of reporting the results.

STEP 1: CONFIRM SPONSORSHIP AND NEGOTIATE PURPOSE AND EXPECTATIONS FOR THE EVALUATION

During Step 1, the training professional partners with a business leader, usually the direct client, to confirm sponsorship and negotiate the evaluation purpose and expectations. Guiding Principle 1 states, "Partner with the sponsor on the evaluation project up front, and reach agreement on the

Figure 3.1   Phase One, Steps 1, 2, and 3

Phase One

Partner and Plan
the Evaluation Project

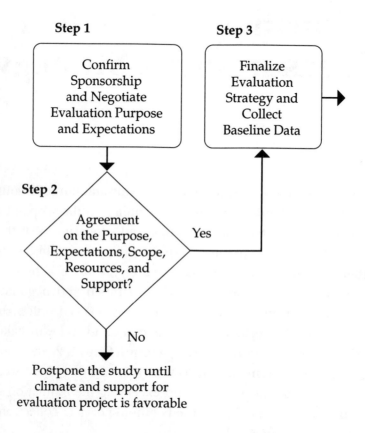

purpose, scope, and expectations for the project, as well as the resources and support required."

Sponsorship involves partnering with a member of the management team who is willing to serve in an influencing and supportive role. Sponsors must concur with the overall data collection strategy and plan. They should have a role in encouraging participants in the data collection effort to provide data in a thorough and timely manner.

Guiding Principle 1

Partner with the sponsor on the evaluation project up front, and reach agreement on the purpose, scope, and expectations for the project, as well as the resources and support required.

While the business leader who is identified as the client for the evaluation is usually the primary partner and sponsor for the evaluation, there can be other key stakeholders as well. A key stakeholder is anyone who seeks to have input into the evaluation or has an interest in reviewing the evaluation data. Interest could be driven by numerous things, such as the high visibility of the training solution, the high cost of the training solution, ownership of the training solution, or interest in a specific business measure and the desire to know how a specific program drives that measure.

The key client can help identify other interested stakeholders. The training director and the senior executive of the business unit that allocates funding for training may be sources as well. Most of the evaluation data required are driven by the needs of the key client. In order to identify the purpose of the evaluation and allow for effective strategy and planning, the planning meeting and discussion with the sponsor should occur before the training solution is implemented. During the Step 1 planning meeting, in addition to confirming sponsorship and identifying the key stakeholders, other issues are discussed and decisions made with regard to the scope of the evaluation and the resources and support required. Each of these topics is addressed in this chapter.

Determine Purpose and Expectations for the Evaluation

When the purpose and expectations of the evaluation initiative are unclear, it's difficult to determine whom to collect data from, the type of data to collect, and when to collect them. Identify the key stakeholders (in addition to the client) who have an interest in the results of the study, and agree on the type of evaluation data that will satisfy their needs. Determine how the client and other stakeholders will benefit from the results of the evaluation and how the data will satisfy their needs regarding information and performance. Determine the different types of data that must be gathered and which sources key stakeholders consider to be credible. Determine the expectations for communicating the progress of the evaluation and final reporting. The training professional may touch base with other stakeholders later to verify this information.

The purpose and expectations go hand in hand because one influences the other. For example, if the client is set on seeing evaluation data that show how people have changed their behavior, the purpose of the evaluation must encompass this requirement, and a plan and strategy must be created accordingly. Occasionally, the initial purpose of an evaluation project may be revised when the client learns that certain data are not readily available or when the planning steps reveal that the resources and time required are greater than was originally anticipated. Once the purpose and success measures of the evaluation project are agreed upon, this drives the remaining evaluation decisions. Table 3.1 includes a few examples of evaluation purpose statements and measures.

An evaluation may include multiple purposes and measures. The client or sponsor must agree to each purpose and measure. It is the purposes and measures that drive all other evaluation decisions. An evaluation should satisfy the needs of stakeholders and the training and performance process, not those of the training department. When the training department is perceived to be the major beneficiary of an evaluation study, it is difficult to build and sustain support for the necessary data collection activities.

Determine How Training Solution Objectives Link to Business Measures

Review the objectives of the program that is being evaluated and identify the performance measures that it is expected to influence. There should be a clear linkage. When either the objectives or the linkage is not clear, the situation must be clarified until there is complete agreement on the aim of the program and the specific measures of success. Review the needs assessment if there is one. Talk with the client and other key people to determine what business driver initiated the program and what business outcome is expected from the solution that is being evaluated. Clarifying these issues helps to solidify the pur-

Table 3.1   Evaluation Purpose Examples

PURPOSE	EXAMPLE OF A SPECIFIC MEASURE
• Determine how often sales representatives are applying cross-selling skills.	Mystery shoppers report that representatives are using discovery questioning techniques to suggest complementary accessory items (target is 90 percent use per sales contact).
• Determine whether the sales target for accessory items is being met.	Sales of complementary accessory items increase by an average of 25 percent per customer.
• Determine whether customers approve of the new service policies.	Customer satisfaction scores improve by 20 percent within three months in categories 6, 8, and 9 on satisfaction surveys.
	There is a 50 percent reduction in customer service complaints.
• Determine successes and disappointments when applying the new decision-making process.	Participants identify the top three successes as a result of applying the decision-making process.
	Participants identify three decisions that they made that did not meet stakeholder expectations.
• Determine customer receptiveness to changes in the new customer service processes.	Before they leave the service department, 20 percent of customers will voluntarily respond to a five-question survey.
• Determine whether a specified return on investment has been achieved.	Achieve an ROI of at least 20 percent with a ROI quality analysis score of "definitely acceptable."
• Determine whether training is relevant to the current job environment.	Achieve at least 4.8 on a 5-point scale for the initial reaction questionnaire at the end of the program (items 6 and 7 on the questionnaire).

pose of the evaluation and ensure that the evaluation project can deliver the type of data needed.

Identify Key Components of the Solution Design

When the decision is made to evaluate a training solution, among the first things to do is to identify what the solution looks like. That is, what are the characteristics of the solution, or, as we say in the training business, "what is the performance design?" It is the performance design that drives the results. As pointed out in Chapter 1, learning strategies may be only one element of the solution design (Table 1.1 gives an example). An evaluation strategy and plan must take the design into account. It is the design that is being evaluated, not just the learning. Changing the design is likely to change the result. When the evaluation reaches the analysis stage, the analysis must determine the extent to which the design influenced the business outcome. Any approach short of this is misrepresenting the dynamic of the cause-and-effect relationship that is being driven by the solution design.

Determine the Scope of the Evaluation

Facilitate agreement with the sponsor on the scope of the study, the population to be sampled, and how data will be collected, analyzed, and reported. The scope addresses such issues as (1) what will be the time span of the evaluation project (a few weeks, a few months, or a year) and (2) how much data will need to be gathered, how often, when, and from whom and how many people? Identify the characteristics (job type, location, working hours, and so on) of the people who will provide the different types of data. Then you can best determine how and when to collect those data from each group. Sample size is often a matter of doing what is practical. In a real work setting, because of the cost, time, and disruption involved, it is often impossible to follow the standards given in a sample size table. Anyway, in this situation, sample size is overrated. We are not inquiring about how someone will vote in the race for a political office, or what TV shows she watches. We are getting in-depth information about performance. Going to the right sources is much more important than sample size as long as the approach is comprehensive. The sampling approach (who should be in the sample) is dictated by the purposes of the data collection initiative, the type of data being collected, and the concern for credibility.

Once the sources and sample size are known, it is easier to decide how to collect the data. We know whether the population to be sampled is concentrated in one location or scattered across a geographic region. We know the type of work these people do, so we can get a feel for how long it will take for the performance cycle to occur. We know the difficulties and approximate cost involved if we decide to conduct interviews or focus groups. We also have an idea about how questionnaires may be able to play a role in collecting large amounts of data.

Determine the Resources Required for the Evaluation

Once we have a full understanding of the purpose, scope, and expectations of the evaluation, the resources needed for the evaluation should be determined. Address how the client organization and others may need to help in data collection and analysis activities. For example, if the organization routinely collects business metrics data that are relevant to the study, access to the custodian of the records will be required, and assistance in interpreting the data may also be needed. Resources may also be required to coordinate the scheduling of interviews or the administration of questionnaires.

Negotiate and Align Support with the Expectations for the Evaluation

Negotiate the sponsor's support role and establish a partnership for the successful completion of the study. Having a full understanding of the purpose, scope, expectations, and resources required, the client or sponsor should make a commitment to provide the necessary support to sustain the evaluation through to completion. This includes a major emphasis on data collection and follow-through on recommendations. Educate the client on the difficulties that are likely to be encountered during the data collection process, such as work priorities usually cause people to view data collection as a disruption, people need encouragement and a good reason to cooperate and provide objective data, people are often suspicious of the reasons for the collection of evaluation data, barriers arise because of the time span required to complete the evaluation, and so on. A good sponsor can help to gain cooperation and reduce many of these difficulties by openly supporting the evaluation and communicating its purpose.

Identify Requirements for Collecting Key Behavior and Execution Data

All follow-up evaluations must collect data on behavior change. Behavior change (execution) is the first hurdle in the chain of impact following delivery of the solution. The objectives and content of the program being evaluated should identify the focus and scope of the behavior change expected from the program. The purpose of the evaluation should address the level of interest in behavior change data. However, even when the main focus of the evaluation project is business outcome data, the behavior change data are still important and relevant to establishing the chain of impact. Experience also shows that executives have a high level of interest in execution data, so it is best to collect them and include them in the analysis and reporting.

During the planning meeting, a discussion should focus on the specific questions that should be asked to determine what behavior data to collect and how to collect them. The client may not be able to respond to all of your questions. Don't hesitate to ask if there are one or more high performers or job experts that the client can refer you to in order to get more specific and relevant information. Determine what people are supposed be doing now (execution requirements) and what they should do differently after the training. This is where you get the information that you will use later in the impact study as you formulate the specific questions you want to ask about execution and behavior change.

STEP 2: GO/NO-GO EVALUATION DECISION

Step 2 of the evaluation process is simply a key decision point to decide whether the evaluation will go forward or whether it would be better to either postpone it until a more favorable time or select another program to measure. When the key elements of the evaluation, such as its purpose and expectations, scope, resources, and support, cannot be agreed upon, it is best to postpone the evaluation until a more favorable climate can be established.

There may be numerous practical reasons to postpone a follow-up evaluation effort or to select a different program for the study. Several possibilities are

- The workload of the organization that must provide the data is excessive.
- The timing is not good because a significant data collection effort was recently implemented in the organization.
- The organization recently announced a restructuring, downsizing, or other such initiative, and people may associate the data collection with these efforts.

- The training solution selected for evaluation has unclear objectives (even after discussion), which leads to lack of agreement on the purpose of the evaluation and the data that should be collected.
- After discussion during the planning meeting, the initial purpose of the evaluation is expanded, but there are insufficient resources currently available to implement the study.

Even in a favorable climate, collecting evaluation data can be difficult. Pursuing evaluation activities in an unfavorable climate is likely to result in frustration, a waste of resources, and possibly calling off the effort while it is in progress. When these things are predictable, it is best to postpone the effort before resources are allocated.

STEP 3: FINALIZE THE EVALUATION STRATEGY AND COLLECT BASELINE DATA

Steps 1 and 2 should provide the preliminary information needed to finalize a specific evaluation strategy and plan. The training professional must now complete the details by making sure that critical questions are answered, a project plan is prepared, resources are identified for allocation, and the evaluation strategy and plan are completed. This plan will document most of the decisions necessary to collect performance data and show a chain of impact. Once the plan and all of its components have been completed, the other detail work begins, such as creating questionnaires and interview guides, tabulating the cost of the solution, and so on. Then the plan and the tools are implemented at the appropriate time, before, during, and after delivery of the solution.

Create an Evaluation Strategy and Plan

The evaluation plan is a road map to collecting the data and making key decisions about data analysis and reporting. The most critical part of the entire evaluation process is collecting the necessary data. Without data, there is no impact study. Figure 3.2 (see page 48) shows a standard form, the Evaluation Strategy and Plan, which is the key planning tool to document data collection decisions.

Figure 3.2 Evaluation Strategy and Plan

Evaluation Strategy and Plan	Your Name:	Company:

Check boxes for applicable type of evaluation: ☐ Initial Reaction ☐ Learning Readiness ☐ Execution ☐ Business Outcome ☐ ROI

Project: _____ Purpose of This Evaluation: _____ Date: _____

Section I. Follow-up Performance Evaluation

A. Guiding Objectives and Strategy	B. Measures	C. Source of Data Collection	D. Data Collection Method	E. Timing of Data Collection	F. Results Will Be Reported To	G. Responsibilities and Notes
Business outcome objectives						
Execution objectives						

Section II Performance Preparation Evaluation

A. Guiding Objectives and Strategy	B. Measures	C. Source of Data Collection	D. Data Collection Method	E. Timing of Data Collection	F. Results Will Be Reported To	G. Responsibilities and Notes
Performance readiness: learning objectives						
Performance readiness: active management reinforcement (AMR) or companion strategy						
Initial reaction objectives						

Method to determine causal influence	Measure 1:	Adjustment for sustained impact	Measure 1:	Method to determine monetary value	Measure 1:	Cost categories
	Measure 2:		Measure 2:		Measure 2:	
	Measure 3:		Measure 3:		Measure 3:	

48

The completed form is your guide as the impact study proceeds. Of course, it is a plan, and plans must sometimes be revised as a result of unexpected events that take place as time progresses. Since the timeline of an impact study often ranges from two to six months, be prepared for unexpected events and the need to consider changes in the plan. At the end of this chapter, Part A of a nine-part case study is introduced. Part A of the case study includes Figure 3.4 (see pages 62–63), which is an example of a completed Evaluation Strategy and Plan. In the upcoming chapters, as the case study progresses through data collection steps, analysis steps, and reporting of results, different parts of the plan and its implementation are explained in more detail.

Adhere to the Five Cs of Data Collection   The five Cs of data collection are provided to help in the planning and implementation of the data collection strategy. As indicated by Guiding Principle 2, "When collecting data, apply the five Cs and collect sufficient data to establish linkages among performance readiness, execution, and business outcome."

Guiding Principle 2

When collecting data, apply the five Cs and collect sufficient data to establish linkages among performance readiness, execution, and business outcome.

You must have good data to analyze in order to develop adequate conclusions and make sound recommendations. Decisions on how to implement the five Cs will play a key role in the thoroughness and quality of the data collected. Since in most organizations, time and resource limitations require a realistic approach, the five Cs, as given here, help in making practical decisions.

1. *Credibility.* Remember that the stakeholders must accept the data as being useful, reliable, and legitimate as they view the source and nature of the data. As you develop your data collection strategy, address questions such as
   - Are the people who are providing the data in a position to know about the results? Are they close to the situation?

- Will people provide the data in an objective and unbiased way? There will always be some bias, but do the best you can here.
- How accurate and reliable are the data? Are the data being collected at the right time? Is there a baseline comparison (before and after the training)?
- During data analysis, what adjustments should be made to the data, and what standards will be consistently applied to do so?

2. *Convenience.* Always consider timing requirements, so that the times when the data are needed coincide with the times when people are easily positioned to provide the data. This helps in gaining cooperation. Address questions such as

- When people must provide data, always ask: is there a place, situation, or time frame that is more convenient for them? How can I adjust my methods to accommodate this convenience?
- If data are available at a time when the timing is not exactly what I would prefer, will the data still be credible and useful if I change my original timeline?
- How can I make the data collection effort easier and more expedient?
- If credible data are already available somewhere in the organization, and those data would serve my purposes, can I gain access to them?

3. *Cooperation.* Consider the willingness of others to take the time to engage in the data collection process. Go into a situation with a strategy to influence the willingness of others to provide the time needed to engage in the data collection process. Consider addressing questions such as

- What strategies will I employ to seek cooperation?
- How will I inform my sources of the benefits of the data collection? How will I communicate "what's in it for them"?
- How can the sponsor of the evaluation project help me with a strategy to overcome resistance to data collection?
- Can I promise participants that the results will be consolidated and that their input will be confidential and protected? If not, how will this affect the integrity of the study?

4. *Comprehensiveness.* Consider the thoroughness with which the data collected meet the approved purpose of the data collection effort. Getting data that touch all the necessary bases is important to the accuracy and credibility of findings, conclusions, and recommendations. Consider addressing questions such as
    *   Which results and types of data are important to which stakeholders? For example, even though the purpose of a specific data collection effort may be to determine the business outcome, the study must show linkages regarding how behavior changed or how the performers executed the required tasks.
    *   Are the data thorough enough to support conclusions that will satisfy stakeholders?
    *   Is the timing of the data collection suitable to allow the complete performance cycle to occur and the business metrics to be affected?
    *   How can "causal influence" of the business outcome be established? How will I establish a linkage between the training and the change in performance so that I will know what really caused the results?
5. *Cost.* Consider the economic impact of data providers' time away from task and any additional cost of collecting the data, and then adjust expectations accordingly. Stakeholders appreciate the attention to saving time and money. Consider addressing questions such as
    *   Does the budget allow for travel and other expenses to collect data? Can I save time and money by using electronic media to conduct interviews?
    *   How do supervisors and team members feel about taking time away from their tasks to respond to data collection activities? How can I make my concern for costs visible and obvious to them?
    *   What compromises am I willing to make in terms of accepting limited data if stakeholders consider the cost excessive? For example, if my preferred method is focus groups, can I settle for a questionnaire and still get the quality of data that I need?
    *   Are there other less costly data collection alternatives that will get me the data I need? For example, can I use social networking

alternatives and still satisfy the purpose with comprehensive and objective data?

Collecting data is about getting people to cooperate in providing credible information in a timely fashion at a reasonable cost. Achieving this can be difficult because everyone is faced with managing her own workload and has her own list of priorities. This reinforces the importance of sponsorship and effective planning. Things do not always go as planned. Good data does not just happen. You have to work hard to get the data you need. So be prepared for a rocky road, but do not let this stop you from achieving your objectives.

Gain Sponsor Buy-in for the Evaluation Strategy and Plan   During Step 1 of the measurement process, there is an initial discussion and general agreement with the sponsor regarding the evaluation strategy. However, the sponsor should be briefed on the actual Evaluation Strategy and Plan after it is completed and documented in Step 3. Depending on the purpose of the evaluation and the visibility of the project to other stakeholders, the sponsor may want to know the full details or may be interested only in certain aspects of the strategy and plan. In any case, it is wise to ensure that you brief the sponsor and obtain buy-in for the plan.

As the study progresses, there could be a need to revise parts of the plan. For example, the data collection timeline may change, certain data may not be available as initially expected, or there may simply be a problem getting cooperation to collect the data. When changes in the plan are necessary or problems occur, the sponsor should be briefed in a timely fashion. The training professional should offer suggestions, communicate the implications for the project, and gain concurrence to make adjustments to the plan.

Plan for Collecting Data on Successes and Disappointments

Guiding Principle 3 says, "Conduct success and disappointment analyses and report both types of data." Data collection should be balanced. First, we are trying to improve the training and performance process. Second, executives are interested in the thorns as well as the roses. They know that things are not working perfectly. They want to know how an expenditure is making a contribution, but they also want to know what is not working so well, what can be learned from it, and what must be done to continue to improve. Training professionals should have the same expectations.

Guiding Principle 3

Conduct success and disappointment analyses and report both types of data.

The success and disappointment analyses should both be approached with a positive attitude. One approach seeks data to identify and understand the successes that may have occurred in the work setting, as influenced by the training and performance solution. The other approach seeks to identify and understand the disappointments or breakdowns that may have occurred in the work setting. It seeks to determine how and why the results fall short of expectations.

The sponsor should take the lead in communicating the need for a balanced approach to providing data and analyzing results. It should be made clear to those who are providing data that a positive approach is being used to discover disappointments so that lessons can be learned and improvements can be addressed as necessary. If the culture does not allow the disappointment analysis to be approached in this positive context, then perhaps the evaluation should be abandoned, since the reported results may be one-sided.

Develop a Project Plan and Identify Responsibilities

There are many things to do during an evaluation project. Usually there is more than one person involved to take on various responsibilities. Some people will have limited involvement, while others may have several responsibilities. As with any project, a plan indicating actions to be accomplished, timelines, and responsibilities should be created. Figure 3.3 (see page 54) is an example of an evaluation project plan. It includes several headings in the first column to illustrate different phases of the project.

Provide those identified as having responsibilities with copies of the project plan and regular updates. Brief the client on the status of the plan as required. One of the biggest issues you will face is ensuring that other

Figure 3.3   Evaluation Project Plan

Evaluation Project Plan   Project Name: Customer Care 101   Client: AJ Hinkle   Date: _____

What is the purpose of the evaluation project? Determine how customer interaction process is being applied and if customer satisfaction improves, and calculate ROI.

Action Steps	Target Date	Responsible	Information Source or Comments
Plan the Impact Study			
1. Determine criteria for comparison group and who is in group.	May 10	Ron and AJ	Cannot use East Div
2. Review customer interaction process and develop draft questions for questionnaire and interview guide.	May 14	Ron and Madison	Must wait on final revision to process
3. Design draft questionnaire and interview guide.	May 15	Ron	
4. Administer field test for questionnaire and interview guide.	May 20	Ron and Stacy	6 to 8 people
5. Client approves final copy of questionnaire and interview guide.	May 24	AJ	
6. Verify timing of data collection.	May 24	Ron and AJ	
7. Coordinate with tech group to arrange online details and portal for questionnaire.	May 24	Jo Ann	
8. Coordinate with person who will provide learning data and initial reaction results following delivery of training.	May 30	Ronda	Check availability of role-play data
Collect the Data (training delivered June 2)			
9. Contact custodian of customer satisfaction data and collect baseline customer satisfaction data.	June 2	Amanda	
10. Administer online follow-up questionnaire.	Sept 5	Amber	
11. Schedule and conduct interviews.	Sept 8	Ron and Amber	
12. Collect follow-up customer satisfaction data from custodian.	Sept 20	Amanda	
Analyze the Data and Develop Conclusions			
13. Analyze data and determine successes and disappointments.	Sept 25	Ron	
14. Analyze data to determine causal influence from comparison group arrangement and make adjustments to data.	Sept 25	Ron	
15. Analyze data and make adjustments for sustained impact and turnover experience.	Sept 25	Ron	Turnover is 20%
16. Tabulate fully loaded costs.	Sept 30	Sam	
17. Calculate ROI and analyze quality of ROI.	Sept 30	Ron	
18. Determine intangible results.	Sept 30	Ron	Interview data
Write and Present the Report			
19. Document findings, conclusions, and recommendations.	Oct 5	Ron	
20. Develop report and schedule presentation.	Oct 10	Ron	

people on the project meet the deadlines they have previously agreed to meet. Missing one deadline will probably affect another timeline date. Place special emphasis on the importance of meeting commitments so that the evaluation project can be completed on time and on budget.

Identify and Collect Baseline Performance Data

Identify how current performance data can be captured so that the results of the study can be compared to the baseline measure to determine any performance change. Baseline data must be captured on a timeline that is dictated by the circumstances. There are three possible times that baseline data can be collected: before the training, during the training, or after the training.

When the data in question are routinely collected by the organization, they should be available for the asking anytime. For example, data on customer satisfaction, complaints, revenue, absenteeism, turnover, and accidents may be routinely available. The difficulty in collecting baseline data occurs when the data are not routinely collected by the organization or when the program being evaluated is an open-enrollment program. In an open-enrollment program, departments are given a limited number of slots, and participants from several different organizations attend.

Participants in open-enrollment programs will not necessarily be influencing the same measures. During the planning phase of evaluation, arrangements must be made to collect baseline data in some systematic way. When practical, participants can bring the baseline measures to the class to be collected at that time. In some situations, baseline data can be collected at the same time the follow-up data are collected, several months after the program. Depending on the measure and the circumstances, people can sometimes reflect back three or four months to recall the status of a measure at an earlier time. For example, people can estimate the amount of time it took them to complete a work process prior to the training, or how much time they spent on resolving complaints prior to the training. Of course, there is a limit on the number of months people can recall a set of circumstances and think about cause and effect. This places some limitations on collecting baseline data after the fact.

Field-Test the Questionnaire

When a questionnaire is used to collect follow-up data, prepare the questionnaire for field testing prior to the training. Field-test it with a small sample of people who are representative of the population that will later respond to the questionnaire. This can be done with a small group of six to eight as follows:

- Explain why the group is reviewing the questionnaire (critical analysis and recommendations).
- Communicate that you are simulating a situation in which the group members would be completing the questionnaire back at their work location.
- Provide a hard copy of the questionnaire to each person and set up a simulation. Allow the group members time to complete the questionnaire. No questions or talking are permitted during the simulation.
- After ample time, stop the simulation and seek input on the strengths and weaknesses of the questionnaire.
- Express appreciation to the group and adjourn.

The process should take about one hour. After the field testing is completed, make the necessary revisions to the questionnaire.

BEWARE THE SILENT EVALUATION

Only one thing is certain about evaluation: training departments and training solutions are being evaluated every day by the users of the services. Some evaluations are ad hoc (impromptu) vocal evaluations, and some may be silent. Fair or not, they all result in conclusions about the training function and its programs and services. The ad hoc vocal evaluation is welcome because it is open and therefore provides an opportunity to address concerns that are brought to the surface. The silent evaluation may seem harmless. After all, if no one expresses his opinion, what is the harm? However, opinions are expressed in different ways. Silence is harmful because people place their own labels on their experience and the brand associated with it—labels such as a waste of money, a waste of time, unimportant, not helpful, not relevant, and so on. These labels may not be of immediate significance, but they are recalled from the deep consciousness of the mind at budget time, or when the C-Suite is making decisions about resources and business strategies.

Rather than allowing informal and silent evaluations to determine their destiny, perhaps training functions should use a systematic and credible approach to find out what is working and what is not. More important, the findings from a systematic and objective evaluation have the ability to determine corrective action so that expectations can be consistently met and reputations can be restored. It is vital that the training function allocate a portion of its resources each year to discovering the kinks in the training and performance process.

Since evaluation resources are always scarce, a strategic approach to decision making works best. Each year, consider the following approach as you determine your strategy in selecting programs for evaluation.

1. Determine which active or new training solutions have the strongest link to the key business strategies of the organization (or the business strategies of a key client department). Consider one or more of these programs for evaluation in the current year to determine whether the expected contribution is being made.
2. Determine where current problems or deficiencies exist in the organization and identify the active training solutions that should already be making contributions to solving these problems.

Discussions with clients will be necessary to identify the programs that fit into these categories and determine evaluation priorities. As an example, I had a client that was being cited by a federal regulatory agency regarding deficiencies that had led to noncompliance issues. The potential for deficiencies had previously been addressed the year before by delivering two training programs. After an analysis of what went wrong and why, these two training programs were redesigned, delivered again, and targeted for evaluation to determine whether they were now making the proper contribution. As you make your own decisions to allocate evaluation resources, perhaps you can add issues to items 1 and 2 that may be unique to your organization.

CASE STUDY INTRODUCTION

The nine-part case study that begins here is presented in Chapters 3 through 11 to demonstrate how the measurement and ROI process is applied. It is recommended that you read each part of the case study as you finish reviewing the corresponding chapter. Each part of the case study reflects the practices and issues covered by that chapter. This is an actual impact study with only two alterations at the company's request: the company name has been changed, and the product revenue and profit numbers were altered slightly to protect proprietary information. The study is presented as it actually occurred, along with all of the difficulties and issues that the evaluation team faced. Since few things in life ever go as planned, presenting the impact study as it actually occurred provides some good teachable moments. It also provides a snapshot of the role that practicality plays when planning and implementing an impact study.

CASE STUDY PART 1: TECH*READ* SMART METERING COMPANY

Background

Tech*Read*, a 14-year-old company, sells smart meters, gauges, and numerous types of measurement instruments in the industrial, commercial, and retail markets. Exceptional success during the last several years has produced significant growth in new jobs and advancement opportunities in the company's six geographic regions. First-line supervisor and management positions have almost doubled as the workforce has grown significantly.

Sam Winston, executive vice president (EVP) of marketing and sales, has expressed concern about a lag in sales and an increase in employee complaints in the six field sales regions during the previous year. He commissioned a Leadership Sales Effectiveness Committee to determine the key problem areas and recommend a solution. The HR and training departments were represented on the committee, along with corporate sales and field sales representation. After appropriate research, the committee presented the following findings and recommendations to Sam.

- *Finding.* Employee turnover combined with rapid company growth has contributed to an inexperienced sales force. The problem is compounded by the promotion of the more experienced sales representatives to sales manager.

- *Finding.* Analysis of employee complaints reveals an average of between 36 and 39 complaints per month in each of the six regions. There is a definite trend in the complaints toward a lack of coaching and reinforcement by sales managers. The most significant complaints are:
  - With the exception of sales targets, performance expectations are rarely communicated or are communicated after the fact.
  - There is limited performance guidance and coaching during call planning and sales calls.
  - Debriefing of field sales calls is almost nonexistent.
  - Performance feedback is mostly negative.
  - There is not much individual or team recognition for anything.

- *Finding.* Employee focus groups reveal that the sales manager deficiencies noted previously are contributing significantly to poor sales call planning and detail sales call deficiencies of field sales representatives. The committee recalled that Tech*Read* had implemented a coaching process nine months ago with little fanfare, and management had elected to forgo any training. Focus groups revealed that the sales managers are not implementing the process. A second round of focus groups with a sample of field sales managers revealed that there is a lack of confidence in applying the coaching skills.

- *Recommendation.* Provide training for sales managers in coaching and team development skills. Consideration was given to recommending sales training for the sales force, but the committee was advised that funding for this was not available.

- *Recommendation.* Track employee complaints and sales to determine how the coaching solution is working.

Before committing to funding for the project, Sam Winston asked three questions: (1) How long will it take to see results? (2) What is the cost estimate to implement the training? (3) Assuming that we succeed, how will we know that our funding is contributing to the results? The committee responded that improved coaching and better performance by sales representatives should begin almost immediately after the training, followed in three to four months by increased sales. The fully loaded cost is estimated at about $3,200 per manager trained.

Sue Brolin, the training manager, suggested a rigorous evaluation process that could measure how the solution influences the business results and even whether it achieves an ROI. She further stated that, to ensure success, the training solution should include a design that is performance-centered. She emphasized the importance of all solution design components being implemented effectively in order to develop successful coaching behavior by the sales managers, which, in turn, will influence the desired business outcome. She reminded the group how difficult it will be to change old performance habits without active management reinforcement from regional managers and the EVP.

She suggested the following solution design, which has been reviewed and endorsed by the committee:

- *Solution design component A.* Prior to the training, regional sales managers conduct a meeting with the sales managers to communicate a summary of the employee complaint analysis and sales status, provide an overview of the upcoming coaching solution, and discuss performance expectations for sales managers in their role as talent developer and coach.
- *Solution design component B.* Deliver performance-centered coaching training for sales managers, including sufficient time for hands-on practice to build their confidence in their coaching duties. Initiate an action plan for sales managers to identify and resolve their ineffective habits regarding their coaching duties.
- *Solution design component C.* Provide a Web-based job aid in the managers' tool kit that is user-friendly and will reinforce the coaching skill set.
- *Solution design component D.* At the beginning of each training session, have a formal presentation by the executive vice president. The EVP

communicates to managers his expectations regarding their talent management and coaching responsibilities.

- *Solution design component E.* Regional sales managers provide active management reinforcement. During the three-month period immediately following the training delivery, regional sales managers follow up with each sales manager (training participant) to discuss progress and resolve any barriers to implementation of coaching duties.

Sam liked what he was hearing and agreed to fund the solution. Sue said, "Sam, in order to develop a reasonable conclusion concerning the causes of any improvement, it will be best if we can compare results across regions during the evaluation. We need to deliver the solution to one region and withhold it from the other five regions until we can analyze and compare the results. This will require withholding the performance solution from the other regions for a period of three to four months." Sam was reluctant to withhold a solution that should increase sales, but he agreed on one condition. "Let's provide the solution to three regions and compare it to the three other regions," Sam said. "This provides an opportunity for an early increase in sales in three regions instead of only one, and it still gives you a comparison group." They agreed that the Southeast, Midwest, and Southwest regions were best suited to be involved in the solution and the study. Sue was elated, since she knew that this would provide the basis for a credible study.

Planning the Evaluation Impact Study

Sue began the challenge of managing the design team to design and deliver the training. She also began the planning for a business impact and ROI study. She met with the committee (a key sponsor for the entire project) on the final details. To ensure greater objectivity, Sue selected an outside consulting organization to assist with the impact study. The firm would work with Sue on the day-to-day planning and implementation of the study, but would actually report to the committee.

Sue and the consulting firm met with the regional sales managers of the Southeast, Midwest, and Southwest regions to obtain their sponsorship of both the delivery of the solution and the impact study. She emphasized the

Figure 3.4 Evaluation Strategy and Plan—Active Coaching for Field Sales Managers at Tech*Read*

Evaluation Strategy and Plan		☒ Initial Reaction	☒ Learning Readiness	☒ Execution	☒ Business Outcome	☒ ROI	Date: _____
			(Check boxes for applicable type of evaluation)				

Project: Coaching Workshop | **Purpose of This Evaluation:** Determine success and disappointments, business outcomes, and ROI

Section I. Follow-up Performance Evaluation: Active Coaching for Field Sales Managers

A. Guiding Objectives and Strategy	B. Measures	C. Source of Data Collection	D. Data Collection Method	E. Timing of Data Collection	F. Results will Be Reported To	G. Responsibilities and Notes
Business outcome objectives 1. Increase quarterly sales 2. Reduce documented employee complaints on coaching related issues	1. Quarterly sales increase at least 20% above comparison group 2. Number of coaching-related complaints reduced by 50% by the end of Month 4	1. Custodian of sales records 2. Custodian of employee complaint records	1. Organization sales records 2. Organization complaint records in HR	1. End of third-quarter sales period 2. Four-month trend before and after program	• Senior executives (summary of report with detailed backup) • Sales force and sales management (brief report) • Leadership Sales Effectiveness Committee (full report)	Program evaluator with assistance from HR staff
Execution objectives 1. Conduct meeting with employees to communicate policy and expectations on coaching process 2. Implement talent management and coaching policy to change habits and improve coaching deficiencies in areas such as • Timely communication of expectations • Performance guidance and coaching • Timely performance follow-up • Providing balanced performance feedback • Giving employee and team recognition	1. Team meeting conducted within 12 days after training; Manager (program participant) communicates coaching practices and roles to be implemented going forward. 2. Sales rep feedback on managers' use of specified skills and behavior in work setting 2. Sales managers feedback 2. Regional sales manager feedback on sales manager use of specified skills and behavior in work setting	1. Team members and HR department 2. Sample of sales representatives 2. All sales managers who complete the training 2. Regional sales managers	1. Completed meeting record with team members responding on key points covered 2. Focus groups with sample of sales representatives 2. Follow-up questionnaire with sales managers 2. Interview with regional sales managers	1. Completed forms sent to HR within 15 days after program delivery 2. Administer sales representative focus groups three months after program delivery 2. Administer sales manager questionnaires three months after program delivery 2. Interview regional sales managers three months after program delivery	• All HR and training staff (full report)	1. HR staff 2. Program evaluator with assistance from HR

Figure 3.4 Evaluation Strategy and Plan—Active Coaching for Field Sales Managers at Tech*Read* (*continued*)

Section II Performance Preparation Evaluation: Active Coaching for Field Sales Managers at Tech*Read*

A. Guiding Objectives and Strategy	B. Measures	C. Source of Data Collection	D. Data Collection Method	E. Timing of Data Collection	F. Results will Be Reported To	G. Responsibilities and Notes
Performance readiness: learning objectives 1. Identify management expectations on coaching responsibilities 2. Demonstrate full range of coaching skills 3. Identify ineffective habits and plan to resolve	1. Score at least 85% on feedback instrument 2. Demonstrated application of skills that meet coaching criteria 3. Action plan	1. Participants 2. Peer participants and facilitator during skill practice 3. Participants	1. Objective questionnaire 2. Observation using criteria during skill practice 3. Follow-up questionnaire	1. Near beginning of session after executive VP presentation 2. During session 3. Three months after training	Training staff and program evaluator	Program coordinator Note: Successes and disappointments for item 3 will be determined during the follow-up evaluation
Performance readiness: active management reinforcement (AMR) or companion strategy 1. Regional sales managers communicate problem, solution, and expectations 2. Executive vice president communicates expectations during session 3. Regional sales managers conduct two follow-up field meetings with each sales manager	1. Subjective observations 2. See item 1 under learning objectives (85%) 3. Sales manager will brief regional manager on how he/she is actively coaching and resolve any barriers to success	1. Regional sales managers 2. Participants 3. Regional sales managers	1. Not applicable; informal discussion 2. Objective questionnaire (same as listed in item 1 under learning objectives) 3. Not applicable; informal discussion	1. Before training as determined by regional sales managers 2. See item 1 above under learning objectives 3. As determined by regional sales manager during the three-month period following training	1. Not applicable; informal discussion 2. Training staff and program evaluator 3. Program evaluator inquires with regional sales managers about progress and issues	Program evaluator Note: Successes and disappointments for strategies 1, 2, and 3 will be determined during follow-up evaluation with the sales managers and interviews with regional sales managers
Initial reaction objectives 1. Participant positive reaction to program and job aid 2. Participant suggestions for improving program 3. Participants identify their ineffective habits and planned coaching actions	90% positive feedback on quality, relevance, achievement of program objectives, and planned performance action	Participants	Initial reaction questionnaire	End of program delivery	Training staff and program evaluator	Program coordinator

Method to determine causal influence		Adjustment for sustained impact		Method to assign monetary value		Cost categories
Measure 1: Increase sales Comparison group arrangement		Measure 1: Increase sales Sales management estimate of recurring impact		Measure 1: Increase Sales Profit margin from revenue		See cost breakdown sheet
Measure 2: Reduce employee complaints Comparison group arrangement		Measure 2: Reduce employee complaints HR staff and management estimate of recurring impact		Measure 2: Reduce employee complaints Historical costs with estimation from HR staff		

difficulty of the data collection phase and stressed the need for support from the management team. The EVP attended the meeting to communicate with the regional sales managers on expectations. Sue had provided the EVP with a checklist and informal coaching on important things to stress to the regional managers. Sue addressed the planning phase of the impact study by confirming the purpose, scope, expectations, and resources required for the study.

The purpose of the study was determined to be to evaluate the complete solution to determine (1) the success of sales managers in implementing coaching responsibilities, (2) the impact on employee complaint reductions, (3) the impact on increases in sales, and (4) return on investment. She informed Sam that he would have the reported results four months after the training and performance solution was delivered. Sue completed the Evaluation Strategy and Plan illustrated in Figure 3.4 and briefed the committee on the evaluation project.

CHAPTER

4

Collect Relevant Performance Data

A training solution to be evaluated for its business impact and ROI has been selected. The planning is complete, and the sample population has been advised of and prepared for its role of providing data for the impact study. While baseline performance data may have already been collected, the delivery date of the learning engagement triggers the timeline for collecting follow-up performance data. This chapter will focus mainly on collecting follow-up performance data, while also giving light coverage of collecting initial reaction and learning readiness data. As illustrated in Figure 4.1 (see page 66), Steps 4 and 5 begin the data collection activities. The remainder of the impact study depends on a successful data collection effort.

COLLECTING INITIAL REACTION AND PERFORMANCE READINESS DATA

As noted in the overview in Chapter 2, the evaluation framework and measurement process addresses two types of preparation data. The first type, "performance readiness," evaluates participants' readiness to execute the targeted objectives (the knowledge, skills, confidence, habits, and other readiness factors identified in the specific solution design). The second type, "initial reaction" (sometimes called a smile sheet), seeks participants' input regarding the relevance and effectiveness of the delivery of the solution.

Learning is an important measure in establishing the chain of evidence for a follow-up performance evaluation. In order to show impact, there

Figure 4.1   Phase Two, Steps 4 and 5

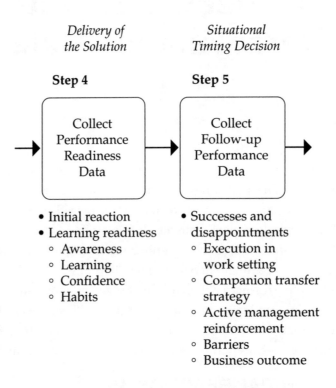

Phase Two

Collect Performance Data*

Delivery of
the Solution

Situational
Timing Decision

Step 4

Step 5

Collect
Performance
Readiness
Data

Collect
Follow-up
Performance
Data

- Initial reaction
- Learning readiness
  - Awareness
  - Learning
  - Confidence
  - Habits

- Successes and
  disappointments
  - Execution in
    work setting
  - Companion transfer
    strategy
  - Active management
    reinforcement
  - Barriers
  - Business outcome

*Analyze and report on the delivery of the complete
solution design, not just the training component.

must be some data to show that the solution actually worked properly at the preparation stage. Successful learning is a major factor that should drive the desired execution in the work setting. This is why the funds are allocated. While successful learning provides no assurance that the participants will perform in the work setting, it provides evidence that the learning engagement has done its job.

There should also be evidence that participants' initial reaction to the solution is positive. Initial reaction is the participants' input on whether the solution satisfied their needs and how it can be refined to make it more rel-evant and effective. Just because the initial reaction is positive does not nec-essarily mean that the solution will be applied in the work setting. However, it can be a leading indicator from participants regarding how effective they think the solution will be when it is applied in the work setting.

Collect Initial Reaction Data

Initial reaction data are useful for the training department in that they help it determine whether a program is on target and well received and how it can be improved. Generally, a questionnaire is administered near the end of a program to collect these data. Figure 4.2 (see page 68) is an example of an initial reaction questionnaire.

There are two types of questions on the initial reaction questionnaire in Figure 4.2. Sections I through IV are seeking a quantitative response, using a scaled rating. Sections V and VI are seeking a qualitative response, such as, "What will you do differently?" The areas labeled "comments" in Sections I through IV are also seeking qualitative information. The example ques-tionnaire also seeks a perspective from three different time frames so that a basic level of effectiveness for the complete training and performance pro-cess can be explored. In Figure 4.2, some questions address issues before the training, others address issues during the training engagement, and still others address issues after the training. Examples are

- Before the training: Section II, "Pre-course discussion with my supervisor was effective."
- During the training: Section III, "Facilitator encouraged deep and analytical thinking about issues."
- After the training: Section IV, "My supervisor will reinforce implementation of these skills."

Questions of these types can serve as an inexpensive needs assessment for the entire training process. The information gathered can be used as indicators to determine where to conduct further assessment of a specific issue that is a barrier to success. For example, suppose that 50 percent of respondents indicate that supervisors will not reinforce the implementation

Figure 4.2   Initial Reaction Questionnaire

Workshop Name: _____   Date _____

Facilitator: _____ Location: _____

Instructions: In Sections I through IV, rate each item on a scale of 1 to 6 using the key shown below and enter your comments for any item. Enter your responses to Sections V and VI.

Strongly Disagree	Disagree	Slightly Disagree	Slightly Agree	Agree	Strongly Agree
1	2	3	4	5	6

Response Rating   Your Comments

I. Workshop Content

1. Workshop objectives were met.   `1 2 3 4 5 6`
2. Workshop was proper length.   `1 2 3 4 5 6`
3. Material presented is important to my job responsibilities.   `1 2 3 4 5 6`
4. Handout materials will be useful for me.   `1 2 3 4 5 6`
5. This training will help me do my job better.   `1 2 3 4 5 6`

II. Key Learning Design Components

1. Pre-course discussion with my supervisor was effective.   `1 2 3 4 5 6`
2. Pre-course Web-based tool kit helped me to get prepared.   `1 2 3 4 5 6`
3. The revised work procedure will result in fewer mistakes.   `1 2 3 4 5 6`
4. Skill practice was sufficient to build my confidence.   `1 2 3 4 5 6`

III. Facilitator

1. Sufficiently led discussion on how this training can be applied in the work setting.   `1 2 3 4 5 6`
2. Kept the topic relevant.   `1 2 3 4 5 6`
3. Encouraged deep and analytical thinking about issues.   `1 2 3 4 5 6`
4. Used examples I could relate to.   `1 2 3 4 5 6`
5. Presented material logically.   `1 2 3 4 5 6`
6. Knows the subject matter.   `1 2 3 4 5 6`
7. Is professional and helpful.   `1 2 3 4 5 6`

IV. Participant Follow-up Action

1. I will work to eliminate ineffective habits that I have identified.   `1 2 3 4 5 6`
2. I will apply this learning to my work.   `1 2 3 4 5 6`
3. My supervisor will reinforce implementation of these skills.   `1 2 3 4 5 6`

V. What are the top three things you will do differently as you apply what you learned to your job?

1.

2.

3.

VI. What do you think will be the most significant barriers to implementing what you learned?

of the skills and behavior targeted by the program. This is cause for concern. Maybe there is something that the training department is doing incorrectly, or maybe the managers are misunderstanding their roles and responsibilities with regard to the training process. Maybe the managers think that the training department is taking care of training and that they don't have to do anything out of the ordinary to make it stick. We may never know unless more focused research is done to determine why this deficiency exists and seek strategies for correcting it.

The initial reaction questionnaire can be a very inexpensive yet powerful and effective tool to indicate what is going on outside the room (or the desktop) where the training is delivered. The corrective action that follows can make a powerful contribution to all training programs. The specific questions that are asked may vary depending on the type of program and whether it is a pilot offering or a long-standing program. When a new program is offered, or when an existing program is offered to a new population, it is useful to solicit feedback through an open discussion involving two-way conversation. This allows a higher quality of information to be captured.

Questions that address what the participant will do differently in the work setting may not be useful in some situations. For example, a new employee who is attending an on-boarding program may not be able to answer this type of question. However, it can be very useful in most situations. Participants may not know what will happen, but they are in a good position to provide an informed opinion. Even though this is a prediction, it is important to ask participants what they think is likely to happen in the work setting following the training. Responses can help to unravel the issues involving transfer that happen to be of significant interest with regard to achieving results.

Collect Performance Readiness Learning Data

An impact study requires performance readiness data so that we know the extent to which the first stage of the chain of performance has occurred. It is early evidence that the expenditures and resources allocated to the design and delivery of the program seem to be working. When the evidence is objective, it should be an indicator that participants are learning and gaining confidence.

With regard to the chain of impact, evidence of readiness is helpful in two ways. First, when transfer to the work setting (execution) eventually occurs, evidence of learning establishes a possible link between the two types of results. It implies that a relationship exists between the solution and the performance in the work setting. Second, if transfer to the work setting (execution) fails to occur, the evidence of successful learning suggests that the breakdown in the process may be somewhere other than the training delivery. Evaluation will help determine where breakdowns occur.

When a follow-up impact study is being conducted, readiness data should be provided to the evaluation team in order to satisfy the chain of evidence. The evaluators may decide to present these data in any number of ways, depending on the purpose of the study and the specific interests of the stakeholder audience. At a minimum, a summary should be provided in the report to show that the data collection was comprehensive and that the expenditure met the test of closing the knowledge and skill gap. Thus, the report demonstrates that Stage 1 of the chain of performance (performance readiness) has been met.

Figure 4.3 is an example of a learning assessment instrument used in a role-play situation. The assessment instrument is used in a training program for managers to learn coaching skills. It is used by table teams during multiple skill practice sessions with either a peer observer, a trained observer, or both.

Peer observers at the role-play tables are given the following instructions as they carry out their rating assignment using the instrument in Figure 4.3.

Peer Observers: Observe the person practicing the assigned role play. Observe the performance in each subskill area (developed rapport, discussed and clarified goals, negotiated expectations and development, and so on). For each subskill area, place a check mark in one of the five columns to indicate the level of performance observed.

Figure 4.3 Role-Play Observation—Active Coaching for Field Sales Managers

Observe the person practicing. Indicate how you observe his/her performance in each skill area below by placing a check mark in the appropriate level. Use the performance criteria provided.

Based on your observations during the role play, document what the person should keep doing, stop doing, and start doing in order to move to the next level and become a more successful coach. Individuals observed to be role models should continue what they are doing and help others achieve that status.

To achieve success in coaching, the person should:

Performance Element / Skill	Levels of Observation (see performance criteria)					Keep Doing	Stop Doing	Start Doing
	Caution	Okay	Good	Great	Role Model			
Reinforce the Relationship								
• Developed rapport								
• Recognized contribution								
• Discussed and clarified goals								
• Negotiated expectations and development								
Provide Feedback								
• Described the performance situation								
• Discussed behavior observed								
• Discussed impact on unit operations								
• Suggested action steps								
Facilitate Discussion								
• Facilitated dialogue not confrontation								
• Actively listened and asked questions								
Explore Needs								
• Discussed the current situation								
• Explored implications and impacts								
• Determined the ideal outcome								
• Identified root causes								
Guide and Support								
• Set goals and support for action plan								
• Brainstormed options and barriers								
• Confirmed commitment going forward								
Follow-up and Encourage Renewal								

For the overall skill area (such as Reinforce the Relationship), based on the performance observed, document what the person should keep doing, stop doing, and start doing. At the end of the role play, share observations in a candid and constructive way.

While this coaching role play is for serious skill-building purposes, the criteria for the performance scale inject a little levity into the situation. The criteria are an attempt to get the peer raters to be more candid and objective in their ratings without the concern of seeming too negative. The performance criteria are as follows:

Caution. Stay calm; you're starting on a new learning curve. Every skill has a learning curve. You'll get better as you practice. Don't get discouraged; keep going.

Okay. Begin using the coaching process, but don't tell yourself that you're completely ready to go. Keep practicing, and you will get better.

Good. You are on your way to being an effective coach. Keep practicing until you feel that you have moved to the next level and aim for role model.

Great. Pat yourself on the back. You are approaching becoming a role model in using coaching techniques. But there is still room for improvement. Continue to fine-tune your skills.

Role Model. Outstanding. Not much else can be said, except that times change, people change, and new and complex situations do arise. Keep your skills sharp. Continue to assess the changing environment and adapt. Help team members achieve at your level.

Training Professionals' Interest in Data That Demonstrate Learning   Training professionals have a keen interest in every aspect of testing and assessing learning. This includes issues such as validity, reliability, legal issues, criterion-referenced testing, performance testing, objective and subjective testing, developing multiple-choice test items, addressing test failure, test item analysis, improving test development—the list goes on and on.

Training professionals also need to know whether learning objectives are being achieved. Pretesting and posttesting is one of the best indicators of learning achievement, but it is difficult to design tests that reflect reality in some soft skill areas. While this book does not address the issues involved and the details of how to test for learning, there are three excellent works included in the References section: *Criterion-Referenced Test Development, How to Measure Training Results,* and *How to Measure Survey Reliability and Validity.*

Participants' Interest in Data That Demonstrate Learning   Participants are interested in data about learning because these data provide personal feedback on their progress. Feedback on successful progress ultimately generates confidence in their ability to perform the task or implement the behavior in real time in the work setting. In a perfect world, learning engagements should build in learning feedback and guidance that ultimately influences satisfactory performance to meet required standards. However, because of the many complexities and issues involved, such as insufficient time for practice to full competency, expense, and difficulties in recreating a performance situation, many learning engagements do not facilitate full competence. Follow-up companion strategies should be employed to continue the learning in the work setting, both formally and informally. Coaching is an example of a follow-up companion strategy to formally continue learning in the work setting.

A less formal companion strategy is to communicate the practical limitations of the learning solution and enlist the immediate supervisor to actively reinforce continued learning in the work setting. In essence, this is asking the supervisor to recognize the complexities of the situation and perform his supportive and reinforcement role by being an active player in helping team members reach full competency over a reasonable period of time. Tools and job aids to assist the supervisor are advisable.

COLLECTING FOLLOW-UP PERFORMANCE DATA—TIPS TO MAKE YOUR JOURNEY EASIER

Collecting data is about getting cooperation so that thorough, objective, and credible data can be collected from the right sources at the right time.

It is hard work, but it will pay off if it is planned and implemented correctly. Since the data collection phase of the measurement and evaluation process is the phase of necessity (no data = no results to report), a few important reminders are in order.

Keep It Simple

In addition to following the 12 guiding principles, keep the following reminders in your thought process throughout your planning and data collection activities.

- Be realistic; do not try to measure everything.
- Keep things simple; identify only a few key measures to track.
- When collecting data, minimize the disruption to the organization.
- Use the most credible sources when collecting data.
- Remember, these are their data; you are the messenger.
- Keep the cost of collecting and analyzing data as low as possible.
- Where possible, use organization records for business outcome data and monetary values.

The most frequent mistake in evaluation is the tendency to measure too much. That is, during the planning stage, determining what to measure for a specific training program often involves a stretch of the imagination. Consequently, a lot of energy and resources are wasted in chasing endless possibilities in the planning and implementation of measurement activities. The key is to quickly narrow down the choices to one to three business metrics that really matter and that realistically can be influenced by the solution. Of course, when a good needs assessment has been conducted, the identification of key metrics should have already occurred. Unfortunately, a good needs assessment sometimes does not exist, and the evaluation planning must address this issue.

Beware of Difficulties in Evaluating Open-Enrollment Programs

An open-enrollment training program is a program that is offered concurrently to multiple departments, with each department having a limited number of slots in each offering (each delivery). This is similar to a public program in which the participants are from different companies or agencies. In terms of data collection issues, e-learning programs also fit the open-enrollment scenario. While open-enrollment delivery has many advantages for the participants, the client, and the organization, it poses serious issues for follow-up evaluation impact studies. Here are a few issues to consider:

- Obtaining and sustaining sponsorship throughout data collection (focus groups, interviews, and so on) is difficult because there are multiple clients in multiple locations.
- Stakeholder expectations for the evaluation project (that is, the expectations of those managers who are sending participants to the program) are difficult to identify. The interest level among multiple stakeholders may vary from a passive interest and no expectations to high interest and high expectations.
- Data from company records have limited use. Since like data do not reside at all locations, participants may be the sole source for data on any change in business measures. Several examples are, (1) not all departments have customers or deal with customers in the same way, (2) quality in the accounting department is not the same as quality in an operations group, (3) employee turnover and employee satisfaction measures in different departments may be at different levels, and (4) cost-saving requirements and opportunities vary considerably.
- Participants from different departments are not likely to influence the same measures in the same way and may not have the same deficiencies on the same measures. For example, employee turnover in Department A may be well within acceptable limits, while it is extremely high in Department B.
- Everyone may be working on a different timeline.
- Baseline data are difficult to obtain because of departmental differences and geographic dispersion, as indicated earlier.

These issues make it difficult to identify specific measures, determine credible sources for the current status and value of business metrics, gain cooperation, and collect and analyze the data. Consequently, consider other alternatives first before evaluating an open-enrollment program. When there is a need to conduct an impact study on an open-enrollment program, however, by all means go forward with it. It is doable, but be prepared for the requirement to plan more carefully and the possibility of a more labor-intensive effort.

Advantages of Evaluating Programs Delivered to Intact Teams

An intact team offering is the offering of a program to a single department, a single business unit, or a single work team. While there may be some drawbacks to evaluating a program that is offered to an intact team, the advantages far outweigh the disadvantages. The major drawback is the possibility that the client may take too much ownership of the situation and may attempt to influence the data collection in a biased way. Careful planning and candid consultation can avoid this. Consider the following advantages of an evaluation project with an intact team as compared to evaluating an open-enrollment delivery:

- There is usually a single client who has "position influence" and the authority and willingness to sponsor the evaluation project.
- There is a single source to identify expectations and business measures associated with the evaluation project and to support data collection efforts.
- There is a high possibility that data from the business records are managed by one source and can be used in the study.
- There is a high possibility that there is a known monetary value for the business measures that are being affected.
- Performance deficiencies and baseline data are easier to identify and collect.
- It is easier to track improvements, identify the business outcome, and establish a chain of impact.
- There is a greater chance that the performance data will be of high quality.
- The timeline for the study is easier to identify, since most of the group are working on the same page, have the same performance cycle, and affect similar measures the same way.

When possible, make your evaluation life easier by selecting a situation that involves an intact team.

Prepare the Audience for What the Evaluation Is and Is Not

When someone comes looking for data, people often become concerned. If they are unsure about what the data may be used for, they may be uncomfortable, guarded, and reluctant to cooperate. Good preparation by the training professional and the sponsor can moderate this situation. Prior to the data collection effort, work with the sponsor to communicate why the data are being collected and explain the approach that is being used. Inform the affected population how the data will be used and reported. Address any confidentiality issues. Make the people involved feel comfortable by informing them of the following:

- The evaluation is reviewing the entire training and performance process with the aim of identifying results and providing recommendations for continuous improvement in the process.
- Evaluating specific programs and how people apply them is an important part of the process.
- This is not an assessment or evaluation of individuals or a team.
- It is not an assessment of the organization or its managers, or of the training department.
- Data will be consolidated and reported in aggregate.

People will usually cooperate when they believe that the objective is continuous improvement that can also benefit them. If they believe that the training organization is trying to justify its existence or put a feather in its own cap, they will resist the data collection efforts.

Share Questionnaires Prior to Implementation

When questionnaires are used for data collection, prepare the target audience. Since the questionnaire has been designed and field-tested during the planning phase of the evaluation project, this provides enough time to prepare the target population for data collection. During the learning engagement, take a few minutes to inform the targeted group of the objectives of the evaluation effort. Set them at ease. Answer their questions about the data collection effort, and gain their commitment to cooperate in providing data.

Share the questionnaire with the group members and let them know when they will be asked to respond. If some members of the group will be involved in focus groups or interviews, let them know how the process will work. The idea is to be completely open about the evaluation initiative. It should be clear that we are not trying to influence the data, but rather are trying to ensure the successful collection of the data. Assure the group that both successes and disappointments are important to the evaluation effort. These preparation steps will pay dividends in getting relevant data and getting them in a timely manner.

Take Action with Data

When people are supportive by providing data, they often wonder if anything really comes of it. If they believe that the data will not be used, they will be reluctant to cooperate. When collecting data of any type, consider adhering to the following policy:

- Ask questions that are important to both the respondent and the organization.
- Analyze trends from the data.
- Do something constructive with the findings.
- Let people know how the data have been used to make important improvements that benefit them and the organization.

When you are involved with others who are implementing data collection activities, use your consultative influence to help them follow this policy. If others violate it, everyone suffers the consequences, because respondents often base their willingness to cooperate on their collective experiences throughout the organization.

CREDIBLE SOURCES FOR FOLLOW-UP PERFORMANCE DATA

During the planning phase of the impact study, an early determination is made about what type of data is needed to satisfy the purposes of the study and meet the needs of stakeholders. This determination is based on the guiding objectives of the training solution and the associated measures that will indicate success. Recall that there are outcome measures, execution measures, readiness measures, and companion strategies. Several are listed in Columns A and B of Figure 3.4, the Evaluation Strategy and Plan for the case study. Once this information is firm, the direction has been set. Now the question in Column C of the plan can be answered: "Who can best provide this information in a thorough and objective way?" Table 4.1 lists 10 categories of sources and a series of six steps that are helpful in determining the best sources for a specific situation.

Answering the questions from the six steps in Table 4.1 helps in narrowing the choices for best sources. In many situations, the evaluator may decide to use several sources for the same type of data. The number of sources used is based on a determination of what it takes to be efficient, yet thorough and objective. Sometimes there is concern that a specific population may be biased in its response, yet you need data from that population. Getting the same type of data from a different source can be helpful in providing a balanced view and analysis. For example, one questionnaire may be

Table 4.1   Determining the Best Sources

TEN CATEGORIES OF SOURCES	SIX STEPS TO DETERMINE THE BEST SOURCES
• Custodians of various organization records	Step 1. What do we (my client and I) need to know?
• Operational managers and direct supervisors	Step 2. Who is best positioned to know what we need to know? Who should know best? Where would my client recommend going to get this type of data?
• Functional group managers or committees	Step 3. Are these sources credible to my client and other key stakeholders?
• Senior executives	Step 4. Will these sources cooperate in providing the data?
• Participants	
• Direct reports of participants	Step 5. Will these sources provide the data objectively?
• Teams or peer groups	Step 6. What is my strategy to gain their cooperation in collecting the data? What's in it for them?
• Coaches	
• Internal and external experts	
• Clients and customers	

sent to the participants, while another is sent to their manager. The 10 categories of sources are described in the following sections.

Custodians of Various Organization Records

There are numerous custodians of data in organizations. Someone in the quality department may be the custodian of all types of quality data related to the products that the company distributes. Every department also has its own quality measures. For example, someone in Accounting manages invoice data and has access to errors made on invoices. Someone in HR manages the database for absenteeism, accidents, employee turnover, and grievances. Data are available in many places, and in each place, someone is responsible for managing them, massaging them, consolidating them, and reporting them. Electronic data management provides an almost unlimited number of ways to analyze and present data for observation, tracking, feedback, and decision making. Custodians are there to make it happen. Sometimes you have to stand in line, so get your order in early.

Operational Managers and Direct Supervisors

Operational managers and direct supervisors of participants are usually very familiar with data reflecting the performance of their unit. They retrieve these data frequently, discuss them in meetings, and act on them to keep their unit or team efficient. Along with the participants, they have the best perspective on how skills, behavior, and work processes are being implemented and the associated problems and issues. They are a credible source for execution data and business outcome data that pertain to their unit. They can usually report objectively on participants' competencies, behavior, and performance before and after a training solution is delivered.

Functional Group Managers or Committees

These are the managers (and staff members) who manage a function that encompasses the entire company—for example, the quality department, the financial department, the IT department, the HR department, and so on. This group also includes functional committees. Functional committees are those that are assigned companywide issues. For example, one government client I work with has committees that serve as a lightning rod for strategic issues. There are separate committees on leadership, talent management, quality of patient care, customer service, political relationships, and so on. These committees are chartered to conduct research, broaden viewpoints (think outside the box), identify problems and issues to be addressed by management, make recommendations, and follow through as necessary. They are sort of a right arm to senior management.

Functional managers and committees can be a rich source of data. They have keen insights into issues as a result of their balanced mindset and the analytical approach that they must take. Because of their responsibility for research into issues, they can also identify other valuable sources of data, both inside and outside the organization.

Senior Executives

While senior executives have access to all kinds of data, they rarely read the details but do ask probing questions to seek more information. Someone else, such as an executive assistant or others in the organization, provides them with information through briefings and formal presentations. Senior executives are a good source of data on policy issues, strategic issues, and a business perspective. When data that span several departments or regions are being collected, senior executives can be helpful in encouraging broad cooperation for the data collection effort. They will be especially willing to do so if they have an interest in the program that is being evaluated or the specific business metrics that are being studied.

The executive assistant who reports to a senior executive is an excellent source of data. The executive assistant spends much of her time finding data both inside and outside the organization so that senior executives have current and historical information. The executive assistant not only understands the data, but also knows the sources to get more data or explanations when necessary.

Participants

Participants are a good source for performance data. They are often asked to self-report on behavior change and implementation of work processes.

While the credibility of self-reported data can sometimes be questionable, participants are often the best source available when data from organization records are inconsistent or not available. People today often work with infrequent supervision or even remote from the office, and they are in a unique position to know what is happening. When the evaluation project is on an open-enrollment program, participants often must provide all of the performance data, including business impact data.

When using participants as a primary data source, it is a good idea to get data from other sources close to the situation who can confirm the results. For example, there could be a coach that floats from team to team. There could be a person from the quality department who spends a lot of time with the group. During an evaluation with a pharmaceutical manufacturing client, the Food and Drug Administration compliance officer was used as a data collection source. She is on the property in the operating department four or five days a week and observes most of the activity. So, there are realistic opportunities to use multiple sources in many instances.

Direct Reports of Participants

Evaluation projects on leadership and supervisory training programs can sometimes benefit from data provided by the participants' direct reports regarding the performance habits and behavior change of supervisors. They may have frequent contact with their supervisor, and they have a unique before and after vantage point. Because of the nature of a supervisor's responsibility to engage, lead, and facilitate individual and group performance, direct reports are excellent sources for behavior-type data.

There are three difficulties with getting input from direct reports. First, they may know that a manager's performance has changed, but they can only speculate on the reason why. Second, they may be biased. Third, they may be self-serving and therefore may report on issues from a narrow vantage point.

Teams or Peer Groups

When a training solution is offered to an intact work team, the peers within the group are an excellent source for data on performance habits and team behavior. Team members are keenly aware of what is going on in the team, from issues with customers, to productivity issues with work processes, to behavior and cultural issues. This is true not only for intact teams, but also for peer positions in an organization, such as all engineers, all IT specialists, all managers, and so on.

Coaches

Designated coaches sometimes work with teams to bring them to a level of competence and productivity. Supervisors also have coaching duties and therefore have a wealth of information on performance and behavior. Executive coaches can provide performance data about key managers and executives who have attended leadership programs or on-campus executive programs. Executive coaches often have confidentiality contracts with their executive partner that prohibit any discussion of the partner's performance with third parties. However, arrangements can be made with an executive for an exception with close control of how the data are used. For example, the data from multiple executives can be consolidated, as it is with many evaluations.

Internal and External Experts

Internal experts typically exist in every department. They are often the go-to people for important data about the department. For example, the safety department has one person who tracks injury data and maintains the database. This person may also have valuable external contacts that have industry data, such as government agencies or professional associations. Industry data can be useful in comparing trends or best practices or identifying typical costs associated with a deficient performance metric (for example, cost of back injuries or cost of absenteeism).

Specialized internal or external groups may have relevant performance or cost data. The training staff has data on training costs, learning data, and possibly performance data associated with competencies. Internal subject-matter experts and external consultants are often a good source, as they observe the application of skills and behavior change. When collecting data from internal or external sources that are directly involved in designing or delivering the solution being evaluated, remember that they have a vested interest in the outcome. Therefore, consider other sources whenever possible.

Clients and Customers

Clients often have useful data or know where to get them. Since clients may be sponsors, they are also helpful in encouraging others to cooperate in providing data for evaluation projects. Their relationship with other managers and other departments is beneficial in opening doors to gain cross-boundary cooperation.

Customers can be a useful source for evaluation data. They can respond to questions such as, Did our representative make you feel welcome? Did she ask you if you knew how to use the accessories with your purchase? Did she ask you to consider a warranty? In some situations, such as relationship selling, customers can recognize a change in behavior before and after a training program. To provide feedback, it may not be necessary for the customer to be aware that the salesperson attended training. His frequent contact with the salesperson during sales and customer service calls may allow him to observe changes over a specified time period. Customer input can be useful for disclosing customers' buying motives, discussing how a representative helped to resolve a complaint or provide service, providing input on employee sales behavior, and other such purposes. Organizations are often reluctant to allow customers to be surveyed other than through the usual corporate-sponsored customer surveys. Evaluation data collection efforts may be able to piggyback (add more questions) on an existing survey or use the data from an existing survey.

EIGHT BEST PRACTICE METHODS TO COLLECT FOLLOW-UP PERFORMANCE DATA

The sources for the evaluation strategy have been identified in Column C of Figure 3.4, the Evaluation Strategy and Plan for the TechRead case study. As illustrated in Column D, the methods to collect data from these sources must now be determined. We know who the sources are, so it is easy to speculate and even confirm how best to acquire the data. We are simply creating the best possible data collection scenario by combining sources with methods and instruments to match the best timing. We know their situation, their interest and willingness to cooperate, the disruption and cost issues, and the availability of the data. Now we can select the methods

Table 4.2   Eight Methods to Collect Follow-up Performance Data

1. Organization records (preferred source for business outcome data)
2. Focus groups (face-to-face or Web-assisted)
3. Interviews (face-to-face, telephone, or Web-assisted)
4. Follow-up questionnaires and assessments
5. Observation/demonstration of the work
6. Learning and performance contracting
7. Learning and performance action planning
8. Shared media and user groups

that are best suited to the constraints and timing issues related to the situation. The eight methods of data collection most frequently used are shown in Table 4.2 and described in the following sections.

Organization Records

Organizations routinely collect data on many types of activities and measures. The data not only provide a trend for what is happening, but may also be examined in depth to analyze relationships, see more details, compare them to similar types of data, and so on. Examples of data that are routinely collected are customer satisfaction, customer churn (turnover), complaints, on-time deliveries, quality (deficiencies, errors, waste, and so on), revenue, number of sales calls, absenteeism, accidents, employee turnover, employee satisfaction, grievances, and time to complete various processes. Since these data are usually deemed to be credible and are readily available, they are the preferred source for business outcome and ROI purposes.

Data from the records can usually be narrowed to organization business units, departments, and even teams working for a specific supervisor so that performance can be tracked at different levels. On occasion, data from organization records may get contaminated in some way or may be erratic or collected and documented inconsistently and therefore of little use. For example, during mergers or acquisitions, much work takes place over a long period of time (months or even years) to merge the processes and data of the two organizations in a compatible way. During this time, the data may not be useful for evaluation purposes.

Focus Groups (Face-to-Face or Web-Assisted)

Focus groups are excellent for collecting qualitative data. They are more economical than conducting one-on-one interviews. Issues and questions can be addressed by the group, and people frequently piggyback on what someone else in the group says. Of course, this can also be a disadvantage if it limits the group's thinking or closes discussion. On occasion, one person in the group may even try to dominate the group, and some people may not be heard. These disadvantages can be minimized by a skilled facilitator. The idea is to tap the synergy of the group so that the quality and quantity of the data are greater than the sum of the parts. Focus groups usually include six to eight people and last one to two hours. When focus groups become too expensive because of the geographic dispersion of the participants, the Web can be used effectively. Software is available to assist in administering and facilitating focus groups online.

Interviews (Face-to-Face, Telephone, or Web-Assisted)

Interviews are very useful for obtaining qualitative data and encouraging success stories. It is easy to probe more deeply or to guide an interview in another direction to get more complete information. Trust and rapport can be developed during interviews, so it is easy to gain access for a follow-up interview if necessary. Some interviewers ask permission to tape-record the interview to help with recalling and tabulating the data. However, organizing and analyzing data from interviews can be very difficult and time consuming. The interviewer should be prepared with methods to make the administrative phase work more efficiently. Interviews are expensive and time consuming. While it can be less expensive to conduct interviews by telephone and through Web assistance, it is more difficult to maintain interest and get rich data using these methods.

Follow-up Questionnaires and Assessments

Questionnaires are generally the most efficient method of collecting data. Large amounts of data can be collected from a large sample of the population in a short time. This is why questionnaires are the most common method of collecting follow-up data. The quantitative data from questionnaires are usually more plentiful than the qualitative data. However, both types of data can be collected, and a wide range of issues can be covered. The length of a questionnaire is the most limiting factor in collecting data. People will usually not commit more than 20 to 25 minutes to complete the task.

There is little ability to influence respondents to complete a questionnaire, and people will sometimes skip questions or give incomplete responses. Questionnaires must be designed skillfully for optimum reliability and validity and to maximize the information that can be gathered.

Questionnaires can be structured to collect data of all types, such as changes in skills and behavior, measurable improvements in business outcomes (quality, revenue, cost savings, and so on), barriers to implementation, disappointments, and even ROI. Questions can be structured in several ways, such as two-way responses (yes-no), open-ended, ranking scales with a range of quantitative responses (1–5 scale, 4–6 scale, 1–10 scale, and so on), rank-ordering choices, or multiple choice.

Observation/Demonstration of the Work

In some work settings, observation is an ideal method for collecting performance data. In other situations, it is expensive, time consuming, or just not feasible. There are numerous types of observation techniques, such as telephone call recording, video monitoring, audio recordings, computer monitoring, and face-to-face observation. Face-to-face observers can be distracting in a work setting when people know the observer is there. It is best if the observer can be casual and go unnoticed. When people notice an observer, they may change their behavior. Therefore, the behavior being observed is not realistic. However, when an observer is always there, such as a video monitor or a telephone call recording during every call, the performer often becomes adapted to it and ignores it. Behavior is usually normal in these situations.

Observation techniques can serve several purposes. One purpose is to observe a worker's performance in order to make improvements. Another purpose is to protect property or to reduce the organization's risk of legal action or unwarranted complaints. Many financial institutions, airlines, and telecommunication companies use call monitoring. In some situations, all telephone calls are recorded, while in others, there may be a third party listening live. Law enforcement agencies use video to ensure that strict policies and protocol are followed, as well as for evidence purposes.

Retail establishments sometimes use secret shoppers to determine how sales associates interact with customers. A famous boutique in New York City uses secret shoppers for two purposes: to ensure that the sales force implements customer service policies and behavior effectively, and to calculate the store's quarterly customer satisfaction scores. The boutique concluded that secret shopper data are just as good as customer satisfaction surveys and can be structured to address important customer issues. So why pay twice? Other retail establishments probably follow this practice as well.

Observation can be effective and efficient in collecting behavior data in some situations. A few examples are

- *Retail settings.* Secret shoppers are an example. Also, the supervisor is in close proximity to employee activities and can easily dedicate time to observe.
- *Call centers.* Telephone calls are monitored. Calls are frequent, and in some situations the representative goes through the complete performance cycle several times a day.
- *Production or assembly lines.* This is a closed work system, so it is easy to see the entire work process from start to finish.

While observation is one of the best ways to know what is actually happening on the job, it can be expensive and disruptive, and it can create trust issues. The use of observation should be carefully planned so that it is not misused or viewed in the wrong way. In most instances, it should be explained to those who will be observed so that they understand why it is happening. They do not necessarily need to know when it is happening unless there are legal, ethical, or safety issues involved.

Learning and Performance Contracting

It is desirable that a participant's immediate supervisor be involved in the training process and support follow-up application in the work setting. When this occurs, there is a notable difference in skill transfer, beginning with learning and continuing with ultimate behavior change. Supervisors frequently observe the participant's performance, and they are involved in negotiating expectations, allocating job assignments, and managing the talent. It makes sense to provide this team of two with a tool that can be used to assist in performance matters. The learning and performance contract is a tool to facilitate agreement between the supervisor and the participant when setting expectations for participating in training. It focuses on performance and encourages a commitment by both parties to address beneficial performance issues during and after training. It can also be used for data collection. Figure 4.4 (see page 90) is a template for a learning and performance contract.

The supervisor and the participant meet prior to the learning engagement to develop an agreement that will satisfy the needs of both the participant and the work unit. For example, suppose an employee is attending a program on project management. During the pretraining meeting, the participant and the supervisor agree on the focus and set a learning objective. They also set an execution objective for what should happen after the training is completed. The supervisor commits to a posttraining job assignment that will place the employee in a project management role so that she can apply her new skills immediately. A performance contract such as the one in Figure 4.4 can be used by the evaluation team to determine how to focus the data collection for the evaluation. This type of tool can be used for any type of training program, and it is useful for open-enrollment programs.

Learning and Performance Action Planning

A learning and performance action plan is similar to a performance contract. Both instruments can be designed to focus on performance execution in the work setting or on achieving business outcomes. The performance contract presented in Figure 4.4 focuses on execution in the work setting. Performance contracts are usually an agreement between the participant and his immediate supervisor. With action plans, the supervisor may or may not be involved. Like the performance contract, an action plan is an integral part of the training design. The action plan form is divided into two parts. One part is the planning component, and it is completed during the training session. The other part is used to document results a few months following the training.

Figure 4.4   Learning and Performance Contract

Learning and Performance Contract		
Performer's Name:	Supervisor's Name:	Date
PART I	Agreement is reached on a learning objective for the training. Agreement is also reached on an execution or behavior objective to be achieved upon completion of the training. Action items should be determined and documented for both objectives. Results are recorded and discussed as they occur.	
A. Learning objective:		
Action item:	Result:	
Action item:	Result:	
A. Execution objective after the training:		
Action item:	Result:	
Action item:	Result:	
PART II	Agreement is reached on an assignment following training that is compatible with the objectives in Part I and will provide an opportunity to use the skills learned. The benefit of the assignment is documented, and mutual commitments are made.	
A. Assignments following training:		
1. We agree that this job assignment will benefit you (performer) and our unit as follows:		
2. My commitment to you		Signature of performer
3. My commitment to you		Signature of supervisor

When the action plan has a strong focus on improving business outcomes and calculating ROI, it must be designed and implemented carefully. The action plan process is a very good tool to use with any learning solution. It works well with open-enrollment situations because it accommodates individual measures and it can be administered to dissimilar groups from multiple geographic areas. Participants who work in different business units can use the process to develop data on performance measures that are specific to their own job and situation. Time must be allocated during the training to explain the action planning process and the data collection component. It is recommended that examples of completed plans be shared with the group during the explanation.

Shared Media and User Groups

Web-assisted user groups employing shared media or online networking groups can provide useful information about issues and behavior patterns of peer interest groups and other types of data. At this writing, use of this method is in its infancy, but significant efficiencies can be gained by using it. The HR profession has significantly reduced the cost of recruiting, screening, and interviewing by using this method. If HR can use this method for job interviews and screening, training professionals can certainly create better ways to use it for data collection purposes.

TWELVE KEY FOCUS AREAS FOR COLLECTING BUSINESS OUTCOME AND ROI DATA

As indicated earlier, the preferred source for business outcome and ROI data is the organization's records. When they are available, these data are usually deemed to be credible, and when they are readily available, they are inexpensive to collect. However, there are numerous circumstances in which the required data may not be available from organization records. Or the data may be available for a specific measure, but they cannot be tracked to the population whose performance we are interested in. Open-enrollment programs pose the greatest limitation to using organization records. This leaves us with the other seven options from which to select a method. Figure 4.5 (see pages 93–96) illustrates several pages of a mock-up questionnaire for a leadership initiative. The 12 questions are designed for use when performance data are not available from the organization's records. The focus is on business outcome and ROI data, with execution data completing the chain of evidence.

While Figure 4.5 is an example from a leadership initiative, slight changes can be made to most of the questions that will allow it to be used in unlimited situations. The 12 key focus areas can be designed as a questionnaire or as an interview guide, or they may be used in various ways with focus groups and learning and performance action plans. The sequence of the questions is important, since each question builds on relevant data from the previous question. This is logical for the respondent and it is necessary in order to organize the data for proper ROI analysis. Each question is briefly addressed in this section.

Question 1: Execution in the Work Setting

If this were an actual questionnaire, the first question in Figure 4.5 would be preceded by instructions, demographic information, and probably a few lead-in questions. Question 1 is the first impact question, and it sets up a sequence that runs through Question 7 to collect the data needed in order to calculate ROI and tell the complete story.

The questionnaire should be field-tested and reviewed with the sample population that will later be asked to complete it. Question 1 is seeking data about behavior change and execution. Since this is a questionnaire and not an interview, examples such as those shown must be used to communicate the full intent of the inquiry. Now that the respondent is thinking about how the learning solution has been applied—and hopefully has provided some successes—it is time to ask Question 2, how the business received a benefit.

Question 2: Specific Business Outcome Improvement

When the respondents are presented with this impact question, we are hopeful that they can link behavior and execution in the work setting to at least one key business outcome. Perhaps some of the participants work with customers, and they have been able to increase sales or improve customer service in some way. Maybe other participants have been able to create quality improvements in areas where there are discrepancies, and so on. It

Figure 4.5 Twelve Key Focus Areas for Collecting
Business Outcome and ROI Data

Example Follow-up Questions for Participants in a Leadership Initiative
Here are 12 key questions to ask to collect sufficient information to show business outcomes and
calculate ROI. Modify these as necessary to suit your specific situation. You may want to ask other
questions as well. Question 1 sets up the sequential flow to the other questions.

Participant instructions: As you respond to these questions, please reflect on how you have applied the
skills learned from the leadership development initiative (LDI) to guide and manage your team effectively
to achieve operational results and reach or exceed business goals.

Questions
1. As a result of participating in the LDI initiative, specifically what are you doing differently as you
   apply leadership principles and skills and support your team to achieve operational results and reach
   or exceed business goals?

   (E.g., specific behavior change such as helped team members with problem solving, increased delegation
   to employees, improved coaching and communication with employees, managed the development and
   potential of your team talent, etc.)

   Please comment specifically on what you have done differently and why you think it is working for you.

   _____

   _____

   _____

2. How has the company gained a *business outcome* improvement from the actions you listed in
   Question 1? That is, what KPIs or other important business measures have improved as a result of
   your actions or your team's actions? (E.g., increased revenue, improved profit margin, shortened an
   account sales or business process cycle, reduced waste, improved on-time delivery, improved customer
   satisfaction or employee satisfaction, decreased costs, saved time, etc.)

   Please comment on the business outcome improvements and indicate how specific business measures improved.

   _____

   _____

   _____

3. Think about the specific business improvements in Question 2 and do your best to determine a
   monetary value and basis for your calculation. A value may be available in your company, or you can
   provide an estimate. Include the time frame, such as per week, per month, per quarter, etc.
   The total monetary amount is $_____ per month (or per_____)

   a. Please check the appropriate box on how you arrived at your monetary value.
      ☐ Known value from company records or acceptable practices   ☐ Estimate   ☐ Other

   b. If "estimate" or "other" is checked above, please explain how you arrived at the calculation.

   _____

   _____

          (continued on next page)

4. Several factors may have contributed to your improvement. Along with the leadership initiative, *which includes the leadership training, Web-based tool kit, and support and reinforcement from your management,* some additional potential factors are identified below. Think about the key factors that helped you to influence the results identified above and assign a percentage of weighting from 0 to 100%. Select only those that apply. The total of the items you select must = 100%.

Factors That Influenced the Business Outcome Improvements	% of Influence
a. The CEO's actions in recognizing leadership competency	
b. LDI initiative (tool kit, leadership training, your management's reinforcement and support)	
c. Feedback from your team	
d. Your prior training and experiences	
e. Other (please specify)	
TOTAL	100%

4a. Regarding the leadership initiative (LDI), rank the three components as they actually contributed to your ability and willingness to execute your leadership responsibilities.
Place a 1 by the highest contributor below, then 2 by the next highest.

_____Tool kit _____Leadership training _____Reinforcement and support of your management

5. How long do you estimate the above business improvement will be sustained beyond today's date? Give serious thought to what may occur down the road and check the appropriate box.

30 days	3 months	6 months	1 year	>1 year	Other (please specify)
☐	☐	☐	☐	☐	☐_____

6. If your improvement is measured through individual time savings, what percentage of the time saved was reallocated toward productive tasks? (0–100%)_____%

7. What confidence level between 0 and 100% do you place on any estimates above? (0 = no confidence; 100% = full confidence)

My confidence level for my estimates is _____%

8. Based on your salary cost while participating in LDI and time away from your job, do you think the leadership training component of LDI represented a good investment for the company?

Yes ☐   No ☐

Please add the reasoning for your response:

_____

_____

9. Reflect on the extent to which you believe your execution of skills and behavior learned through the leadership development initiative had an influence on improving the following business outcome measures in your work unit or company.

Check the appropriate response to the right of each item.

Business Measure	Not Applicable	Applies but No Influence	Limited Influence	Moderate Influence	Significant Influence	Very Significant Influence
A. Sales or revenue	☐	☐	☐	☐	☐	☐
B. Cost reductions	☐	☐	☐	☐	☐	☐
C. Work efficiency or output	☐	☐	☐	☐	☐	☐
D. Quality measures	☐	☐	☐	☐	☐	☐
E. Cycle time of products/services	☐	☐	☐	☐	☐	☐
F. Response time to customers	☐	☐	☐	☐	☐	☐
G. Customer retention	☐	☐	☐	☐	☐	☐
H. Customer complaints	☐	☐	☐	☐	☐	☐
I. Customer satisfaction	☐	☐	☐	☐	☐	☐
J. Employee satisfaction	☐	☐	☐	☐	☐	☐
K. Employee complaints	☐	☐	☐	☐	☐	☐
L. Employee retention	☐	☐	☐	☐	☐	☐
M. Other (please specify)	☐	☐	☐	☐	☐	☐

a. Please provide any specific examples along with details:

_____

_____

_____

b. In your best estimate, how long will the top two business improvements above be sustained beyond today's date? List the measure and check the appropriate box.

Measure 1	30 days	3 months	6 months	1 year	>1 year	Other (please specify)
_____	☐	☐	☐	☐	☐	☐ _____

_____

Measure 2	30 days	3 months	6 months	1 year	>1 year	Other (please specify)
_____	☐	☐	☐	☐	☐	☐ _____

_____

(continued on next page)

10. As you reflect on your execution of leadership skills, what would your team say that you did to
"actively reinforce" their ability to perform, and how successful would they say you were in doing this?

Below, list what your team would say that you personally did to reinforce their ability to perform.	Level of Success: Your Team Would Say				
	Unsuccessful	Limited Success	Moderate Success	Successful	Very Successful
A. _____	☐	☐	☐	☐	☐
B. _____	☐	☐	☐	☐	☐

11. As you reflect on your execution of leadership skills, what are the one or two habits that you most
wanted to change and how successful were you at changing these habits?

List the habits below.	Your Level of Success				
	Unsuccessful	Limited Success	Moderate Success	Successful	Very Successful
A. _____	☐	☐	☐	☐	☐
B. _____	☐	☐	☐	☐	☐

12. As you reflect on the LDI initiative and your execution of leadership skills, what are your biggest
disappointments and why?

Please comment specifically on your disappointments:

_____

_____

_____

Note: These questions may be used for interviews, focus groups, team discussions, or on a questionnaire.

would be wonderful if all the participants set business improvement goals before participating in our learning engagement. If so, they may have a greater chance of achieving results and providing some evidence to show it. This is a key reason why performance contracting and action planning works so well. Okay, what about the money?

Question 3: Assigning a Monetary Value

When identifying a monetary value, it's easier to find the value for some improvements than it is for others. Known values are sometimes plentiful in organizations. Values often exist for quality measures, work output measures, accidents, complaints, absenteeism, and so on. When a known value is not available for a specific measure, estimates are acceptable as long as the right sources are used and an adjustment is made for confidence level (addressed later in this section). Note that item "a" under Question 3 asks whether the value is an estimate, and if it is, item b seeks an explanation. When the explanation does not make sense, the evaluator analyzing the data would elect not to use this value for the ROI calculation. Otherwise, it could become a credibility issue.

Occasionally a respondent will provide a range for a monetary value. For example, the cost of customer complaints ranges from $125 to $150 per complaint. Of course, this would be an estimate. Guiding Principle 4 states, "Choose the most conservative alternative when analyzing data and reporting results."

Guiding Principle 4

Choose the most conservative alternative when analyzing data and reporting results.

In the customer complaint example, since the improvement is a benefit, $125 is more conservative than $150. When the value cannot be resolved, the lower value of $125 is used in developing the ROI calculation. This is just one of many steps that can be taken to help ensure that the ROI will not be overstated. Estimates are more prevalent in organizations than most people believe. Engineers use estimates; accounting and finance professionals use estimates; executives make decisions using data that are based on estimates. Everyone in the organization uses estimates at one time or another.

I am not advocating the use of estimates. However, it is important to know that they are acceptable as long as more objective or hard data are not available, a proper basis for the estimate exists, and adjustments are made for confidence level. Even many of the so-called known or standard values are based on estimates. More data are based on soft calculations than are based on hard calculations. For example, when a company produces and/ or sells multiple products or services (which is usually the case), the company's indirect costs must be allocated across all product lines. These allocations are frequently based on estimates rather than actual utilization, and they must also rely on truthful and accurate timekeeping or reporting (we know how that goes). In many instances, the numbers are used to play games for political purposes, accounting purposes, or market advantage purposes. These games result in indirect costs being shifted from one product line to favor another product line. So, the real cost of making a product and getting it to market is often skewed by the use of estimates.

Question 4: Causal Influence

When a business impact is achieved, the central question is, "What caused it?" Question 4 shows one way to capture this through an estimate. Note the way in which this question is focused. It addresses the entire solution—the complete design, which includes the companion strategy of active management reinforcement. In Chapter 5, you will learn more about why it is a serious mistake to isolate the effects of "only the training or learning component."

When analyzing the response to this question, an adjustment is made to the data. Only the percentage attributed to the complete solution design (item 4b) will be carried forward with other data to develop the ROI. Should there be an interest in how participants view the three design components, Question 4A is used to report this relationship.

Question 5: Sustained Improvement

When an evaluation is conducted, the follow-up performance data are captured at a predetermined time, usually weeks or months after delivery of the solution. Not many people want to ride out an evaluation for a year or longer. This raises the issue of sustainability. How long will the improvement continue beyond the data collection period? Can the improvement be annualized? Are there other issues? Some measurement and evaluation processes automatically annualize data that are captured a few months after the program. The assumption is that when training solutions influence an improvement, the improvement may last for a year or even longer.

Some improvements may be sustained for a long period of time, while others may not be. Rather than letting the evaluator decide this, the people who achieve the results should develop a conclusion about this issue. They are in a position to know, although even they cannot be sure. But their take on sustaining an improvement is far superior to that of someone who is completely removed from the situation. It is their data. Question 5 captures the likelihood of an improvement's being sustained. The response set of 30 days, 3 months, and so on makes it easier to tabulate the data. Chapter 6 addresses sustained impact in detail.

Question 6: Time-Savings Adjustment

Some improvements are a result of reducing the time required to perform work processes or serve customers. Time is money. When time is saved and other things remain equal, it will ultimately take cost out of the business because the time can be reallocated to productive tasks. It is the job of managers and team leaders to see that this occurs. Of course, time that is saved is not always reallocated to productive tasks or to things that matter. Question 6 captures this so that an adjustment can be made during the analysis. For example, suppose that an individual saves 6 hours per week and responds that 80 percent of that time was reallocated to productive tasks ($6 \times 0.8 = 4.8$). The adjusted 4.8 hours is used in the analysis.

Question 7: Confidence Level

As Guiding Principle 5 states, "When sources estimate results, make an adjustment for the potential error of the estimate." This helps to keep the analysis conservative and minimizes the possibility of inflating the results. When the data are being analyzed, an adjustment may look like this:

- Estimated improvement of 30 additional on-time deliveries
- Confidence level of 80 percent
- $30 \times 0.8 = 24$ additional on-time deliveries

When the data are analyzed and conclusions are developed, the adjusted improvement of 24 is reported. When the confidence level question is asked, the respondent is replying with the possibility of error. Complete confidence is 100 percent. In the example given here, the respondent is replying that there is a 20 percent possibility of error. The error possibility could be on either side of 100 percent. It could be lower (80 percent) or higher (120 percent). A conservative adjustment of 80 percent reduces the result by 6 deliveries (from 30 to 24). A liberal adjustment of 120 percent increases the result by 6 deliveries (to 36). To remain conservative, the 80 percent adjustment is used in the analysis.

Guiding Principle 5

When sources estimate results, make an adjustment for the potential error of the estimate.

Technically speaking, Question 7 should be asked after each of the preceding questions that involves an estimate. But when this question is used in a questionnaire, it would be unwieldy to repeat it multiple times, and it would discourage the respondent from completing the questionnaire. It is much easier to inject the confidence question multiple times during an interview. Question 7 is the last of the 12 questions that contributes to the development of the ROI calculation. Data from the remaining five questions will be reported, but do not provide sufficient information for ROI analysis.

Question 8: Investment Perception

This is a straightforward question that yields very useful information. Some may think that this is a risky question, but it will quickly point out either that the solution is on target or that something is lacking. Additional comments are sought to clarify the respondents' reasoning.

Question 9: Generic Business Outcome Measures

The items listed in Question 9 cover a large range of measures. The idea is to list the measures that are appropriate for the specific population that will provide the data. When the solution being evaluated is an open-enrollment offering, the list of possibilities is lengthy, as seen in this example. This makes the measures more generic, since some measures will not apply at all to an individual respondent. For an offering to an intact work group that routinely affects similar measures, the list is customized and will be shorter and more focused.

Question 9 is an important question because the data will provide insight into the scope of the solution's impact beyond the detailed analysis in Questions 1 through 7. However the data do not provide enough detail for ROI analysis. Questions 9a and b are used to probe slightly and give more depth and credibility to the response. When Question 9 is used during an interview, additional probing can solicit success stories and more qualitative information.

Question 10: Reinforcing Team Performance

Question 10 is important for gaining insight into how the leader (participant) interacts with her team. Based on the content of the leadership solution, this question could be changed and even expanded. A self-report question of this type that seeks only limited information on one's own behavior may not seem credible to some. However, the direct reports should be asked the same question, either through a questionnaire, in an interview, or in a focus group setting. The analysis can compare the results much like a 360-degree analysis.

Question 11: Changing Ineffective Habits

This follow-up question should be used when the participants were asked during the learning engagement to identify their ineffective habits. More learning engagements should do this by requiring participants to reflect on aspects of their behavior that may be limiting their own performance and the performance of their team. A participant action plan usually accommodates the activity. Question 11 seeks to determine progress on the commitment to correct the ineffective habits.

Question 12: Disappointments

It is advisable to seek balanced information during a follow-up evaluation. Executives know that things are not perfect. In essence, the entire work experience in an organization is an experiment to determine what works best, make midcourse corrections, and keep tracking toward a moving target. That's kind of like life. Why should the results from a learning engagement be any different? Explore the thorns as well as the roses so that continuous improvement can thrive.

All 12 of these questions have one thing in common: they are performance-centered. There is ample opportunity during the learning engagement to seek information and collect data on learning. The follow-up evaluation should focus on follow-up execution, how it is influenced by the complete solution design, and how the business is affected.

The next chapter addresses the details of determining the causal influence of improvements in business measures. Before proceeding, review the case study given here to see how data collection is applied to a real situation. The case study began with planning in the previous chapter and continues throughout the upcoming chapters.

CASE STUDY PART 2: TECH*READ* SMART METERING COMPANY

Delivery of the Solution—Active Coaching for Field Sales Managers

The 12-hour training solution, "Active Coaching for Field Sales Managers," was implemented three weeks before the end of the second quarter. The experimental group—the Southeast, Midwest, and Southwest regions—implemented the solution, while the other three regions (Northwest, West, and Northeast) served as a comparison group. Five sessions were delivered, with 12 sales managers in each session (60 managers total). This accommodated all the sales managers in the three experimental regions and provided four table teams for role plays in each session. Two skilled facilitators were used for each session. The sessions were treated like a pilot offering so that the training solution could be withheld from the comparison group without raising issues. The three comparison regions were informed that they would receive the training after there was assurance that the pilot was successful.

Sue and the Leadership Sales Effectiveness Committee felt good about the design of the training solution. The needs assessment had provided good insight into the problem, identified why the business deficiencies existed, and helped to identify a good solution that could put things on track. A good companion strategy was included in the design that should encourage effective follow-through after the training. Everyone seemed to be focused on a results-centered delivery.

Implementing the Evaluation Strategy

The purpose of this impact study is to evaluate the complete solution to determine (1) the success of sales managers in implementing coaching responsibilities, (2) the impact on reductions in employee complaints, (3) the impact on increases in sales, and (4) the return on investment. Now that the solution has been delivered, attention turns to implementing the Evaluation Strategy and Plan (for details, see Figure 3.4 of the case study in Chapter 3).

Tech*Read*'s product sales do not involve seasonal fluctuations, and the sales cycle from sales call to sales closing is short. This makes the follow-up data collection easier, and results can be reported after only a few months. Sue implemented several data collection activities to meet stakeholder expectations, satisfy the objectives of the program, and establish the chain of impact. The program objectives and data collection strategy are summarized here for convenient reference.

Assessing Performance Readiness   After the committee challenged Sam (the EVP) about the need for management support, he agreed to open each session to discuss three things: (1) revenue requirements to sustain operations, (2) coaching expectations, and (3) the relationship between team performance and good coaching by sales managers. After the EVP departed, the participants completed a short assessment questionnaire on expectations.

The role-play performance guide shown in Figure 4.3 (near the beginning of this chapter) was used by the facilitators and by peers at each table to assess performance and give candid and constructive feedback. Every participant had his turn both as performer and as rater. The role-play scenarios were repeated multiple times to allow for ample skill practice of each competency, observable progress, and building confidence.

Toward the end of the session, the members of each table team discussed managers' ineffective habits related to coaching and developing employees that they had observed on the job. The table teams then reported these observations on a flip chart to the larger group. Following this exercise, each individual identified her own tendency toward ineffective habits and developed a personal action plan to eliminate these habits. Plans were shared at each table, and participants made commitments to their team to implement the plan following training. A few questions were inserted into a follow-up questionnaire to get input on successful implementation of the action plan.

Collecting the assessment data from the role plays and the data from the initial reaction smile sheet is generally the responsibility of the program manager. Sue coordinated with the program manager to get these data for later analysis and consolidation into her evaluation report. The data were to be consolidated and reported for the group as a whole to show evidence of learning and establish a basis for the chain of impact. It is not usually necessary to report individual data. Should there be deficiencies in readiness, this will show in the report as x percent of participants being assessed as having a continuing need to improve. The areas of need would be identified, along with a plan to address continuous improvement.

Active Management Reinforcement and Companion Strategies   Companion strategies should be considered for all training solutions unless there is a compelling reason that no such strategy is needed. Training professionals know that solutions designed with a stand-alone learning component face serious odds against achieving success. The coaching training initiative included three companion strategies. One strategy was implemented before the training (regional sales managers communication), one during training (the EVP session), and one after the engagement (regional sales managers follow-up and active management reinforcement).

Companion strategies are part of the solution design. They are put in place to influence participants to initiate and sustain behavior change. The follow-up strategy can subside a few weeks or months after the new behavior has taken hold and participants have the willingness and confidence to continue to apply the new behavior or skill.

While evaluation data are not always collected on companion strategies, it often becomes evident when these strategies are not working. In the Tech*Read* case, successful application of the companion strategies is determined by a few questions added to the follow-up evaluation questionnaire for sales managers and the interviews with the three regional managers.

Execution in the Work Setting   A credible impact study requires comprehensive data from the work setting. Executives want to know what people are doing to influence the business outcome. Not only does this indicate what caused the success, but it is a key source of information to help replicate the success in other situations or with other programs. Readiness, or learning, is the first indicator that the training solution is working. Execution is the second indicator in the chain of evidence that the solution is working. Execution is the bridge between the delivery of the readiness solution and a successful business outcome. Without execution, the impact on the business will not occur. This is why companion strategies and active management reinforcement are so important.

The first execution objective required the sales managers to conduct a meeting with their team within 12 days following the training. This helped the team members understand how the coaching process should work. It placed added pressure on the sales manager to follow through, since expectations became public knowledge. The other execution objective focused on the nuts and bolts of implementing the coaching competencies to meet expectations. If all went as planned, communication of expectations, active coaching, feedback, guidance, development, and recognition should be in alignment with the work processes. The evaluation strategy was designed to collect evidence that this was happening.

The data were to be collected through interviews with the three regional sales managers, focus groups with a sample of sales representatives, and a questionnaire administered to the 60 sales managers. After much discussion about sample size for the focus groups, it was determined that the size of the sample was not that important. The evaluation team felt that two considerations were important:

1. Since there were not enough resources and time to have all sales teams represented, enough focus groups had to be conducted to cover the three regions. Since there were two other data collection efforts (questionnaires to sales managers and interviews with regional managers), the decision was made to conduct one focus group in each of the three regions, using a random sample of sales representatives to select the participants. Each focus group had eight participants.
2. The second consideration was that, given that so many of the sales representatives were inexperienced, the evaluation team felt that it would be a good idea to get input from some experienced sales representatives who fully understood the process and were in a position to observe the coaching activities in their region. The team decided to conduct three more focus groups and designate the members, with perhaps only four or five people in each focus group.

Because of the short sales cycle and the number of repetitive times that the planning and sales call process could be implemented during the course of a normal workweek, the team felt that the three-month window for collecting performance data would be sufficient to show results. The regional managers agreed.

Business Outcomes   As the team planned the evaluation strategy and made decisions about the business outcome measures that would be affected, it seemed as if the discussion would never end. After the needs assessment, it was agreed that the key measures were sales and employee complaints. However, some people on the committee wanted to include other measures, such as employee satisfaction, turnover, and customer satisfaction. After a lot of discussion, the committee decided that even if these measures were affected by the training, they were not likely to change during the short three-month window. The team agreed that quarterly sales and employee complaints were the significant measures that would be affected. Sales data were to be collected from custodian records at the end of the third quarter. The HR records custodian would provide the pre- and posttraining trend for employee complaints.

Problem with Retail Sales.   There was discussion about how long it would take before the business measures changed and exactly how much of a change should be targeted. The team deferred to the regional sales managers on the issue of sales. After meeting with the three regional managers, the definition of sales was refined further. The regional managers suggested taking retail sales out of the study because sales representatives no longer sold retail. Retail sales had shifted exclusively to online several years ago, and they basically involved taking an order. Consequently, retail sales were dropped from the study.

Another Surprise.   Just before the training was delivered, as the detailed planning for the impact study was coming to an end, a slight problem emerged. After the regional managers fully understood how the three regions would be compared to determine the causal influence, one of them suggested rethinking the approach. It turned out that the Northeast region had a significantly different sales mix between industrial and commercial sales, and the baseline sales were significantly different from those of the other five regions. The baseline sales for the last three months and projected sales were similar in only five of the six regions. There were also other significant differences in the Northeast region that did not make for good comparisons. Therefore, the decision was made to drop the Northeast region from the study. Two regions would be used as the comparison group, with their sales averaged together. The three experimental regions to be trained would also be averaged together for the comparison.

Decisions, Decisions.   The regional managers were reminded of the solution design, including the companion strategies. The evaluation team then asked them what factors would determine the change in sales during the three-month timing for the pilot training. The regional managers reflected for a few minutes and responded that the sales opportunities in the pipeline would be a major factor. Sales are projected monthly based on historical data, competitive strategies, and market conditions. Since the managers had good historical data and the market situation was not too volatile, the historical numbers seemed like a good source to use in making this decision. But even then, how much the coaching would influence sales reps in their sales planning and sales calls to close the deals was a guess. Although there were a lot of unknowns and a lot of variables, a target of a 20 percent increase in revenue was recommended by the regional managers as an estimate.

5

Analyze Results and Adjust for Causal Influence

When a business outcome measure changes, executives and other stake-holders are interested in what influenced the change. There may be multiple variables—some internal and some external—that act on a specific measure during a given time frame. Therefore, it is difficult to develop conclusions concerning what actually caused a change in a business measure. When there is an expenditure on an intervention to close a performance gap and the results are evaluated, there are three options for addressing the causal influence issue: (1) ignore the issue, (2) when reporting the results, claim that all performance improvement was caused by the intervention, or (3) apply a practical and credible method to distinguish among the influences on performance improvement. The measurement and ROI process addresses the third option, as it includes methods for determining causal influences. This is a step toward answering the "why" question: why did the results happen? As illustrated in Figure 5.1 (see page 110), Step 6 begins the follow-up data analysis and addresses causal influences.

SENDING THE RIGHT MESSAGE TO STAKEHOLDERS

When a business outcome deficiency exists and the root cause has been identified, resources are allocated to determine the best solution design. With today's performance issues, it is rare that learning alone will close a performance deficiency gap. There may be other significant causes of the business deficiency, along with learning needs. In addition, as seasoned

Figure 5.1   Phase Three, Step 6

Phase Three

Analyze Data and Make
Conservative Adjustments*

Step 6

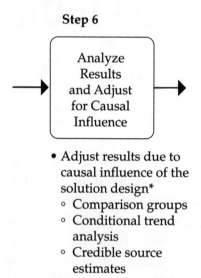

- Adjust results due to
  causal influence of the
  solution design*
  ○ Comparison groups
  ○ Conditional trend
    analysis
  ○ Credible source
    estimates

*Analyze and report on the delivery of the complete
solution design, not just the training component.

training professionals have discovered, even when learning is the primary
solution required, design features that aim at transferring that learning and
sustaining performance in the work setting must be included. Research has
indicated that as much as 90 percent of what is learned is not applied to the
job (Kaufman, 2002). When training is appropriately identified as part of
the solution, attention must be given to various aspects of the design. The
learning itself is only one aspect. That is, strategies are developed to ensure
that learning is optimized before, during, and after delivery. The other
aspect is to develop companion strategies that influence and sustain execution in the work setting.

The bottom line for any learning solution is, if there is no transfer to the
work setting, there is no learning. Part 1 of the Tech*Read* case study illus-

trates a solution design that includes built-in companion strategies to influence transfer. These include the skill practice during training delivery, the action plan to eliminate ineffective habits, the pre- and posttraining reinforcement by the regional sales managers, the job aid, and the involvement of the EVP.

Historically, by delivering training without requiring the necessary management support and reinforcement, we have conditioned stakeholders to believe that training is a magic wand. Instead, we must send the right message by including support and reinforcement for training solutions and analyzing how the complete solution design influences the business outcome. When solutions are designed and evaluated this way and we report results that are influenced by the complete design, we educate stakeholders and build confidence in what really causes the outcomes. This evidence becomes a strong message to convince stakeholders that a partnership can design solutions that achieve the intended performance outcomes. When evaluating training solutions to obtain this evidence, two crucial issues involving the causal influences on business measures must be considered.

Crucial Issue 1: The Solution Design

When determining the causal influences on a business measure improvement, it is important to view the complete solution design, instead of isolating the effects of a single component, such as training. The design represents the complete solution that the partners created to influence performance and the desired outcomes. For example, a pharmaceutical company in Asia implemented a high-potential development program that included the following companion strategies as design components:

- *Prior to the learning engagement.* There were 360-degree assessments, 360-degree feedback and development plan, dialogue with the manager prior to the learning engagement, and pre-reading.
- *During the learning engagement.* The two-week learning engagement focused on leadership and strategic issues (a one-week engagement was followed by another one-week engagement six months later).
- *Between week 1 and week 2 of the learning engagement.* This six-month time frame included a cross-boundary job assignment, continued coaching

by the sponsor, a midterm progress review, monitoring by HR, a project team work assignment, and a personal dinner with the CEO.

- *Following the learning engagement.* There was post-360-degree feedback, continuous coaching and learning, and follow-up on the action plan from ineffective leadership habits.

These companion strategies are an example of a complete solution design to drive a desired outcome. The solution designs for many learning engagements may be much simpler and may be in place over a shorter term. For any training solution or intervention, changing any one of the design components is likely to have an effect on the outcome. When a good design is engineered, the training professional should protect it from being watered down by others. It could be the difference between success and failure.

During the impact study, it is important to determine successes and disappointments for each key component of the design. This can be done through focus groups or other methods simply by getting evaluation input on each design component. However, when determining the causal influences for business outcome and ROI analysis purposes, it is inappropriate, cumbersome, and unmanageable to try to isolate any individual component. It is the complete design that affects the results. One can imagine trying to set up a comparison group or asking participants to slice and dice estimates on the causal influence of each of the factors in the high-potential program listed earlier. Good luck on the credibility of that one. Plus, there are variables in the work environment that represent even more influencing factors that need to be considered.

Crucial Issue 2: Other Influencing Factors

When a business measure improves, it is possible that factors other than the solution design may be influencing the improvement. These variables may be internal or external to the organization. For example, in the Tech*Read* case study, the solution is expected to improve revenue through increased sales. External factors such as the economy, actions by competitors, marketing and promotions, reduced product demand, and quality issues with products or services are just a few of the things that can influence a change in revenue. In order to determine the contribution of the solution design, these variables must be accounted for when applying methods to evaluate the causal influence. While we may never be able to determine the influences with certainty, we must apply practical methods to make the causal influence decision.

During the planning phase of the evaluation, the key variables that influence the targeted business outcome measures should be identified. Even when the needs analysis identifies these influencing factors, the sponsor or client should be consulted to verify them. Executive management may have a viewpoint that includes additional variables. Participants and their immediate manager are also credible sources to identify these variables. Training professionals should never be the single source identifying these influencing factors. Identifying these variables is necessary in order to develop an effective evaluation strategy to determine causal influences. One of three practical methods can be used to determine the causal influence of an improvement relative to all influencing factors. These three methods are addressed in the following sections. Figure 5.2 (see page 114) illustrates the chain of impact relationship that we are trying to establish when determining causal influence.

CREDIBLE METHODS TO DETERMINE CAUSAL INFLUENCE

Let's be emphatic here. There is no method that will provide an exact answer for why an outcome measure changes. Why? Because the answer will be an estimate no matter what method is used to address the issue. There will be more in the next section on why the use of a comparison group (sometimes called a control group) is far from a precise method. No one has devised a method that is precise. However, the issue cannot be ignored, nor can the full improvement be claimed unless there is compelling evidence to support such a conclusion. Guiding Principle 6 of the measurement and ROI process states, "Identify the key factors that influence business outcome measures and apply the appropriate method to adjust for causal influence." Making an adjustment for causal influence is a fragile issue because so many internal or external factors can cause a measure to change. The goal is to establish a linkage between the solution and the business outcome with an acceptable degree of accuracy.

Figure 5.2 Chain of Impact

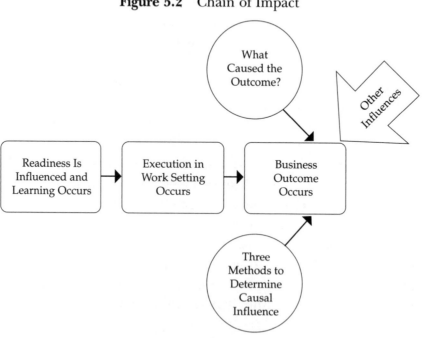

Guiding Principle 6

Identify the key factors that influence business outcome measures and apply the appropriate method to adjust for causal influence.

We are trying to provide evidence that establishes a contribution relationship between the solution design and the business outcome. Leaving this question unanswered and assuming that the solution is 100 percent the cause of the business improvement will seriously overstate the results and the ROI. It will also damage the credibility of the impact study, the training professional, and the training department.

Comparison Group Method (Sometimes Called Control Group)

Many people consider a comparison group arrangement to be the method of choice for determining causal influence. Although there are many variations in establishing a comparison group arrangement, in its simplest form it works like this:

- A group is selected to be involved in the solution. Specific criteria are developed to apply in selecting the group (see the discussion of criteria later in this section). This group is the *experimental group.*
- Another group that has the same or similar characteristics and that influences the variables in the same way is also chosen. Specific criteria are developed to use in selecting the matching groups (see the discussion of criteria later in this section). The selection process may also be random. However, when there are multiple variables and issues, it is easy for random selection to lead to a mismatch unless the sample is very large. The solution is withheld from this second group. This is the *comparison group.*
- The two groups together form the *comparison group arrangement.* Neither group should be aware of the comparison, as this awareness could influence a change in performance.
- The comparison group arrangement must be intact for the duration of the data collection period. This is the predetermined time allowed to collect the follow-up performance data. After this point has passed, the arrangement can be dissolved.
- Baseline and follow-up performance data from each group are analyzed. The results are compared, and the difference between the two groups is attributed to the solution.

Scheduling to allow time for the data collection to be completed can be addressed in two ways: (1) communicate that a pilot program is being conducted and that if it is determined to be successful, others will be offered the program, or (2) when allowed by the size of the eligible population, schedule the delivery of offerings to the experimental group first, and then schedule the comparison group after the data collection time frame.

Practical Issues with Comparison Group Arrangements   Many issues may arise in establishing a comparison group arrangement that may make it impractical to use this arrangement in some situations. It is not always acceptable to withhold a solution from part of the population for a time period when management is convinced that the solution will help solve an operational problem. The time frame of the impact study is a major factor in making this decision. When the data collection window is two months as compared to six months, it is easier to gain agreement for a comparison group arrangement.

Another key factor that often prevents the use of a comparison group arrangement is the number of key variables identified that can influence the business outcome. The more variables there are the more difficult it is to find or create two groups that match across all variables. When a comparison group match does not exist, the comparison group arrangement cannot be used.

Contamination can easily occur with a comparison group arrangement. When one or more members of the comparison group become aware of the solution or when the two groups are in the same location and teaching or coaching bleeds over from the experimental group, this spoils the arrangement. Employee transfers can also spoil the arrangement. Care must be exercised to keep the groups separated. This can be aided by selecting groups that are in different geographic locations or situated in different buildings.

As discussed in detail earlier, it is more accurate and makes more practical sense to determine the causal influence of the complete solution design rather than "only the learning component." When there is a compelling reason to break out the learning component to analyze its influence, the comparison group is the best method to use. An example may be when new technology is implemented and there is a training component to the technology solution. The client may believe that the technology is not complex enough to warrant the training and therefore may want to implement the technology without paying for the training. When the partners are agreeable, a pilot training session and a comparison group can be used to determine the value of the training component. The experimental group's solution would include both the technology and the training. The other group would be given the technology without the training. The evaluation would analyze the difference between the two groups in terms of time to productivity, number of errors, and any other metric that may be of interest in the specific situation. For example, maybe the user group interacts with customers and the proper application of the technology may affect customer satisfaction or customer complaints.

Criteria for a Comparison Group Arrangement   The key element in developing credible comparison groups is the criteria used to select the groups. Figure 5.3 gives an example of the steps to follow in developing the criteria for a comparison group.

Figure 5.3   Steps to Determine Comparison Group Criteria—Example

Steps to Determine Comparison Group Criteria—Example	
Identify the solution being evaluated, the population involved, and the nature of their work environment. *Active Coaching for Field Sales Managers (from TechRead case study). Sales manager manages geographic territory sales operation. Directs and facilitates sales reps to plan and make sales calls in regional field environment. Manager and reps located in field offices. Reps often travel and work alone.*	
Step 1	Select only one of the business outcome measures that your solution should influence (sales, quality, complaints, customer satisfaction, etc.). The measure is: *Sales of smart metering devices.*
Step 2	Identify the time frame necessary to monitor progress and collect data to determine if the selected measure has changed (must be sufficient to allow the targeted performance cycle to occur). The time frame is: *Three* (months)
Step 3	Identify the key internal and external variables—other than the solution being delivered—that could influence a change in the measure in the performance setting during the established time frame. The key variables are: a. *Customer churn experience (turnover).* b. *Sales rep turnover experience.* c. *Sales opportunities in pipeline.* d. *Market conditions (economy, sales promotions, strength of competitors).* e. *Experience and training of sales reps and sales managers.* f. *Density of customer base, mix of customers, and number of customers per sales rep.*
Step 4	Use the factors identified in Step 3 as a basis (criteria) to select the comparison group arrangement. Select the groups by matching those with characteristics and job situations having these factors in common.

The results from Step 3 in Figure 5.3 become the criteria for selecting the comparison group. The goal is to determine the best fit for the comparison group. The fit will never be perfect, and it will always be somewhat deficient. We are looking for a reasonable fit that will satisfy key stakeholders as being credible when developing conclusions as to how the solution influenced the business outcome. When determining the criteria for developing a comparison group arrangement, it is important that the steps be followed in the exact sequence shown in Figure 5.3. A different set of variables is likely to develop in Step 3 when the time frame in Step 2 changes, and this affects which groups will be a reasonable match. After the variables are identified in Step 3, it is a matter of finding the right match for the arrangement (Step 4). If an acceptable match does not exist, another method must be used to determine causal influence.

As can be surmised from a review of the example in Figure 5.3, it can be very difficult to arrive at a good match. Compromises in the criteria almost always have to be made. For example, item e in Step 3 (experience and training) will not be easy to match. You just have to decide if the differences might influence small or large increments of performance (at least 70 percent confidence level is recommended for this decision). You will probably never know with certainty. With every compromise in the criteria comes a weakening of the comparison group match. This in turn skews and waters down any conclusions about the causal influence, which may ultimately be no better than a bystander's estimate. To paraphrase an earlier statement at the beginning of this chapter, "Comparison groups are an estimate even in the best-case scenario." Add in another issue: when a solution is targeted to influence more than one outcome measure, the steps in Figure 5.3 must be repeated for each measure. This further complicates the ability to use comparison groups if additional measures require different time frames and/or different comparison groups. It is always tempting to make compromises in the comparison group criteria. Do your best to find a good match.

Review Part 3 of the TechRead case study at the end of this chapter to see an example of a causal influence analysis using the comparison group arrangement method. You will also see how a surprise variable entered the picture when the final sales data were being collected and analyzed. Surprises do happen, some good and some bad.

Conditional Trend Analysis Method

Just as the comparison group method is an estimate, so is the conditional trend analysis method. Trend-line analysis is often used to show how data have changed (or might change) during a specific time frame compared to a previous comparable time frame. Sometimes, those who display or view such data assume that the intervention being discussed is the single factor that is influencing the measure being portrayed. While this could be true, it may not necessarily be the case. Trend lines may be used at any time to show a before and after snapshot of an event or intervention. However, using trend analysis to show a cause-and-effect relationship is another matter. Two conditions must be met in order to use trend analysis to determine causal influence. This is why it is called conditional trend analysis.

Trend Analysis Condition 1   There must be sufficient historical data available from which to establish a reasonable trend for comparison purposes. The historical data must be stable enough to establish a reasonable trend, as opposed to there being significant erratic movements in the data (for example, a measure is extremely high one month and extremely low the next month). The acceptable historical and posttraining time frame (three months, six months, or some other period) is dictated by the specific measure (sales, quality, complaints, customer satisfaction, and so on) and the stakeholders' comfort level that the specific pre- and posttraining time period reflects stable conditions acting on the measure. An example of an unstable situation may occur when sales are cyclical because of a holiday, distinguishing characteristics of a product, or because of consumer buying habits during a posttraining time period that differ from the pretraining time period.

Trend Analysis Condition 2   During the follow-up time frame from delivery until the data will be collected, there must be no new influences on the measure being analyzed, other than the solution design. In effect, this means that the pretraining solution trend will continue on the same path unless it is changed by the training solution. If it holds true when the follow-up data are collected that no other variables influenced the measure, any change in the trend during the post-data collection time frame is deemed to be caused by the training solution.

Unless the two aforementioned conditions are met, the trend analysis method cannot be used to determine causal influence.

Example of Conditional Trend Analysis Method   When conditional trend analysis meets the test for use, the post-solution data are plotted and compared to the pre-solution historical trend to show how the measure changed. Figure 5.4 illustrates an example of the conditional trend analysis method.

Figure 5.4 shows the DigitalWave Cellular monthly report on order fulfillment, which is being reviewed during the month of September. The report shows a steady upward trend in errors in filling customer orders. The

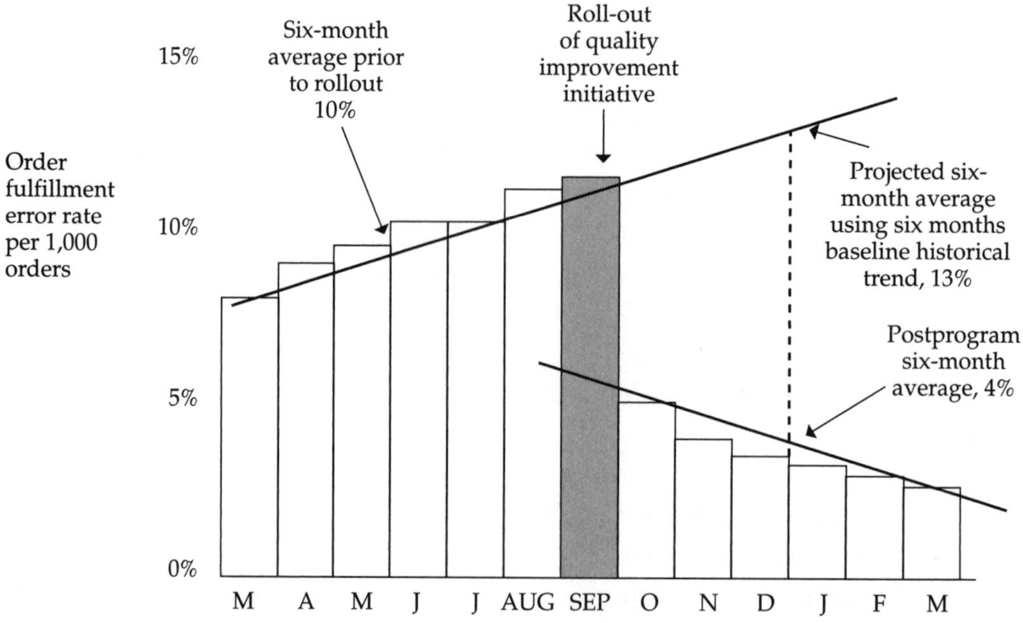

Figure 5.4   DigitalWave Cellular—Example of Conditional Trend Analysis Method

previous six-month trend is 10 percent errors per 1,000 orders filled per month. The most recent month (August) is at 11.5 percent. This trend in discrepancies is costly. The rework cost averages $100 per error. That's $10,000 per month waste (10 percent pretraining is 100 errors × $100 value). A quick analysis of performance issues has pinpointed the major reasons for the upward trend in errors. In order to improve cost efficiency and deliver more error-free order fulfillment, management has sponsored a quality improvement initiative based on the findings.

The quality initiative included three key design components: (1) a hands-on four-hour training session focusing on capturing and documenting the specifications of customer orders, (2) follow-up supervisor coaching to encourage thorough communication and proper documentation of orders, and (3) management focus on reducing errors through a monthly recognition program.

All employees participated in the initiative, which was rolled out in September. After the program was completed, the training staff was asked to measure the impact that the quality initiative had on proper execution and the reduction of order fulfillment errors. Figure 5.4 shows the relative trend of errors six months before and six months after the quality initiative was implemented.

The analysis reveals an improvement influenced by the quality initiative. The discrepancies would have been at 13 percent had we done nothing because this was the pretraining trend. The 13 percent projected trend minus the 4 percent posttraining actual = 9 percent.

With 1,000 orders per month, a 9 percent error rate = a reduction of 90 errors. A more conservative estimate would be to use 6 percent (10 percent pretraining trend minus 4 percent posttraining), or a reduction of 60 errors.

A reduction of 60 errors × a value of $100 per error = $6,000 per month savings. If it is appropriate to annualize the full amount, this is $72,000 annual savings influenced by the quality initiative.

Conditional trend analysis may be used to determine causal influence as long as the two aforementioned conditions are met. It is likely that this method may have limited use, since one of the conditions is that the post-intervention data collection period cannot be influenced by any variable except the solution design. While there are situations where the use of trending may be appropriate, it will usually be used in closed performance systems. Assembly lines or manufacturing operations are examples of closed performance systems. In a closed performance system, it is usually easier to determine the variables that influence performance, as there is limited influence from outside factors, and performance is usually influenced mostly by the immediate surroundings of the performers.

Situations in which there is a short window for follow-up data collection (weeks and not months) may also be candidates for use of the conditional trend analysis method. A shorter time window for collecting data can mean that fewer variables enter the picture. Some call centers may fit both the closed performance system and the short window scenarios.

Credible Source Estimates Method

When the comparison group and conditional trend analysis methods cannot be used, estimates from credible sources may be an acceptable method. This estimation method may utilize any source that key stakeholders consider to be credible.

Sources for Estimates   While the use of estimates is only one method for determining causal influence, this method can be varied through the use of numerous sources and techniques. When estimates are used, it is important to use the right source to match the needs and circumstances of the situation. Table 5.1 lists the possible sources and a possible basis for using each one. These sources are generally considered credible as input to determine the causal influence.

Sources can be combined in any way that is practical in order to provide multiple inputs. It is often useful to see and analyze a situation from different vantage points. It is important to remember that one source may have a better vantage point than another and therefore may be both more credible and more accurate. Always ask for a confidence level with estimates, and make the necessary conservative adjustment.

Advantages to Using the Credible Source Estimates Method   There are actually some advantages to using the estimation method rather than the com-

Table 5.1   Credible Sources

SOURCE	BASIS FOR USE IN DETERMINING CAUSAL INFLUENCE
Performers (participants)	They are often uniquely positioned to answer the "why" question. The participants' execution in the work setting should be at least partially responsible for the business outcome improvement.
Immediate supervisor of participants	Immediate supervisors are often close to the action and can provide key input. In some scenarios, the participants' immediate supervisor may be more familiar with the other factors that influence performance and therefore can assist in allocating influence among the key variables.
Management	Department heads, senior managers, and executives can sometimes offer a broader viewpoint and address variables that others may not know about. Management also may be allowed to make adjustments to participants' or supervisors' estimates when it is considered necessary.
Experts	Experts can provide insight, but they should rarely be used as the only source. Observations from experts must be impartial in order to combine their estimates with those from other sources that will be used for adjustments to the data. Experts who are routinely involved with a specific measure can offer insight into how other factors and the training solution may influence that measure. For example, custodians of business records can often provide impartial insight into factors that influence a measure. Conversely, it is inappropriate to use vendor input when it is the vendor's program that is being evaluated.
Customers	Customers can sometimes offer insight, but with limitations. They may be aware that an individual's performance has changed. However, when addressing causal influence, we are trying to answer the "why" question. Customers usually do not have a way of knowing why performance changed. Therefore, customers can provide credible input in situations in which they are able to observe before and after performance. Using this customer input, other credible sources can then link the change to the training solution that is being evaluated.

parison group or conditional trend analysis method. Consider the following advantages when using credible sources to estimate causal influence:

- There is the flexibility to determine the best sources depending on the scenario.
- More than one source may be used to add to the credibility.
- When estimating is used, the human element can include a wide range of potential influencing factors and unusual circumstances that the other methods will not identify.

- Estimates can always be used as a backup to the comparison group and trending methods. A backup is always advised when comparison groups and trending are used because the unexpected may happen, such as spoilage of the arrangement or a new variable entering the picture.

While there are many advantages to using estimates, the disadvantage of how they may be perceived is a significant drawback. Estimates are often viewed as "guessing with no realistic basis." Therefore, when using estimates, it is of extreme importance that a basis for the estimate be provided and that Guiding Principle 5 be followed and an adjustment for confidence level be made to account for the possibility of error. Guiding Principle 4 is also applied to ensure that the most conservative alternative is chosen for calculations.

Approach When Using Estimates to Determine Causal Influence   When estimates are used to determine causal influence, a systematic approach must be applied that sets the context and allows the sources to think through the possibilities. Briefly refer to Chapter 4 for an example. Chapter 4 includes a 12-item questionnaire, illustrated in Figure 4.5. The questionnaire is an example of systematically setting the performance context and collecting data. The full set of 12 questions is often used to collect performance data from participants and their immediate supervisors. Only some of the questions would be used with other sources. For example, most of these questions would not be used with a customer. Customers would simply be asked how or when the participant's skills or behaviors were used and how effective they were in performance situations such as providing satisfactory service, making the customer feel valued, influencing the customer's confidence in the company or a specific product, influencing the customer to return or make additional purchases, or closing a sale.

Estimates Using a Questionnaire with Forced Allocation   Figure 5.5 is an abbreviated version of the questionnaire from Chapter 4. It is used as an example to illustrate how to apply the forced allocation method to make the necessary adjustment for causal influence. In this example, department managers were engaged in a leadership initiative. During the learning en-

Figure 5.5   Estimating Causal Influence—Abbreviated Questionnaire Example

2. How has the company gained a *business outcome improvement* from the actions you listed in Question 1? List your business objective here and provide input on how it changed and the basis of that change. *Objective is to reduce monthly service call discrepancies, which began at 30 per 100 calls.*

   Monthly deficiencies in service calls have been reduced from 30 per 100 to 5 per 100. Our new customer engagement process is getting better input on the nature of service problems, and a greater focus on troubleshooting is getting it right the first time. More frequent feedback is being provided to service representatives, and on-job coaching by supervisors is raising competency levels.

3. Think about the specific business improvements in Question 2 and do your best to determine a monetary value and basis for your calculation. The total monetary amount is:
   $3,000 per month (improvement of 25 per month X $120 value for a repeat service call).

   a. Please check the appropriate box on how you arrived at your monetary value.
      ☒ Known value from company records or acceptable practices   ☐ Estimate   ☐ Other
   b. If "estimate" or "other" is checked above, please explain how you arrived at the calculation.

4. As discussed during the training, several factors may have contributed to the improvement in your selected measure. Referring to the example provided to you during the training, think about these key factors and enter them in the table in b, c, and d below. The leadership initiative is listed in item a in the table (*includes the leadership training Web-based problem-solving kit, and support and reinforcement from your director or vice president*). Think about all of the factors that helped influence a change in the measure and assign a percentage of weighting from 0 to 100%. Select only those that apply. The total of the items you select must = 100%. Consider using an objective approach to get your team's input into identifying the contributing factors and allocating the percentages.

Factors that influenced the business outcome improvement	% of influence
a. Leadership development initiative (tool kit, leadership training, director's reinforcement and support)	40%
b. The new customer engagement process recently implemented	20%
c. Supervisors' consistent and frequent feedback to team regarding performance	10%
d. Prior training and experience	30%
e. None	0%
TOTAL	100%

4a. The input for Question 4 above is: ____My input only ____Input from my team only _X_ Combination

5. How long do you estimate the above business improvement will be sustained beyond today's date? Give a serious thought to what may occur down the road and check the appropriate box.

30 days	3 months	6 months	1 year	>1 year	Other (please specify)
☐	☐	☐	☒	☐	☐ _____

6. What confidence level between 0 and 100% do you place on any estimates above?
   (0 = no confidence; 100% = full confidence)

   My confidence level for my estimate is 85%

gagement, each participant was asked to set objectives to improve at least one business metric that was deficient in his own department. The objective of the participant responding in this example questionnaire was to eliminate or reduce deficiencies in the quality of service calls. Prior to the leadership initiative, service calls were experiencing only 70 percent effectiveness. That is, 30 service calls out of 100 did not resolve the customer's problem, and a repeat call was required to correct the problems.

The response to Question 1 (not shown) established a change in leadership behavior that resulted in performance improvement toward achieving the objective of reducing service call deficiencies. The participant's explanation in response to Question 2 provides some indication of what occurred. The participant documents the business outcome improvement in her feedback on Question 2. As indicated, the deficiencies in quality of service calls have been reduced from 30 per 100 to 5 per 100 per month. This is an improvement of 25 deficiencies, or an 83 percent improvement in effectiveness ($25 \div 30 = 83\%$). At this point, it is not certain what caused the change.

Question 3 seeks a monetary value for the improvement. The participant provides a total amount of $3,000 per month ($25 \times \$120$). This is based on the known value of $120, which is the cost of one repeat service call. Having this as a frame of reference, Question 4 asks the participant what might have influenced the improvement in the discrepancies.

The draft questionnaire was presented to participants for review during the training. Since this was an open-enrollment program, each participant was asked to develop a list of possible influencing factors that might cause his specific measure to change. The participants were given examples and informed that they would need to enter these influencing factors when they received the follow-up questionnaire several months later. The participant in Figure 5.5 provided three influencing factors in addition to the leadership initiative. Item 4a indicates that she used her team's input to address this issue. Question 4 sets up a response that requires the respondent to allocate percentages from 0 to 100 percent to each of the factors, as deemed appropriate. The total must equal 100 percent.

Since "prior training and experience" received a 30 percent weighting in Question 4, we can assume that this participant is a somewhat seasoned manager who came to the training needing something to boost her leadership skills. The department implemented a new customer engagement process during the same time frame in which the leadership initiative was delivered. This received a 20 percent allocation, and supervisors providing consistent and frequent feedback to their teams received another 10 percent. Considering all relevant factors, the participant attributes a 40 percent contribution toward the improvement to the leadership initiative.

Now that this participant has provided the contribution of the leadership initiative, the result can be analyzed and calculated. A monthly reduction (improvement) of 25 discrepancies $\times$ 0.4 contribution of the leadership initiative = 10 per month. The improvement is expected to be sustained for one year (Question 5), therefore it can be annualized. The monthly improvement of 10 $\times$ 12 months = 120 per year. Question 6 captures the confidence level of any estimates in the process: 120 $\times$ 85 percent confidence = 102. The annualized improvement is a reduction of 102 discrepancies. The monetary value of one discrepancy (from the response to Question 3) is $120. Therefore, the total monetary value is $12,240 (102 $\times$ $120).

Questionnaires from all participants will be tallied, and the $12,240 will be added to the monetary results from the other participants to arrive at the total benefits. Each participant may provide a different type of measure with a different monetary value, a different causal influence contribution percentage, and a different sustained impact and confidence level. When the final values from all participants are tabulated, they are simply added together for the total monetary benefit.

Use of the forced allocation method to determine causal influence is practical and enhances the credibility of estimates because the participant (or other respondent) is provided or develops the other possible factors. An additional factor labeled "other" can be provided in case the respondent knows of additional factors. Even though the questionnaire was field-tested during the planning phase, other factors could be present that were not present at the time of the field test, or an individual could have influencing factors that are not present for others involved in the process.

Using a Questionnaire with Straightforward Causal Influence Questions
Sometimes there is not enough room on a questionnaire to do all that is necessary to gather data in the way that is preferred. A short version of the

question can be used to determine causal influence. One approach is discussed here.

Q. Considering all components of the training and performance solution, what influence did it have on your ability to execute and achieve the business outcome results? (100 percent = it was the only influence, and 0 percent = it had no influence)

On a scale between 100 and 0 percent, the percentage influence factor is: _____ %.

Q. What is your level of confidence in the above estimate? (100 percent = I am sure; 0 percent = total uncertainty)

My confidence factor is: _____ %.

This straightforward approach relies on the respondent to recall the potential factors that are not associated with the solution. While it is of some value, and we have captured the confidence level, it lacks the degree of accuracy of the forced allocation approach. When this approach must be used, it is highly recommended that multiple sources be used. For example, have the estimate completed by both participants and their supervisors. The two estimates could be averaged to determine the contribution value, or the source that has the most conservative (lowest) estimate could be accepted.

Using Focus Groups and Interviews to Answer the "Why" Question   No matter what methods or sources are used, determining the causal influence is a best effort to answer the "why" question. Why did the measure change, and how much of the change is due to the implementation of the solution design? When using participants or their immediate supervisors as the source for estimates in focus groups or interviews, the following approach and steps are recommended.

I.   During evaluation planning and prior to collecting the follow-up performance data, implement the following steps.

   A.   Consider the solution being evaluated, the measure(s) in question, the circumstances, and the work environment. Determine who is in a position to know, who is most capable, and who can best provide the estimation.

B. When possible, the members of the group that will respond with their estimates should know in advance that they will be asked to provide this information. When the planning step is completed in Phase One of the measurement and ROI process, the group should be selected and notified.

C. Communicate (preferably face-to-face) to inform the group of the details and how the process will play out.

These steps will help to avoid a lot of confusion and will also allow the group to be thinking about the issue as the calendar advances toward the time for data collection.

II. During the process of collecting follow-up performance data, proceed as follows. (*Note:* The steps given here use a focus group as an example of how to proceed. Interviews can also be used.)

A. Remind the group of when the training solution was implemented (dates) and that it was expected to improve one or more business measures.

B. Inform the group that in order to determine business contribution and to focus on continuous improvement, it is necessary to determine any linkage between the training solution and any business improvement.

C. Explain to the group members that, since they have been involved in (or close to) the training or the follow-up performance, their task is to help establish this linkage. Explain any confidentiality rules and the way the focus group will work. Communicate the importance of establishing the linkage and that it will be an acceptable estimate.

D. Communicate the business improvement to the group and explain the source of the improvement, such as the business records. The circumstances could be such that the group or a certain individual has provided the business improvement. If so, explain this and proceed with the next steps.

E. Present the business outcome measure, the beginning status (baseline), and the improvement. List the various key factors and explain that they could have caused the improvement. Explain how you arrived at these factors (the client, sponsor, experts, and so on). Allow the group to offer input and other possibilities and make any necessary revisions in these factors before moving forward.

F. Provide the context to the group and share the tool to be used to make the causal influence decision. For example, provide copies (or display a slide) of the forced allocation process, such as the one covered earlier in this chapter that was used with a questionnaire in Figure 5.5. Be certain to make changes to the tool from the group's input in Step 5. Explain the confidence level process and how it will be used in conjunction with the estimate.

G. Briefly discuss the solution that was delivered and all of the key design components. Point out that this is one of the choices on the tool. Discuss each influencing factor thoroughly so that the group understands how each could also have influenced the business outcome measure, but do not provide an opinion. The facilitator should be neutral.

H. Allow time for the focus group participants to reflect on the issues, and ask each person to make his choices and provide a confidence estimate.

I. Ask participants to calculate their final percentages after adjusting for confidence level.

J. Average the scores together to determine the group average and communicate it to the group.

K. Inform the group that its response may be combined with that of other focus groups and will be used to determine the contribution of the training solution.

THE CAUSAL INFLUENCE DECISION: USING A FAIL-SAFE TOOL TO CHOOSE A METHOD

At some point during the evaluation planning process for the impact study, the decision is made as to what method is to be used to determine causal influence. There are three possible choices (comparison group, trending, or estimates) and multiple possible sources. The worksheet in Figure 5.6 is

Figure 5.6 Worksheet to Select Method to Identify Causal Influence

Use this job aid to make a decision on the most feasible method(s) to use
to determine the causal influence of a business outcome improvement

Step 1

Select one of the business outcome measures that your solution should influence.

The measure is:

_____

Step 2

Identify the time frame necessary to monitor progress and collect data to determine if the selected measure has changed.

The time frame is:

_____

The time frame must be sufficient to allow for performance change and normal influences in the operational environment.

Step 3

Identify the key internal and external variables (other than the solution being delivered) that could influence the measure in the performance setting during the established time frame. The key factors are:

a.	d.	g.
b.	e.	h.
c.	f.	i.

Who is best positioned to know and assist in identifying these factors? Seek their input.

Step 4—the Decision

Is it feasible and appropriate to establish a comparison group arrangement?

Given the time frame in Step 2 consider logistical issues, ethical issues, contamination issues, ability to withhold the solution from some groups, best-fit method, etc.

Yes

No

Can a trend be established on the selected measure using historical performance data, and are the criteria for using the conditional trend analysis method met?

No

Yes

Use comparison group arrangement to determine causal influence.

Use the factors identified in Step 3 as a basis to select the comparison group. Select groups by matching those with characteristics and job situations having these factors in common.

Who is best positioned to identify the groups that have these factors in common? Ask them to assist in determining the comparison group.

Use estimates from credible sources to determine causal influence.

Use conditional trend analysis to determine causal influence.

Identify who is best positioned to estimate causal influences based on the impact of other influencing factors from Step 3 and the solution design. Ask: are they positioned to know, are they credible and objective, and will they cooperate?

If using trend analysis, be certain there are no influencing factors other than your solution design.

a useful tool to help in making a quick and effective decision. Follow the steps in the worksheet to make the decision as to which causal influence method to use.

The four steps in the worksheet in Figure 5.6 are the same as the four steps used to determine the comparison group criteria in Figure 5.3, presented earlier in the chapter. To use the worksheet, simply follow these same steps. The variables identified in Step 3 are the factors that will be applied when using estimates to consider causal influence. As you arrive at Step 4 of the worksheet, it should be easy to make a yes or no decision and progress through the other steps. When using this worksheet, if the answer to the first question in Step 4 is "no," consider using the conditional trend analysis method. However, when considering this method, if the two conditions for using trend analysis cannot be met, then the "no" decision leads to the option of using estimates.

CASE STUDY PART 3: TECH*READ* SMART METERING COMPANY

Preparing to Analyze the Results

The readiness data and the performance data have been collected, and the analysis has begun. The evaluation team has four points of coordination in order to pull all the data together and analyze them.

1. The program coordinator for the solution, "Active Coaching for Field Sales Managers," provides the summary of the learning readiness data and the initial reaction data. This is not an objective predictor, but it is a reasonable indicator of the success that is expected to occur as participants return to the work setting.
2. The data from the participant questionnaire, the interviews with the three regional managers, and the focus groups with sales representatives are collected and analyzed by the evaluation team.
3. The HR department, the custodian of the employee complaint data, provides the business outcome regarding complaints and acts as the expert to provide insight on the analysis.
4. The custodian for the sales data and the three regional managers are the expert sources to interpret the business outcome sales data.

It is not unusual to have issues with the consistency, accuracy, and reliability of the business outcome data from an organization's records. As the evaluation team analyzes this type of data (Steps 3 and 4 in the previous list), it must rely on insight and observations from the experts to make the final analysis decisions. It is these same experts that executive management routinely relies on to make decisions with the same data.

The data collection methods and instruments accounted for the fact that we would need to make an adjustment to the business outcome data for causal influence. At the end of this section, we will see how the causal influence analysis works out. Now, beginning with the training solution, let's briefly address each type of data that establishes the chain of impact.

Results—Readiness Solution

During the learning engagement, several assessments were administered. The most prominent in terms of determining readiness is the assessment from the multiple role-play exercises. Even though it is subjective, it is the best indicator of learning that we have for this initiative. The consolidated results are shown in Table 5.2 (see page 134).

While the evaluation team carried out a more in-depth analysis, only a summary is shown here. The summary, from the facilitators' observation, shows that at least 70 percent of the participants (42 of 60) scored at a readiness level of 4 or higher on a 1–5 scale. Details on the assessment scale and the instrument are given in Chapter 4. This is a strong indicator of the success of the program to this point.

The initial reaction questionnaire, as its name implies, gives initial input from an end-of-program perspective that provides an indicator of success in terms of relevance and expected application when participants return to the work setting. Because of space limitations, these results are not shown.

Execution in the Work Setting—Performance Results

Clients, sponsors, and senior management usually have many questions in this area when a report is presented. Therefore, the collection and analysis of this type of data serves two purposes: to establish the chain of impact and to satisfy questions that will surely arise. That is why an impact study requires

Table 5.2   Learning Readiness—Consolidation of Skill Practice Assessments for the Active Coaching Solution

	SUBJECTIVE ASSESSMENT OF HANDS-ON SKILL PRACTICE				
	PERCENTAGE OF PARTICIPANTS SCORING IN EACH ASSESSMENT LEVEL (OBSERVATION BY FACILITATOR)				
ITEM	CAUTION 1	OKAY 2	GOOD 3	GREAT 4	ROLE MODEL 5
1. Reinforce the relationship	0%	20%	20%	50%	10%
2. Provide feedback	0%	0%	10%	70%	20%
3. Facilitate discussion	0%	10%	10%	50%	30%
4. Explore needs	0%	10%	30%	40%	20%
5. Guide and support	0%	0%	30%	40%	30%
6. Follow up and encourage renewal	0%	0%	30%	30%	40%

comprehensive data and even success stories on what happens in the work setting. Three sources were used to collect this execution data: the regional managers, a sample of sales representatives, and the 60 participants. Each is addressed in the following sections.

Input from Interviews with Regional Managers   The regional managers from the three regions that formed the experimental group were interviewed for their input. The comments and examples provided during the interviews support the conclusion that most of the sales managers are doing quite well at applying coaching behavior. The regional managers reported that about 30 percent of the sales managers seemed to be deficient in communicating expectations. There was some discussion about this during the interviews, and it is an issue that can be addressed.

The sales managers could be biased in their responses, but everyone is usually biased in some way. It would be impractical to place a full-time objective observer in all of these locations to observe 60 sales managers. Perfection is not our goal in data collection. Our goal is to get reasonable input from sources that are credible and are in a position to know what has happened. Certainly there are trade-offs, but they are reasonable and practical.

Input from Focus Groups with Sales Representatives Data were collected from sales representatives using two focus groups in each region. Table 5.3 shows the consolidated data.

Table 5.3 Sales Representative Follow-up Focus Groups—Consolidated Results

PART A: Assess the behavior/actions of your sales manager over the last three months.				
EXTENT TO WHICH YOUR SALES MANAGER HAS	NOT AT ALL	OCCASIONALLY	OFTEN	VERY OFTEN
1. Helped you realize and take advantage of the value of a good market analysis	15%	55%	30%	0%
2. Worked through call planning problems and issues with you	0%	10%	40%	50%
3. Helped you create sales opportunities	0%	15%	50%	35%
4. Helped you to improve customer relationships	10%	30%	30%	30%

PART B: Assess the behavior/actions of your sales manager over the last three months.				
EXTENT TO WHICH YOUR SALES MANAGER HAS PROVIDED	NOT AT ALL	OCCASIONALLY	OFTEN	VERY OFTEN
1. Timely communication of expectations	0%	40%	50%	10%
2. Performance guidance and coaching	0%	30%	60%	10%
3. Balanced performance feedback	5%	45%	40%	10%
4. Employee and team recognition	10%	35%	40%	15%

PART C: Please respond as appropriate below.

1. Did your individual sales improve during the quarter just ended? ❏ 85% Yes ❏ 15% No
2. Are you satisfied with how your sales manager has recognized your progress and contribution during the last three months? ❏ 55% Yes ❏ 30% To some extent ❏ 15% Not at all

PART D: Please comment as requested below.

1. Provide an example of how these actions helped you achieve success in your market territory.	
2. What disappointments did you experience throughout the coaching process with your sales manager?	

Three of the focus groups (one in each region) had a random sample of sales representatives. The other three focus groups used input from experienced sales representatives from the regions. As the data were analyzed, it became clear that there was very little difference in the input. The results are combined in Table 5.3. The weakest areas of guidance were market analysis and customer relationships. Call planning and sales opportunities were the strongest. There was room for improvement in all areas of coaching.

Successes.   The top three examples of success are (1) planning the sales call, (2) how to position the sales call, and (3) the significance of and how to follow up with the customer to build relationships. The group was unanimous that more time needed to be spent on how to build customer relationships. They related that the time spent on this has been very advantageous.

Disappointments.   The most frequently mentioned disappointments were (1) lack of sales manager help in market analysis, which can help in creating strategies to outsell the competition, and (2) that more than half of the focus group participants felt that the three-month time period was insufficient time to allow the coaching process to completely play out. They stated that when they are in the field, communication with the sales manager is limited unless she is on the sales detail with them, which happens less than once a month.

The experienced group of sales representatives suggested that they could be used as peer coaches, especially in the area of call planning, when the team is together in the office. This would free the sales manager to do more one-on-one work in the areas of market analysis and building customer relationships.

Input from Sales Managers' Questionnaires

Even though the sales managers may not be as objective as we would like, their input is essential because of their perspective as participants. They are the focal point and the center of the intervention. The solution was designed to prepare and influence them to change their behavior. Even though the questions asked are in areas that are the sales managers' responsibility, many of them are not about the sales manager, but about other aspects of performance. This nullifies some of the concern about objectivity. Table 5.4 includes the consolidated feedback from the follow-up questionnaire.

Part A of the questionnaire in Table 5.4 is an assessment to determine the sales managers' view about the regional manager's support and reinforcement. Recall that support and reinforcement from the regional manager is part of the solution design. It is a companion strategy to influence

Table 5.4   Sales Manager Follow-up Questionnaire—Consolidated Results

PART A: Assess the actions of your regional manager over the last three months.				
EXTENT TO WHICH THE REGIONAL SALES MANAGER HAS BEEN HELPFUL THE LAST THREE MONTHS IN	**NOT HELPFUL**	**SOMEWHAT HELPFUL**	**HELPFUL**	**VERY HELPFUL**
1. Clarifying my expectations with regard to actively coaching my team to achieve results.	0%	30%	50%	20%
2. Supporting and helping me as I provide coaching to my team.	0%	0%	40%	60%
3. Influencing me to sustain my focus on creating sales opportunities through my team.	0%	0%	50%	50%
4. Offering advice to overcome barriers to coaching my team.	0%	10%	70%	20%

PART B: Please comment as requested below.
1. How did these actions by your regional manager help you achieve success?
2. What disappointments did you experience in the sessions with your regional manager?

PART C: Assess your sales team's improvement during the last three months.								
WHAT PERCENTAGE OF YOUR SALES REPS HAVE IMPROVED DURING THE LAST THREE MONTHS IN	**0 TO 5%**	**5 TO 15%**	**16 TO 30%**	**31 TO 45%**	**46 TO 60%**	**61 TO 75%**	**76 TO 90%**	**> 90%**
1. Market analysis	10%	20%	40%	20%	10%	0%	0%	0%
2. Sales call planning	0%	0%	0%	5%	15%	10%	60%	10%
3. Closing sales	0%	0%	0%	20%	10%	30%	40%	0%
4. Customer relationship behavior	10%	5%	10%	15%	20%	30%	10%	0%

(continued on next page)

Table 5.4   Sales Manager Follow-up Questionnaire—
Consolidated Results *(continued)*

PART D: Please comment as requested below.

1. Provide an example of your
   coaching success with your team.
 	
2. What disappointments did you
   experience throughout the training
   and coaching activities?

PART E: Please respond to the questions below to provide further insight into your coaching relationship with your team and its sales performance.
1. Provide specific examples of how your team responded to your coaching in sales call planning. 2. Provide specific examples of how your team responded to your coaching in closing sales. 3. Provide details on how you changed your ineffective habits to allow you to succeed in coaching.

the sales managers' coaching behavior. The actual coaching performance of the sales manager is evidence that the strategy worked. These follow-up questions simply provide more evidence.

Part C in Table 5.4 is seeking the sales managers' view and evidence on the performance of the sales representatives as they respond to the coaching. The whole idea is to develop sales representatives, reduce employee complaints about coaching and style of management, and influence an increase in sales by coaching in the key areas of sales performance. The consolidated responses in Part C appear to closely track the input from the focus groups with the sales representatives.

Successes. The top three examples of success reported by sales managers were (1) helping sales representatives one-on-one with sales call planning, (2) receiving useful help and advice from the regional manager on overcoming barriers that often got in the way of coaching my team, and (3) helping sales representatives with actual call behavior.

Disappointments. The most frequently mentioned disappointments were (1) lack of time to work with sales teams to coach and improve performance and (2) inability to provide much help and coaching to sales teams in market analysis because of a personal lack of knowledge and experience in this area.

Changing Ineffective Habits.   During the learning engagement, sales managers identified their ineffective habits in the areas of coaching and management style. Prior to the end of the session, they created an action plan to correct these habits. The top three habits sales managers reported as changed, from Part E, item 3 on the questionnaire, are

- Become more proactive in scheduling time with each sales representative to discuss expectations and ongoing performance.
- Give each sales representative more quality time and coaching by riding with him on a sales detail each month.
- Focus on learning how each team member makes different and unique contributions to the team and find more ways to recognize them.

Business Outcome Results and Adjusting for Causal Influence

The training solution focused on two types of business outcomes: a reduction in employee complaints related to coaching and an increase in sales. Both types of data exist in company records. The HR department is the custodian for employee complaint data, and the corporate marketing and sales department is the custodian for sales data.

Since outcome measures such as complaints and sales can be influenced by numerous variables, any success with these two measures must be adjusted for causal influence. This is why the comparison group arrangement was put in place. Recall that the criteria for selecting the comparison group were established as shown earlier in this chapter in Figure 5.3. The two business measures are analyzed in the following sections.

The Solution's Impact on Employee Complaints Related to Coaching   About six weeks after the training was delivered, the evaluation team received a telephone call from the HR analyst who was custodian of the HR complaint data. The HR analyst had been in the job for only about a month, replacing an analyst who had recently resigned.

Trouble in Paradise.   The HR analyst revealed to the evaluation team that the employee complaint data are unreliable. The initial analysis of employee complaints several months ago revealed an average of between 36 and 38 complaints per month in each of the six regions. The average for the three regions in the experimental group showed 38 complaints per month. The average for the two comparison regions showed 37 per month.

The new analyst had discovered that something was not right and began a detailed analysis of the four-month pretraining data. Many of the complaints were double-counted from month to month. Others were classified in the wrong region, and still others were misclassified and should have been in the manufacturing business unit, not the sales function. The issues were caused by both computer and human error (recording of data had been handled by three different HR people during a six-month period). The origin of much of the data had been lost.

Conclusions.   The HR department's best estimate is that baseline complaints are at least 30 percent less than initially reported. The data are inaccurate and incomplete, and some data have been lost. This prevents a conclusion that would be considered credible based on the historical data. Since the contaminated database was discovered, the HR analyst has kept a separate record. Since the training was delivered, an average of 6 coaching-related complaints have been reported in the three experimental sales regions during the three-month posttraining time period. Since there was low confidence in the baseline data and there were more questions than answers, for purposes of the ROI analysis, the evaluation team decided to abandon the comparison of employee complaints. Consider it a lesson in bad data.

The Solution's Impact on Sales   The custodian of the sales data provided the reports from the two comparison groups to the evaluation team. After some initial analysis to develop conclusions, the team met with the three regional managers to determine if there were any inconsistencies in or issues with the data. Since they get reports weekly, the regional managers had already studied the data, and they saw only one issue that raised any questions. While sales had been deficient in all regions before the solution was implemented, now sales were up for both the comparison group and the experimental group. Table 5.5 shows the before and after revenue from sales in the five regions.

Why did the sales of the comparison group also improve? The answer to this question is important for one key reason related to the impact study: did something occur that would contaminate the comparison group arrangement and therefore render any comparison invalid? There are several obvious possibilities. Maybe a few sales managers who were trained got transferred to a comparison region during the three-month analysis period. Maybe there were marketing promotions implemented in the two comparison regions that differed from those in the experimental group, thereby having the effect of increasing sales. Maybe the regional managers in the two comparison regions somehow became informed that they were being compared to another group and began to step up their efforts so that they would not look bad.

Conclusions.   Many factors both internal and external to Tech*Read* could cause a change in sales. The evaluation team and the regional managers studied the issue and could find no plausible reasons for the 8 percent sales increase in the comparison group. The fact is, irregularities occur often with comparison groups. We must remember that the two groups are not exact. They are a reasonable comparison. There will always be faults with comparison groups. The evaluation team and the regional managers of the experimental group decided that the comparison was valid enough to use in the analysis.

Table 5.5   Sales Data Pre- and Post-Comparison Group Arrangement

COMPARISON GROUP ARRANGEMENT	NORTHWEST AND WEST REGIONS: *COMPARISON GROUP*	SOUTHEAST, MIDWEST, AND SOUTHWEST REGIONS: *EXPERIMENTAL GROUP*
Three-month follow-up data: average sales per month	$15,228,000	$15,960,000
Baseline data: average sales per month	$14,100,000	$14,000,000
Change per month	$1,128,000 (+8%)	$1,960,000 (+14%)

In Table 5.5, the average monthly sales for all regions in each group are used to enable a uniform comparison of the data. The total sales increase per month for the experimental group is $5,880,000 (3 regions × average of $1,960,000).

While there is a definite increase, the target of a 20 percent increase in sales was not reached. Perhaps this was an aggressive target. In order to find the true gain, we must compare the difference between the two groups. There are two ways in which the gain can be calculated.

1. 14 percent minus 8 percent = 6 percent difference by the experimental group over the comparison group. Therefore, 6 percent of the experimental group baseline of $14,000,000 = $840,000 difference per month.

2. Experimental group increase of $1,960,000 minus comparison group increase of $1,128,000 = $832,000 difference by the experimental group. This answer is more conservative than the previous one, so an average of $832,000 per month is used as the gain.

Since the five regions in the comparison group arrangement (two in the comparison group and three in the experimental group) are considered to be an acceptable match, the conclusion is that the $832,000 monthly increase is caused by the delivery of the solution design, "Active Coaching for Field Sales Managers." The total monthly revenue increase is $2,496,000 per month ($832,000 per month × 3 regions in experimental group = $2,496,000 total per month).

More Decisions Ahead.   Now there are additional decisions to make. The sustained impact, Step 7 of the measurement and ROI process, must now be considered. The analysis must determine how long this monthly increase in revenue is likely to continue. Do we claim the amount just for the three-month period where we have a known increase in revenue? Can we project the monthly sales forward and annualize the revenue? Will the same level of sales continue? Part 4 of the case study in Chapter 6 will answer these questions and more.

6

Analyze Results and Adjust for Sustained Impact

It is sometimes relatively easy to initiate a change, such as a change in behavior. Sustaining the change over a given time frame, even in the short term, is another matter. When an intervention is evaluated, the performance data are usually collected within a two- to six-month time period. Any improvement in performance shown by the data analyzed represents only what happened during the time period for which the actual results data were collected. This sets up the question, can the improvement from the abbreviated performance period be annualized, and if so, under what conditions? As illustrated in Figure 6.1 (see page 144), Step 7 continues the follow-up data analysis phase and addresses an adjustment for sustained impact.

THE VOLATILITY OF MODERN-DAY ORGANIZATIONS AND ITS EFFECT ON SUSTAINING PERFORMANCE

Modern-day organizations are volatile and subject to frequent change. This volatility often creates changes in expectation, breakdowns in communication, disruption in coordination, reallocation of resources, and loss of productivity and effectiveness. Some of these frequent changes include intervening variables such as the following:

- A new manager with a different focus, agenda, and expectations takes over.
- The competition steps things up a notch and makes our processes and activities ineffective.
- New competing products are introduced into the market.

- The needs of customers change.
- New technologies are introduced.
- Negative changes in the economy reduce product demand.
- Strategic initiatives and business processes shift frequently.
- Mergers or acquisitions create disruption and change in business processes and jeopardize job security.
- A performer or a key support member of a team transfers to another department.

These and other factors often act to create deficiencies in important business measures. Likewise, they may shorten the effective life of any business outcome improvement that has been influenced by training solutions or other performance interventions. Whether the performers still retain the skills or know how to exhibit the expected behavior that was learned

Figure 6.1   Phase Three, Step 7

Phase Three

Analyze Data and Make
Conservative Adjustments*

Step 7

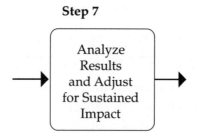

- Adjust results for
  sustained impact
  - One-time impact
  - Recurring impact
  - Turnover loss
    adjustment

*Analyze and report on the delivery of the complete
solution design, not just the training component.

from a training solution is not the issue in this scenario. The question is whether the performers will be effective when they apply the skills under the new conditions and whether performance will even occur in a way that matters, or whether these skills will make a difference in the new situation. Will the performers overcome the new obstacles that are being presented, or will they be reluctant to apply the skills and behavior in a situation with unknown conditions and consequences? The answers to questions of this type and the many intervening factors determine whether improvements resulting from training solutions can be sustained beyond the initial data collection period.

IF IT CAN'T BE SUSTAINED, IT CAN'T BE CLAIMED

The time frame for collecting performance data is often condensed to a two- to six-month period so that results can be reported before additional money is spent to deliver the solution to a larger population. This always raises the question, will the performance continue to be sustained following the abbreviated data collection period? Many of the questions about sustained performance cannot be answered with certainty. But the possibility of performers reverting to ineffective habits or the likelihood of intervening circumstances causing a change in future performance cannot be ignored.

The volatility of organizations can often work against any performance improvement being sustained for a long period. Thus, the improvement may be temporary. If you can't sustain it, you can't claim it. When data are collected and business outcome improvements are identified during an abbreviated time frame, such as two to six months after a program is delivered, any decision to annualize the impact must be questioned.

Annualizing Improvements for the First Year

Can the actual business outcome improvement achieved during an abbreviated time frame be annualized? Some practitioners, as a matter of routine, will annualize business outcome improvements with little to no concern about the expected life of these improvements. Annualizing improvements resulting from training solutions for the first year is acceptable, but not as a matter of routine. Careful consideration must be given to the feasibility of the business outcome improvement continuing beyond the abbreviated data collection period. Annualizing a business outcome must also take into account any additional costs that may be incurred to sustain the performance during a 12-month business cycle.

Annualizing Improvements beyond the First Year

When calculating the ROI, some practitioners annualize business outcome improvements two or three years into the future. Most training solutions are short-term in nature and should not be annualized beyond the first year. The practice of annualizing improvements beyond the first year is acceptable only when there are compelling reasons to believe that the improvement associated with the intervention will continue over the longer term without being diminished. Annualizing beyond one year should be a rare occurrence and should be used with great caution. There are so many intervening variables that can enter the performance picture beyond one year that the credibility of any such calculation is in serious question. As demonstrated in the next section, annualizing a business outcome improvement, even when only for the first year, can result in the serious flaw of overstating the results and the ROI.

THE SERIOUS FLAW OF OVERSTATING THE ROI

Those who are conducting a ROI analysis are easily tempted to annualize any performance improvement without questioning the reality of the situation. Look at the two scenarios given here to see the implications for calculating ROI.

Scenario 1: Sustained Impact According to Cautious Carol

Carol is evaluating the business outcome and return on investment from a three-day leadership program that was delivered four months ago to managers and supervisors in the customer service department. The primary focus of the program was on managing the development and performance of the team's talent. The short-term business outcome measures are improved quality and reduction of customer complaints. Carol has collected the performance data after four months and has made the adjustments for causal influence. Complaints were reduced, and quality has improved. The total improvement (benefits after causal influence adjustments) has been valued by management at $95,000 per month. The fully loaded cost of the leadership program is $210,000.

Carol is always cautious when analyzing data and reporting results, especially ROI. Realizing that she has only four months of actual results, Carol thinks about how she should treat the total benefits. Being of a cautious and conservative nature, she decides that the total benefits are $380,000 ($95,000 × 4 months). Carol's ROI calculation is shown here.

$$\text{ROI} = \frac{\$170,000\ [\$380,000 - \$210,000]}{\$210,000} = 0.81 \times 100 = 81\%$$

Since the minimum acceptable return for most business investments is usually in the range of 10 to 20 percent, Carol's calculation of 81 percent represents a very good return on the training investment. Perhaps the return is actually greater than 81 percent, since the improvement could continue beyond the abbreviated four-month period during which the data were collected. However, Carol will be able to consider this assumption only if her client or the managers participating in the leadership program offer their insight and recommendations about the likelihood of the improvement being sustained.

Scenario 2: Sustained Impact According to Generous George

Let's suppose that Carol planned and implemented the evaluation of the leadership program in Scenario 1. However, Carol takes an extended leave of absence before the performance data are collected. George steps in at the end of four months and is responsible for collecting and analyzing the data.

George has his own guiding principles for analysis and believes in making the most of everything. He also likes to be the one to make all the decisions. He treats the data as if they were his own. Unlike Carol, he is quite liberal in his analysis of the improvement data. George talked with three people before making the decision on how to calculate the sustained impact of the monthly improvement. The problem is, the three people that George talked with were "me, myself, and I." Based on his singular input, George proceeds to annualize the monthly improvement. He decides that the total benefits are $1,140,000 ($95,000 × 12 months). George's ROI calculation of 443 percent is shown here.

$$ROI = \frac{\$930,000 \; [\$1,140,000 - \$210,000]}{\$210,000} = 4.43 \times 100 = \mathbf{443\%}$$

The significant difference between the 81 percent calculated by Cautious Carol and the 443 percent calculated by Generous George raises some interesting issues, as noted here:

Issue 1: Who is correct, Carol or George?

Issue 2: How can this type of adjustment be made realistically with any degree of comfort and credibility?

Issue 3: Should the ROI of any program always be suspect, since there can be such an extreme difference in the conclusions about an improvement?

Issue 1 asks, who is correct, Carol or George? The sustained impact adjustment could have the result shown by Carol, the result shown by George, or something in between. It is difficult to say who is correct because neither Carol nor George is in a position to know how long the improvement may continue. Actually, they are both wrong because neither of them went to the right sources to determine the adjustment. Both of them relied on their own knowledge (or lack of it) and instincts. At least Carol's conclusion did not overstate the ROI, which is one of the worst things an analyst can do. Guiding Principle 7 states, "In determining the sustainable impact of improvements, use only credible sources and make adjustments accordingly."

Guiding Principle 7

In determining the sustainable impact of improvements, use only credible sources and make adjustments accordingly.

The client, the management closest to the work situation, and the participants are in the best position to know what is likely to happen with the improvement measures. Rather than letting the evaluator decide this, the people who achieve the results should develop the conclusion about this issue. They know the nuances of the job, the customers, the organization environment, and other factors that may affect the performers and the measures. All of these factors and more will influence their ability to sustain any improvement. In any case, casually or routinely assuming that improvements that are influenced by a solution will be sustained beyond the initial data collection period is faulty analysis. The scenarios involving Carol and George illustrate how the ROI can possibly be understated (Carol) or highly overstated (George). The adjustment should be made using information from those sources that are in the best position to know.

Issue 2 asks, how can this type of adjustment be made realistically with any degree of comfort and credibility? While credible sources are in the best position to know, even they cannot be sure because they are looking into a crystal ball to determine the future. The good news is, an adjustment is being made for the near term rather than the long term. Credible sources can usually determine the sustainability of improvements in the short term (one year or less) with credibility and some degree of comfort. They have already seen the performance change. The question is, can the performance be sustained? Table 6.1 (see page 150) includes a series of recommended steps to help credible sources think through the issues of sustained impact and arrive at a reasonable decision. Use it as a job aid with clients to make the sustained impact adjustment.

Using the job aid in Table 6.1, credible sources can make a reasonable decision about sustained impact. Since this is a projection (an estimate), the confidence level is provided in Step 6 so that another adjustment can be made to the calculation. For example, an improvement of $95,000 per month annualized for one year is $1,140,000 ($95,000 × 12 months). When asked about confidence, the source responds with an 80 percent confidence level. Recall that an 80 percent confidence level means that the estimate could be in error by 20 percent on either side of $1,140,000. Thus, the adjustment could be $912,000 ($1,140,000 minus $228,000), or it could be as much as $1,368,000 ($1,140,000 plus $228,000). Since the guiding principles tell us to be conservative, $912,000 is used for the confidence adjustment.

Issue 3 asks, should the ROI of any program always be suspect, since there can be such an extreme difference in the conclusions about an improvement? Absolutely and emphatically, yes! When someone claims an

Table 6.1 Accounting for Future Intervening Variables and Performance Factors

1. Identify the specific business outcome measure and the improvement captured during the evaluation.	• The business outcome measure is _____ . • The monthly improvement is _____ .
2. Communicate to the source(s) why a decision on sustained impact is needed and how the decision process will work (next steps).	• Have a candid discussion about why the sustained impact adjustment is necessary and how the result of the analysis will affect the ROI calculation. • Discuss the need for objectivity and a realistic conclusion after considering the proper factors.
3. Ask the sources to consider the performers and their job environment and determine the likelihood of the performers continuing to execute as they are doing now.	• What have the performers done during the previous _____ months to influence the improvement in the measure identified in Step 1?_____ • Are the job environment and the performers' situation such that they are likely to be able to maintain their performance at the same level?
4. Ask the sources to reflect on the job and organization environment and think about any internal or external intervening variables that may enter the picture during the next 12 months.*	• Since you are considering whether the improvement in the business measure will continue over the next 6 to 12 months, think about any factors (internal or external) that may reasonably occur that would eliminate, nullify, or retard the improvement. What would these factors be?
5. Ask the sources to reflect on their answers in Steps 3 and 4 and provide their best answer on sustained impact (up to one year).	• Considering your reflection in Steps 3 and 4, and the likely impact of any intervening variables, how long do you believe the monthly improvement in the business measure will be sustained (up to one year)? _____
6. Ask the sources to provide a confidence level for their projection.	• What is your level of confidence in the projection in Step 5? (100 percent = I am sure; 0 percent = total uncertainty) Confidence level is _____%.

* Sustaining a performance effort or a business improvement can be dependent on avoiding or overcoming adverse actions in the future such as
  • Changes in the competitive environment. For example, competitor actions can negate an improvement in sales or customer service.
  • Changes in the regulatory environment. For example, a new federal, state, or industry requirement can add cost to the business or render historical improvement actions ineffective.
  • Conflict and debate on controversial or sensitive issues in the political or social environment. For example, legislative, government agency, or public debate can influence a delay or reversal in a company's decisions or improvement actions.

150

ROI, the methodology and the analysis standards that drive the decision, plus the type of data used to develop the calculation, are very significant and relevant factors. After all, those who hold the chalk can write what they desire on the board (or the flip chart or the PowerPoint graphic or the sales brochure for the vendor training program). The truth is, unless we can examine how an ROI is derived, there is no way of knowing whether it is snake oil analysis or whether it represents a truly magnificent result. Understanding the systematic ROI methodology presented in this book, including adjusting for sustained impact, will go a long way in helping to determine the quality of anyone's ROI calculation.

Hopefully, this explanation also helps to clarify one reason why it is not wise to compare ROI calculations from one program to another, one organization to another, or one vendor to another. A comparison of ROI calculations is anything but objective. The sustaining impact adjustment is only one of a multitude of reasons that ROI calculations should not be compared. The best course of action is simply to question every phase of how the ROI is developed. Subsequent chapters will clarify this issue further.

MAKING ADJUSTMENTS FOR SUSTAINED IMPACT

When decisions about sustained impact are made, there is one type of situation that requires no adjustment and two types of situations that require consideration of a sustained impact adjustment. Each situation is treated based on the way the sources consider the facts and conditions.

One-Time Impact

A one-time impact occurs when an improvement will not be realized beyond the time frame in which the improvement is initially reported. The improvement will not recur from week to week, month to month, or quarter to quarter. No adjustment is made for a one-time impact because the result will not recur. The improvement is calculated in the analysis as a one-time improvement, just as it is reported by the source.

Example of a One-Time Impact   Sam completes a training course in negotiation skills. Several months later, he applies what he learned. When negotiating with an outside supplier on a large quantity purchase of file cabinets that he will not purchase again for several years, he saved $50,000. Sam attributed half of the $50,000 savings to the new skills he had learned and applied from the course. How much is the saving attributed to the course, and should it be annualized?

Answer to Sam's One-Time Impact Example   Sam saved $50,000 while negotiating with the outside supplier. He says that half of the savings resulted from his use of the skills he learned during the negotiation training; $50,000 ÷ 2 = $25,000 savings attributed to the training solution. The number used for Sam's savings is $25,000. It is not annualized because it is a one-time savings that is not sustained beyond the data collection period. Sam reports that it will not recur this year.

Recurring Impact

A recurring impact is an improvement that can be reasonably expected to be sustained or to repeat itself continuously or for a given period of time as reported by the source. When a recurring improvement is expected to continue for at least one year, it is acceptable to annualize the improvement. In the ROI analysis of training and HR initiatives, recurring improvements are generally not annualized beyond the first year, unless there is a compelling reason to believe that the improvement will be sustained in the longer term and the additional longer-term variables can be identified and reasonably accounted for in the adjustment.

Example of a Recurring Impact Adjustment   After three months on the job, a group of new junior accountants was making a significant number of processing errors. At the end of the third month, they completed a classroom training course, followed by coaching during the next 30 days, allowing them to apply their work processes correctly by the end of one month. After one month, they are no longer making the costly processing errors that they had been making during their first three months on the job.

The total cost of these errors was $20,000 monthly. This cost is completely eliminated one month after the accountants return to the job. Kristen

Green, the accounting supervisor, says that without the training and coaching, these errors would have been eliminated anyway, but it would have taken another three months of working on the job before the accountants eliminated all of the errors. What is the sustained impact of the elimination of errors by the accountants as a result of the training and coaching?

Answer to Recurring Impact Example   The errors before the training and coaching were costing the company $20,000 per month. One month following the training and coaching, the performers are no longer making these errors. Kristen, the supervisor, says that without the training and coaching, it would have taken an additional three months to eliminate the errors.

Only the three months of savings following the delivery of the solution can be claimed, because our credible source determines that at the end of that time, the errors would be eliminated with "no intervention."

The sustained impact is three months. Total savings from the sustained impact is $60,000 ($20,000 × 3 months). The savings cannot be annualized. Another way to think about this is, the training and coaching improved effectiveness by shortening the amount of time required to achieve 100 percent quality with no errors.

Turnover Loss Adjustment

When an improvement is annualized for 12 months or longer, it must also be adjusted for the employee turnover experience of the organization that is being studied. A turnover loss adjustment is calculated to account for the average turnover of a population that achieves an improvement. This adjustment is considered when any type of improvement has a recurring impact that is annualized.

Since annualizing predicts that an improvement will be sustained beyond the abbreviated data collection period, the performers must be on hand to actually contribute to the sustained improvement in the future. Circumstances will dictate when it is appropriate to make a turnover loss adjustment.

When an adjustment is necessary, it can be made to either the benefits or the cost side of the equation, whichever is appropriate. The evaluator should be consistent in the way the adjustment is applied.

Example of Turnover Loss Adjustment   A call center routinely trains new representatives before they are allowed to staff a desk and receive customer calls. This practice has proven effective because historically, new reps make costly mistakes with accounts and usually do not know how to interact with customers properly. A significant number of errors occurred following a recent routine change in the center's operating process. The center redesigned the training program to be compatible with the new process, with the goal of eliminating the errors.

Stacy Hinkle evaluated the redesigned program for effectiveness and ROI. A recent group of 30 new graduates was used as a sample group for the evaluation. Prior to the training, the error count was 40 per month at an average cost of $100 per error. After the training, all 40 errors were eliminated. The training and performance solution was 60 percent responsible for eliminating the 40 errors, and the result will be sustained for one year.

40 errors per month $\times$ $100 per error = $4,000 per month cost of errors

$4,000 $\times$ 12 months = $48,000 a year

$48,000 $\times$ 0.60 causal influence = $28,800 a year benefits

The fully loaded cost of the training is $600 per employee. The annual turnover in the call center is 20 percent. How should the turnover loss adjustment be calculated, and what is the ROI?

Answer to Turnover Loss Adjustment Example   There are two ways to make the adjustment for turnover loss. It can be made to the cost side of the ROI formula (the denominator) or to the benefits side (the numerator).

Using the cost side of the ROI formula, an adjustment can be made by increasing the training cost to account for the necessity to train the replacement employees, as 20 percent of the 30 employees who were trained will no longer be with the company at the end of 12 months.

- The fully loaded cost of the training is $18,000 (30 graduates $\times$ $600 per trainee).
- The turnover experience is 20 percent annually; 30 employees $\times$ 0.20 = 6 employees who leave each year.

- 6 employees × $600 each to train = $3,600 to train 6 replacement employees.
- $18,000 plus $3,600 = $21,600 new training cost basis.
- Annualized benefits influenced by training solution = $28,800.
- ($28,800 – $21,600) ÷ $21,600 = 0.33 × 100 = 33% ROI adjusted for turnover.

Using the benefits side of the ROI formula, an adjustment can be made by decreasing the benefits to account for the amount of improvement that will not be realized as a result of the 20 percent turnover experience.

- The sustained benefits must be adjusted for the 20 percent turnover because the benefits are being annualized for 12 months and only 80 percent of the 30 employees who were trained will still be with the company at the end of that time.
- $28,800 annualized benefits × 0.80 = $23,040 sustained benefit value after the adjustment for turnover.
- The fully loaded cost of the training is $18,000 (30 graduates × $600). Even though because of turnover, there are only 24 employees remaining at the end of one year, we must count all 30 employees in the training cost because 30 were trained.
- ($23,040 annualized benefit adjusted for turnover – $18,000) ÷ $18,000 = 0.28 × 100 = 28% ROI adjusted for turnover.

The adjustment using the benefits (28 percent) is more conservative than the adjustment using the training costs (33 percent). However, there could be circumstances that would dictate that the training cost be used for some turnover adjustments. There could also be situations in which an adjustment may not be made even when there is turnover in the group. For example, review the following situation:

- The turnover experience is 10 percent, and 30 employees are trained.
- The performance data are collected after three months.
- The improvement is annualized; therefore, a turnover adjustment must be made to account for a loss of 3 employees (30 × 0.10 = 3 employees).

- However, it is determined that the 3 employees left the group at the end of the first month following the training. Two resigned, and one transferred to another group.
- Since the three employees left after one month, they have no improvement data represented in the data that were collected after three months.
- Conclusion: the turnover has been accounted for, and a turnover adjustment is not necessary.

When making an adjustment for turnover, it is important to consult with the client to gain agreement on how to make this adjustment. When an improvement is annualized, there may be additional factors or circumstances that require an adjustment to be made. For example, an adjustment may need to be made to account for the time value of money. Money that is available at the present time is worth more than the same amount in the future because of its potential earning capacity. The chief financial officer (CFO) can advise whether this adjustment needs to be made based on internal practices. There is a simple way to make the adjustment, as shown here:

- The current cost of funds, according to the CFO, is 5 percent.
- The fully loaded cost of the training program is $100,000.
- Add the current cost of funds to the cost of the training program.
- 5% of $100,000 = $5,000.
- $100,000 + $5,000 = $105,000 cost of training program adjusted for the future value of funds at the end of the first year.

Any time it is necessary to depart from the principle of making an adjustment for sustained impact, be certain of three things: (1) there is a compelling reason to depart from the principle, (2) key stakeholders, such as the client, the sponsor, and the executive management, agree with the decision, and (3) the analysis treats any variation in the adjustment consistently. Adjusting for sustained impact protects the credibility of the impact study and is a key factor in developing an ROI that represents reality and the truth.

CASE STUDY PART 4:
TECH*READ* SMART METERING COMPANY

Adjusting Business Outcome Results for Sustained Impact

About six weeks after the training solution was delivered, the evaluation team and its HR partner made the decision to eliminate the employee complaint data from the ROI analysis because the baseline data were unreliable. The revenue from sales is the remaining measure that can be used to evaluate business impact and prepare the ROI calculation. During the evaluation team's meeting with the regional managers (three months posttraining) to analyze the sales data, the decision was made concerning how much of the revenue could be attributed to the training solution. As reported in Part 3 of the Tech*Read* case study, the predetermined comparison group arrangement was the basis for this decision. The total monthly revenue increase for the three regions that participated in the training solution is $2,496,000 per month ($832,000 average per month $\times$ 3 regions in the experimental group = $2,496,000 total per month).

Choices for the Sustained Impact Adjustment   The sustained impact, Step 7 of the measurement and ROI process, must be addressed. Since the business outcome improvement data were collected only three months after the intervention, there is an issue about whether the improvement will be sustained. Some practitioners automatically annualize a business outcome improvement as a matter of routine. This practice is "generous analysis" that almost always grossly overstates the results and the ROI. The analysis must answer the question: how long is the monthly increase in revenue likely to continue? There are two extreme choices:

Extreme choice 1. Assume that the sales improvement will not continue beyond the three months of the evaluation period for which actual results data were collected. Thus, the revenue increase would stand at $7,488,000 total for the three-month period ($2,496,000 per month $\times$ 3 months = $7,488,000).

Extreme choice 2. Annualize the revenue for maximum impact. This calculation gives $29,952,000 for the first year ($2,496,000 $\times$ 12 months).

These two extreme alternatives would certainly make a huge difference in the calculation of the ROI. The conservative decision is to go with choice 1. However, the sustained impact decision should be made only after conferring with the sources that are in a position to address this issue. Can the monthly sales be projected forward to annualize the revenue? Will the same level of sales continue?

When determining sustained impact, the key issue is the effect of other intervening variables as the timeline moves forward for three months, six months, nine months, and so on. The issue could be resolved more easily if the actual results were collected and reported after six months or after one year. However, the nature of solutions and evaluation is that no one is willing to wait that long to see the results and apply the lessons learned. In the case of Tech*Read*, the training solution was withheld from three regions until the results could be analyzed. Therefore, waiting for more data is not an option.

Since the evaluation team is not involved in day-to-day sales, it is not a credible source to answer the sustained impact question. The credible sources at Tech*Read* are the regional sales managers. They are in the business of reviewing historical data (actual sales versus projections), analyzing the market, considering potential intervening variables, and forecasting sales. They know their customer base. They are involved in these activities every week, so they are in a position to forecast what should happen, based on both facts and their subjective analysis. This is not a science (it involves estimating, projections, and opinion), but it is the best way to do this. Business decisions—including sales projections—are frequently made in this manner. It would be a serious mistake to assume that the revenue can just be annualized as is.

A Critical Turn of Events   As the evaluation team was meeting with the regional managers to analyze the sales data, some critical information was revealed. The regional managers related that, one week earlier, they had been informed that new federal environmental legislation was certain to be passed by Congress this week. The legislation, which initially was not expected to pass, will have a near-term negative impact on Tech*Read*'s metering sales. Tech*Read*'s customers will be required to make substantial new capital investments as a result of the legislation. Tech*Read*'s internal business operations will not be affected by the legislation, but any effect on its customers' cost of doing business directly affects orders for metering devices of all types. The ripple effect has already begun. The field sales force in all regions is reporting that customers say that they are cutting back on their orders to help them find funding for the new investment requirements. Customers will not upgrade their outdated metering devices for at least another budget year. Customer plant and equipment upgrades represent about 30 percent of metering sales, and maybe more.

After considering all the information at hand, the three regional managers agreed that the new behavior of the sales force in call planning and sales call behavior is likely to continue, and sales would therefore continue. There is no reason to think otherwise. Therefore, the sales can be annualized. However, because of customer cutbacks, the regional managers were extremely uncomfortable about annualizing the sales at 100 percent. They agreed that the cutbacks by customers could have a significant negative effect on sales, but there is no way to determine the exact impact. They ultimately agreed that only 60 percent of the current sales should be annualized, meaning that they expect up to a 40 percent reduction in revenue.

When asked about their confidence (0 to 100 percent) in the estimate, the regional managers discussed it and agreed on an 80 percent confidence level. The sustained impact adjustment of 60 percent of the projected revenue is shown in Table 6.2. Since the projection is an estimate, the confidence level adjustment is also shown.

Table 6.2   Sustained Impact Adjustment

1. Sustained impact adjustment	Average monthly sales $2,496,000 × 0.60 = $1,497,600
2. Confidence level adjustment	$1,497,600 × 0.80 confidence level = $1,198,080
3. Annualized improvement	$1,198,080 × 12 months = $14,376,960 benefits first year

The annualized increase in revenue is $14,376,960 after the required adjustments shown in Table 6.2. Most training solutions are short-term in nature and should not be annualized beyond the first year.

Addressing the Effects of Turnover   Since the sales improvement was annualized, even though at a reduced amount, the improvement must be adjusted to account for the turnover within the experimental group. This adjustment is the responsibility of the evaluation team after acquiring the necessary information. A lengthy debate occurred regarding how this should be done. Should the adjustment be based on the turnover of the sales representatives or on the turnover of the sales managers, who were the participants in the training solution?

The sales representatives influenced the increase in sales by actually closing the sales. But they were not the group that had been trained. Sales managers influenced the increase through their managerial and coaching actions. After much deliberation and looking at the pros and cons, it was decided that the turnover experience of the sales representatives should be used to make the adjustment. The logic was that (1) they are the individuals that work the territory and close the sales, and (2) when new sales representatives are hired as replacements, it will take an extended period of time for them to affect sales while the sales manager coaches them to get up to speed on the territory, the products, the customers, and the Tech*Read* sales process. This will negatively affect sales during the window of time in which the improvement is annualized.

The annual turnover experience of the sales representatives at Tech*Read* is 20 percent. Therefore 80 percent of the annualized improvement is used to calculate the results. Table 6.3 shows the final results after the adjustment.

The total annualized benefits of $11,501,568 are carried forward in the study and used to calculate the ROI. As monetary values are assigned in the next chapter, another adjustment will take place.

Table 6.3   Sustained Impact Adjustment for Turnover

ADJUSTMENT FOR TURNOVER EXPERIENCE	
1. Annualized improvement from earlier adjustments	$14,376,960
2. Turnover experience	Turnover experience of sales representatives is 20 percent. Therefore, 80 percent is used to calculate the improvement.
3. Turnover adjustment	$14,376,960 × 0.80 = $11,501,568 total annualized benefits from revenue after turnover adjustment.

7

Go/No-Go: Assign a Monetary Value to Business Outcome Data

In evaluating training solutions to determine their contribution, the sustainability of one or more business outcomes is the most significant measure. The next most significant measure is sustained execution in the work setting—that is, knowing what the performers do to cause the business outcome and how the funding of a performance readiness solution influenced their execution. Some studies may only evaluate performance readiness to determine whether the performers learned a new skill or behavior. Other studies may examine execution in the work setting, but stop short of examining the business outcome. A business impact study evaluates all of these, plus it identifies how business outcomes are influenced by the solution.

Assigning a monetary value to the business outcome provides additional insight into the contribution of the training solution and allows for calculation of the ROI. The return on investment of a training and performance solution answers the question, did the solution pay for itself? The ROI can be calculated only when a monetary value is assigned to one or more business outcome measures. Values can be assigned to both hard and soft measures. As illustrated in Figure 7.1 (see page 164), Steps 8 and 9a address data analysis and assigning monetary values in preparation for calculating the return on investment.

Figure 7.1   Phase Three, Steps 8 and 9a

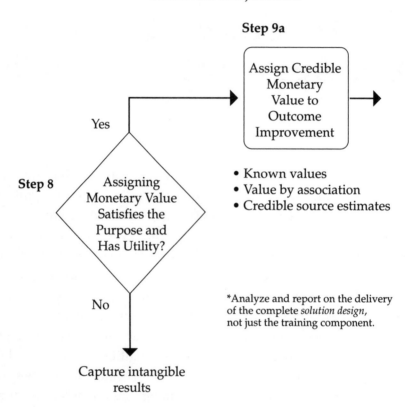

Phase Three

Analyze Data and Make
Conservative Adjustments*

Step 9a

Assign Credible
Monetary
Value to
Outcome
Improvement

Yes

Step 8   Assigning
Monetary Value
Satisfies the
Purpose and
Has Utility?

- Known values
- Value by association
- Credible source estimates

No

*Analyze and report on the delivery
of the complete *solution design*,
not just the training component.

Capture intangible
results

IN SEARCH OF VALUE—TRAINING IS NOT ALONE

Every function and every department is expected to provide value to the organization. For most of those who acquire or create the organization's products or services, and those who engage the customer to deliver and service the products, the value and contribution is direct and relatively easy to define without jumping through a lot of hoops. For others, such as staff functions like marketing, HR, learning and development, information technology, public relations, governmental affairs, and so on, the contribution and value is usually indirect and more difficult to demonstrate. Several prominent factors such as those shown here contribute to management's interest in and "need to know" about the contribution of the training function.

1. The size of the overall budget allocated to training as an indirect expense. *Indirect expense* generally means a cost that is not attributed directly to a particular product or service of the company.

2. The ongoing visibility of employees' absence from the job at hand because of their participation in training programs.

3. The lack of a clear line of sight between the funding and delivery of training solutions and the business outcomes influenced by those solutions.

4. The lack of current information and data that indicate the impact of training on the business.

5. Personal experiences participating in some training programs that seem to have limited connection to the organization's goals, strategies, or business problems.

6. The availability of inexpensive alternatives to formal training and development, such as hiring experienced personnel, implementing supervised on-the-job training exclusively, relying on learning through social networking, and self-learning initiatives.

7. The appearance of or actual duplication of training initiatives.

These factors place training professionals in a precarious position. Key stakeholders will always question the real value of training and development initiatives. This issue will not go away. Executive management will be at the head of the line with questions. If it is not the executive who is in place today, it will be her replacement tomorrow. Coupled with the seven factors just listed, a key reason that executives will always question the value of training is that training is considered a business expense, not an investment. Sure, we talk about training being an investment all the time. Some executives will even nod their head in agreement. We may not like it, but here's the bottom line: when the books are balanced in the accounting department and when profit is officially calculated in the CFO's office at the end of each fiscal year, training is treated as an expense that falls into the category of reducing profitability, not adding to it. From the perspective of the C-Suite, this is the picture that is clear, and this is the way the executives connect the dots.

The moral to this story is, while funding any operation (training included) takes away from profitability on the expense (cost) side of the business, there needs to be a corresponding way in which the funding contributes to adding value. This is even more vital for an operation like training, whose funding is usually treated as an indirect expense on the financial books. As illustrated by Table 7.1, there are two ways in which training can make a business contribution. One way is associated with revenue or funding, and the other is associated with cost savings.

Table 7.1   Two Ways in Which Training Can Affect the Business

BUSINESS IMPACT	EXAMPLES
1. Increase revenue, other income, or funding	• Profit margin from increased revenue • Higher profit margin resulting from the sale of products and services that have a higher profit • Increased income or funding from other sources

2. Cost reductions or savings	• Not associated with revenue, income, or funding. Value contribution created by cost savings resulting from numerous types of improvements in areas such as
	
	  ○ Quality improvements (reductions in discrepancies, waste, errors, rework, defects, spoilage, and so on)
	  ○ Savings resulting from improvements in time utilization
	  ○ Reduction in turnaround time to customer
	  ○ Increase in customer or employee retention
	  ○ Increase in customer or employee satisfaction
	  ○ Reduction in complaints
	  ○ Increases in output of products and services (quantity, efficiency)
	  ○ Various business process improvements
	  ○ Cost savings by eliminating a current business expense
	  ○ Cost savings by avoiding an imminent business expense

The examples of income or funding in item 1 in Table 7.1 apply to the public sector and nonprofits as well as to for-profit organizations. Government agencies, educational institutions, and nonprofits must acquire funding or a stream of income in some way. No organization operates without funding unless it is a 100 percent volunteer entity. If training engagements can influence the readiness of performers, and as a result the performers' actions increase revenue, funding, or income streams, then this provides a business contribution. Revenue is generally associated with goods and services sold by an entity. For a state government or municipality, funding is received from taxation, license or other fees, fines, intergovernmental grants or transfers, and any sales made.

Regarding item 2, all organizations, whether profit or nonprofit, must keep costs and waste under control in order to remain financially healthy. Hence, when training is responsible for the ultimate improvement in any of these measures, then this represents a business contribution. The following sections address considerations and ways to assign a monetary value to contributions or savings that training typically influences.

THE DISTINCTION BETWEEN HARD AND SOFT DATA

There is often a great deal of debate about the distinction between hard and soft data. There are extremes and many variations in the definitions of the two categories of measures. The distinction is important for two reasons. First, with soft data, it is often more difficult to establish a monetary value, and organizations may not have an assigned value. Second, when reporting soft data, the recipient of the communication will often raise questions about the credibility of the monetary value and how the improvement is associated with or links to a business contribution.

Hard Data

Generally there are four categories of hard data (Phillips and Stone, 2002). Measures in the hard data category are usually described as

1. *Output measures.* Orders filled, shipments, items sold, revenue collected, services provided, patients visited, medical procedures per-

formed, loans closed, customers called, customers served, tasks completed, forms processed, customers billed, and so on.

2. *Quality measures.* Errors, rejects, waste, scrap, rework, defective packages, product failures, baggage lost, orders filled incorrectly, bidding or proposal hit rate, stoppages, spoilage, deviation from standard, product batch contamination, theft, security breach, noncompliance, product defects, flaws, over- or underbilling customers, and so on.

3. *Time measures.* Processing time, length of customer calls, customer wait time, time to complete a task or project, meeting time, time to full competence, repair time, downtime, on-time shipments, overtime, and so on.

4. *Cost measures.* Unit costs, variable costs, fixed costs, cost savings, cost per hire, sales expense, cost of goods sold, cost per patient, cost per procedure, cost per customer, overhead costs, costs per complaint, cost per bed day, cost of supplies, cost per bid or proposal, and so on.

Hard data are more likely to have an assigned or standard monetary value. The source of this value could be an industry standard or a value that has been determined internally by tracking or estimating the associated costs in some manner over a period of time. The monetary values assigned to hard data may be used for multiple purposes and are usually accepted within the organization as credible values.

An important characteristic of hard measures is that every employee influences each hard data category every day. There are no exceptions to this. Each employee, from the CEO to the janitor, influences output, quality, cost, and time as she goes about her own activities. This is significant because there could be deficiencies in each category that may be caused by lack of knowledge or skills. Therefore, training has an opportunity to make a business contribution through improvements in these deficiencies.

Soft Data

Soft data are more subjective in nature. Generally, there are six categories of soft data. The number of measures in each category is too long to list here. Measures in the soft data category can be described as

1. *Customer service measures.* Customer satisfaction index, customer loyalty, customer complaints, churn rate (turnover), mystery shopper scores, and so on.

2. *Work habit measures.* Availability at workstation, tardiness to work, tardiness to meetings, excessive breaks, extended breaks, and so on.

3. *Work climate effectiveness measures.* Employee engagement, workload distribution, workplace conflict, employee stress, employee complaints or grievances, discrimination charges, job satisfaction, employee turnover, absenteeism, litigation, morale, effectiveness of coaching, effectiveness of meetings, effectiveness of leadership, and so on.

4. *Work climate opportunity measures* (the first three are measures of supervisors). Providing clear and reasonable expectations, constructive performance feedback, and reinforcing desired performance; access to coaching, access to mentoring, diversity of assignments, number of promotions and pay increases, number of training programs available, number of training programs attended, cross-functional training availability, and so on.

5. *Job attitude measures.* Cooperation, compatibility with team, acceptance of responsibility, respect for others, inclusiveness of others, informing others, professionalism, attentiveness to detail, and so on.

6. *Initiative measures.* Goals identified on personal development plan versus goals achieved, evidence of performance improvement, evidence of giving effort, successful completion of projects, keeping commitments, follow-through, and so on.

Soft data may not have an assigned monetary value. They are likely to be more difficult to quantify and measure. They are sometimes intangible or behavioral in nature. Soft data will be questioned more frequently when they are presented as evidence of results. Some of the soft measures given in the previous list are in the soft category not because they are difficult to measure, but because of the difficulty in assigning a credible monetary value to them (for example, turnover and absenteeism).

An important characteristic of soft data is that each soft measure always influences one or more categories of hard measures. Stated another way, under each hard measure lie multiple soft measures. So, even though the soft measures may not have an assigned monetary value, or the value may be more subjective than objective, efforts can be made to trace their linkage to one or more hard measures. When this linkage can be established, it makes the soft data more useful and credible.

As an example of linking soft measures to hard measures, let's review item 3 in the previous list, work climate effectiveness measures. If these types of measures can be improved, then the work climate improves. There could be a follow-on business improvement as a result of the improved climate. For example, when there is unnecessary conflict within a team, the team members are distracted from their work. They spend excessive amounts of time addressing the conflict in ways that take time and take their attention away from important tasks. They may become so concerned or stressed by the conflict that they lose concentration on their work and make mistakes. Mistakes require rework. So, just with this one soft example of conflict, at least three hard data categories are directly affected: time, output, and quality.

An analysis of such a situation can determine how much time is wasted as a result of the conflict and how much rework must be done because of poor-quality work caused by it. The time it takes to do the rework represents the minimum cost of the deficiency in quality. The hours wasted as a result of distractions represent lost output. If employees are talking about or debating the conflict, they cannot be doing the important work that they were hired to do. These costs now become hard data and are easily measurable by assigning the percentage of salary and benefits represented by the lost hours. For example:

- A team of 10 people wastes a total of 15 hours weekly on the unnecessary conflict. That's lost output or productivity.
- Another 10 hours are required to rework errors resulting from the conflict.
- Both figures are adjusted for an 80 percent confidence level. That leaves 20 total hours of unproductive time caused by the unnecessary conflict.
- 20 × $50 per hour (the cost of salary and employee benefits) = $1,000 weekly. If the employees can be trained to handle conflict appropriately, and as a consequence 80 percent of the conflict can be

eliminated, this is a savings of $800 weekly, or $3,200 for a four-week month. And this is a conservative adjustment.

The distinction between hard and soft data does not necessarily imply that hard data are more important than soft data. That is, paying attention to only the hard data will not necessarily contribute more to the organization's success, since the soft data lurking underneath can be the root cause of problems. The previous example illustrates that issues arising from soft data can easily undermine the success of the organization and directly affect the hard data categories. Perhaps we should look at the hard data for indicators of deficiencies (because they are easier to see and measure), then look underneath toward the soft measures as a possible source of the root cause. In the previous example, if the team manager is observant, he will see the poor quality and the drop in output. In reality, it may take him weeks to discover both deficiencies in today's world of knowledge and service workers.

TO BE OR NOT TO BE—ASSIGNING A MONETARY VALUE

Guiding Principle 8 states, "Calculate ROI only when it satisfies the purpose of the evaluation project and has utility for one or more interested stakeholders." Step 8 of the measurement and ROI process shown in Figure 7.1 is a key decision point in the methodology to determine whether a specific measure will be utilized to calculate ROI. A single question must be answered for each business outcome measure: does this measure have an existing known monetary value? If the answer is yes, the journey for that measure will continue down the path of Steps 9a, 9b, and 9c to calculate the ROI. If the answer is no, a second question must be asked: should resources be dedicated to assigning a monetary value to this measure? If the answer is yes, the journey for that measure continues to Steps 9a, 9b, and 9c to calculate the ROI. If the answer is no, the journey for that measure continues on a different path to Step 9d, and the improvement is reported as an intangible outcome.

Guiding Principle 8

Calculate ROI only when it satisfies the purpose of the evaluation project and has utility for one or more interested stakeholders.

In essence, Step 8 of the measurement and ROI process can be considered the gateway to calculating ROI. A decision at Step 8 to go down the path to assign a monetary value does not require that the ROI be calculated. The monetary value may be useful without the ROI calculation. However, once a value for a specific measure is determined, it is easy to proceed to calculate ROI.

Compelling Reasons to Assign a Monetary Value

The decision to assign a monetary value is initially made during the evaluation planning stage. However, the situation may be quite different several months later, when the improvement data are actually being collected and analyzed. During the decision-making process at Step 8, there are compelling factors that must be taken into consideration to determine whether a monetary value is to be assigned and the ROI calculated. The following are the compelling factors in favor of a yes decision to assign a monetary value at Step 8.

Compelling Factor 1 Leading to a Yes Decision *A specific measure has a known monetary value that is credible to key stakeholders, and the information is easy to retrieve.* Since the data are readily available and credible, there are few resources needed and very little cost to analyze the data and calculate the ROI. This provides an extended level of beneficial information to communicate to stakeholders that shows the contribution of training.

Compelling Factor 2 Leading to a Yes Decision *Assigning a monetary value satisfies the purpose of the evaluation project and has utility for one or more key stakeholders.* When one of the stated purposes of an evaluation is to calculate the ROI, and when the monetary value is known, as in Compelling Factor 1, then the study normally moves forward to calculate the ROI. However, consider a situation in which the value of a measure is not known.

When the value is not known, a quick assessment of the time and resources that it may take to establish a credible value should be made. If the time and resources are determined to be considerable, then a question should be asked about utility. That is, considering both the time and resources required and any expected benefit from knowing the monetary value, will the information be sufficiently useful to the key stakeholders? The client or sponsor should be approached, and a decision should be recommended: go or no-go?

The client may decide that the information is necessary and that the analysis should continue as initially planned. Or the client may decide that the journey would cost more than any expected benefit from knowing the value, and therefore the ROI calculation is abandoned. When it is abandoned, the business improvement is routed through the path of Step 9d and reported as an intangible. The same results are carried forward, but the monetary value is not known.

Compelling Factor 3 Leading to a Yes Decision   *A specific measure is important to the organization.* When a specific measure is important to the organization, everything about that measure becomes important. It may be extremely important to the organization to know the monetary value of that measure, even when considerable amounts of resources and time are required to identify that value. For example, think about the monetary value of customer satisfaction or employee satisfaction. Perhaps the organization will benefit by applying the value in multiple situations and in numerous ways. Therefore, the client or sponsor may be very supportive of proceeding with a calculation, even when doing so was not the original intent, and even when it requires significant amounts of resources.

Compelling Factor 4 Leading to a Yes Decision   *A key stakeholder demands to know the ROI, regardless of other considerations.* There are times or situations when a key stakeholder insists on certain things. This sometimes happens with ROI. Stakeholders may want to see the value, even though calculating it may consume considerable time and resources. Sometimes this happens after the fact. A program is delivered, and a key stakeholder sees something that raises questions and asks for a study to determine the ROI. This is not the advisable way to calculate ROI, but it can certainly be done.

Compelling Reasons That a Monetary Value Should Not Be Assigned

During the decision-making process at Step 8, just as there are compelling reasons to assign a monetary value to improvement data, there are also valid reasons to report an improvement without assigning a monetary value. The following are the compelling factors in favor of a no decision, and therefore not assigning a monetary value, at Step 8.

Compelling Factor 1 Leading to a No Decision   *Key stakeholders have no interest in knowing the monetary value of a specific measure.* While stakeholders are interested in achieving a return on investment, they are not always interested in allocating resources after the fact to determine whether it was actually achieved. The business outcome improvement can often show a compelling result that satisfies stakeholder expectations without the need for a monetary value and a ROI calculation.

Compelling Factor 2 Leading to a No Decision   *There is limited utility to assigning a monetary value because of the amount of resources it would require to determine a credible value compared with the benefit of knowing the value.* When this circumstance prevails, consult with key stakeholders to explain the difficulty and communicate the amount of resources it would require to proceed with a calculation. If the measure is important to the stakeholders and they believe that a credible value can be determined, they will support the additional time and resources required.

Compelling Factor 3 Leading to a No Decision   *The credibility of the approach used to determine a monetary value would be seriously questioned by key stakeholders.* Key stakeholders usually have a standard when it comes to accepting any type of research data. When the credibility of an approach used to assign monetary values is not certain, key stakeholders should be consulted before continuing the process.

Compelling Factor 4 Leading to a No Decision   *Key stakeholders are unwilling to wait as long as it would take to determine a monetary value.* If it is important to wrap up the evaluation project and you have the business improvements identified, present the data as is, with the stipulation that perhaps an ROI can be calculated later. Gauge the interest level and determine whether to proceed with the calculation at a later time.

Compelling Factor 5 Leading to a No Decision   *The monetary value will probably not be used again (it is a one-off measure, or it will be used only in limited situations).* This one is difficult to call and can go either way. Keep Compelling Factor 1 (interest level) in mind when making the decision based on Compelling Factor 5. If the value is easy to assign and it helps the credibility of your project, then it may be useful to proceed by assigning a monetary value.

Business outcome results that are not assigned a monetary value are often called *intangible results.* The results may be evident: there is an improvement over the baseline status of the measure, and the causal influence and sustained impact are known, but for various reasons, a monetary value has not been determined. Intangible results are addressed in more detail in Chapter 10.

CREDIBLE METHODS FOR ASSIGNING A MONETARY VALUE

In order to calculate the return on investment of training, a monetary value must be assigned to one or more business outcomes that are influenced by a training solution. Calculating ROI is important for one significant reason: assigning a monetary value and calculating the ROI helps to show that training is more than a business expense. To the extent that training is successful in improving business outcomes, the ROI demonstrates that training also contributes to the bottom line of the business by covering its own cost. There are three methods of assigning a monetary value that can then be compared to the costs to develop a ROI:

1. Known values
2. Values by association
3. Credible source estimates

Known values, when they exist, are available in the records of the organization. Guiding Principle 9 states, "When they are available, use organization records as a first source to report outcome improvement data and to determine monetary values, then resort to other credible sources." Known values do not always exist, or sometimes the data may not be useful for purposes of a specific study or may be contaminated in some way. When this is the case, the other two methods may be used to assign a monetary value. While there are only three methods for assigning a monetary value, there are a multitude of sources and types of measures to which these methods can be applied. Each method is discussed in the following sections, with examples.

Guiding Principle 9

When they are available, use organization records as a first source to report outcome improvement data and to determine monetary values, then resort to other credible sources.

Using Known Values

Known values exist for many types of business outcomes, from sales, to output of products and services, to various kinds of quality measures. The status of these measures is usually tracked monthly, weekly, or even daily, depending on the metric. For example, in an automobile dealership, customer satisfaction is tracked with each transaction. Someone in the organization acts as custodian for each type of metric, and this individual may also know the monetary value that the organization places on the measure. If not, he may know where to go to get useful information about the value. Table 7.2 shows examples of output and quality measures that typically have a known or standard monetary value.

When you approach a database custodian, be prepared to answer a series of questions. The custodian usually guards the data as though it were his own creation. He is likely to want to know the answer to questions like: (1) Why do you need these data, and how are you going to use them? (2) Who will this analysis be reported to? (3) Will I be able to see your conclusions about the data? (4) Will you provide me with feedback on how your audience responds to the data and conclusions? The questions that a custodian asks are actually very useful in determining whether the data suit your

Table 7.2   Measures That Typically Have Known Values

TYPE OF MEASURE	HOW THE VALUE MAY TYPICALLY BE DETERMINED
1. Increase in sales (sales is a type of output)	Profit margin is used to determine the contribution and value of revenue from sales. The finance department will provide the proper percentage to use for the profit margin on revenue.
	The finance department may do the calculation of the margin a couple of different ways. Ultimately, the calculation will yield a small percentage of the revenue.
	Example: Revenue from sales influenced by the training is $2,000,000. The CFO provides a profit margin of 8 percent. Revenue of $2,000,000 × 0.08 = $160,000 contribution.
2. Increase in output of a product or service (production or creation of goods and services)	The value of output is usually determined by the total fixed and variable costs required to produce one unit of output. When an improvement occurs that reduces the cost of output or increases the actual amount of output for a specific timeframe, the contribution becomes the new standard when the improvement is sustained. The resulting cost savings or increase in output is the value of the improvement.
	Example: An expensive production process for refrigerator doors has a scheduled stoppage twice a month to change out patterns so that a different type of door can be manufactured. The average time for a scheduled stoppage is 2 hours. The office of the CFO says that the loss of productivity costs the company $200,000 for each scheduled stoppage.
	A problem-solving workshop results in cutting the scheduled stoppage from 2 hours to a sustained 1½ hours.
	Using $200,000 as a known value and 2 hours as the baseline prior to the workshop, the sustained improvement of 30 minutes per stoppage is valued at $50,000. The $50,000 savings per stoppage is used to calculate the ROI.
3. Improved quality of a product or service	One way to view the value of quality is to determine the value of eliminating unnecessary costs associated with errors, rework, discrepancies, and so on.
	This includes time, materials, supplies, and other such expenses.
	Example: Employee time for rework is valued at $50 per hour wages and benefits. Wasted materials are valued at $100 replacement cost. Rework consumes 10 employee hours.
	10 hours × $50 = $500 + $100 materials = $600

purposes, how to interpret the data, and how to present the data. Data custodians are allies and partners. Cooperate with them in every way because they are a useful and credible resource. They will also help you to interpret the data.

The Value of Sales   Sales is a type of output. In item 1 of Table 7.2, when calculating the ROI for a training program, the contribution (value) of revenue from sales is treated differently from the contribution of other types of output. Where revenue from sales is the benefit from an intervention, the contribution to profit from the revenue is used in the ROI formula. As an example, to determine the value of an improvement in sales, assume that a training program for sales personnel influences a $2,000,000 annual increase in commercial sales, as shown in Table 7.2. The finance department provides a profit margin of 8 percent for the commercial sales in question.

Thus, $2,000,000 \times 0.08 = \$160,000$ contribution to profit. The $160,000 is carried forward to the numerator of the ROI calculation to determine the net benefit from the training program. The fully loaded cost of the training is $115,000. The ROI for the training solution is 39 percent, as calculated here:

$$\text{ROI} = \frac{\$45,000 \; [\$160,000 - \$115,000]}{\$115,000} = 0.39 \times 100 = 39\%$$

The total $2,000,000 revenue from sales cannot be used as a benefit in the numerator of the ROI formula because all the costs involved in generating that revenue must be accounted for first. The finance department's calculation of the profit margin accounts for these costs. All expenses, such as parts, materials, electricity, building space, and total compensation for the labor involved in creating the products that are sold, are accounted for when the finance department calculates the 8 percent profit margin. Therefore, the amount of the revenue that represents profit is used in the ROI calculation.

The Value of Output   Output, such as producing a product or creating a service, has a value that is associated with the cost to produce one unit. Unit cost can be calculated for any type of product or service in profit, nonprofit, and government entities as long as someone takes the time to do it. Known values often exist for output, in particular for the products and services that an organization markets to sustain the business. A cell phone manufacturer knows the value of producing one cell phone (one unit of output). It knows both the value of producing one new cell phone and the value of one refurbished cell phone. A new and a refurbished cell phone each has a different market value. Each is priced on the basis of what it costs to move the phone through the company's assembly process to become a marketable product. Before pricing the products, administrative and general expenses are added to the cost of the process to account for the indirect costs of those departments that are not directly involved in producing the cell phones.

A consulting company knows the value of a unit of output, which may typically be one consulting day. A consulting company generates revenue through the billable time of consultants. There is an average of 21⅔ workdays in a month. A typical consultant is expected to bill 12 to 15 days per month. This leaves the consultant ample time to travel to client sites, develop proposals, attend meetings, assist in selling the company's services, take vacation and personal days, and so on. The value (price) of a billable day must account for the consultant's total workdays (21⅔ days per month) and other costs that the consulting company must recover through the billable days. Suppose a consultant's personal take-home paycheck is $500 per day. The billable rate to clients must be 5 to 10 times that amount (or even more) if the company is to earn enough revenue to pay all the costs associated with supporting the consultant and managing and sustaining the consulting business.

A municipality knows the value of issuing city licenses of various types. If the municipality is operated like a business, the cost that citizens pay for the various types of licenses must be enough to keep the respective license departments financially solvent. A city will often subsidize one department with the revenue from the services of another department. For-profit companies sometimes do this too, but it is preferable for them to keep profit centers self-sustaining.

Because placing a value on a unit of output is not always precise, the value of a product, service, or process may be overstated or may even be understated. Values are not always designed to withstand close scrutiny, but rather are intended to provide a basis for allocating resources, making investments, pricing products, and making other business decisions. Of course, the more precise the value, the more accurate and efficient all of the organization's decisions will be, especially pricing. Once value is determined, it is used for many purposes throughout the organization.

The Value of Quality Quality represents effectiveness and is a significant measure in any organization. The more effective or the more accurate a product, process, or service is, the more likely it is to be helping to achieve the organization's objectives. Certainly most organizations want 100 percent quality. However, the cost to maintain 100 percent quality may be prohibitive. Therefore, each type of industry or government agency has a built-in tolerance level for quality. When improving quality equates to reducing costs, or serving customers better (up to a point), or sustaining or improving revenue, most organizations will make an investment to do so.

Poor quality can have a negative impact on an organization in two ways. It can increase the cost of doing business through waste, scrap, spoilage, discrepancies, errors, and the cost of rework. It can also result in a decrease in revenue when it goes undetected and reaches the doorsteps of customers. Even the most loyal of customers can be unforgiving and resort to alternatives in the marketplace for their products and services. Item 3 in Table 7.2 illustrates one of numerous ways to determine the value of an improvement in quality. The following example illustrates another way to determine the value of a quality improvement.

Example. Electronics manufacturer XYZ determines the cost of quality by calculating the cost of customer returns from all retail stores and online outlets. The value is developed from the cost of repair on returns, plus average discount on resale, plus transportation and overhead. Repairs are outsourced in local markets.

The average cost of repair per unit is $150. The average discount on resale is $200. Transportation and internal overhead expenses are $30 per unit. Therefore, the average cost of poor quality is $150 + $200 + $30 = $380 per unit returned.

An internal quality improvement program at XYZ reduces returns from 500 per month to 200 per month. Improvement of 300 returns × $380 = $114,000 per month savings in the cost of quality.

Many training programs can influence improvements in quality. It can be relatively easy to determine the monetary value of an improvement. Improvements in quality ultimately lead to sustained customer satisfaction and increased profitability. Use credible sources in the organization, such as participants, immediate supervisors of participants, managers, custodians of quality data, or client input, to determine the impact and value of improving quality.

The Value of Employee Time Savings   It is interesting to note that in Item 3 of Table 7.2, "Measures That Typically Have Known Values," time savings is one element used as a means of determining the monetary value of quality. Time savings is also frequently used to determine the value of a unit of output or the value of an improvement. Time is money. All activities require time. Activities that are unnecessary, are wasteful, or are a duplication of other activities are unproductive. Unproductive tasks rob time from productive tasks that employees should be doing to achieve company objectives.

An improvement in employee time savings can be determined through estimates, observation, or the use of technology, such as computerized management systems that track the status of a measure. The value used for employee time savings is salaries and benefits, a known value. For example, suppose the time required to resolve a typical customer complaint is reduced by one hour. The mid-value of the salaries of those involved is used for the calculation. Mid-value is the salary that would be earned by a fully competent employee in a specific job. The HR department can provide this mid-value for any job.

For simplification, in this example, let's assume that only one person is involved in handling and resolving customer complaints. The midpoint salary is $20 per hour. The employee benefits factor provided by the HR department is 32 percent (employee benefits are always given as a percentage of salaries); thus, 20 × 0.32 = $6.40. The total value of $26.40 per hour is used for the employee's time. Typically, 60 customer complaints are handled per month; $26.40 × 60 = $1,584 cost per month. The result of eliminating all complaints would be a savings of $1,584 per month. Of course, in reality, there is likely to be more than one person involved in hearing and resolving customer complaints. Some complaints are reviewed by a manager. The manager may also get involved in the resolution and communication with the customer. The same calculation would be done for the manager's time, and this would be added to the cost shown here for a typical complaint.

When the value of time saved is used in a ROI calculation, two adjustments may be necessary. The first adjustment is to reduce the time saved by the amount that is not reallocated to productive tasks. For example, suppose that a team of junior accountants saves 20 total hours in a typical workweek. When asked how much of the saved time is being reallocated to productive tasks, the response is 90 percent. The adjustment is 20 hours × 0.9 = 18 hours adjusted time saved. The 18-hour savings is used for the ROI calculation.

A second adjustment is made if the reported time savings is an estimate. In this case, the respondent would be asked, what is your confidence level in the estimate, based on a scale of 100 percent to 0 percent (100 percent = I am sure; 0 percent = total uncertainty)? A response of a 95 percent confidence level on the savings of 18 hours = 17 hours adjusted time savings. The total savings is then determined by multiplying the salary and benefits of a junior accountant by 17 hours.

When time savings are used to determine the value of an improvement, be certain that the time of everyone involved is captured. For example, the cost of an employee grievance would include the time of the employee who files the grievance, those hearing the grievance, those resolving the grievance, and those involved in reviewing and communicating the resolution. As you can imagine, the costs can add up considerably, especially when resolving a grievance involves several levels of management. There can be other costs as well, such as disruption in the work setting within the team and additional loss of productivity.

Direct Cost Savings   When there is a straightforward cost savings, there is little calculation to do other than determining how much money was saved.

Once it is established that a specific amount of money has been saved as a result of the training solution's influence and the sustainability of that savings is confirmed, then that amount of savings is documented for inclusion in the benefits. For example, an e-learning solution on negotiation skills is implemented for the buyers in the purchasing department. The participants complete action plans to apply what they learned. When the action plans are completed four months after the training, 12 of 20 participants provide data showing a business outcome improvement of some type during negotiations with vendors. One participant provides a one-time savings of $20,000 when negotiating with a vendor for a large contract for batteries and lightbulbs. She credits the e-learning solution with half the savings. Thus, $10,000 is carried forward to add to the results from the other 11 participants. This is a direct cash savings that is not annualized because it is a one-time savings.

As can be seen from some of the other types of measures already provided here, and as noted in Table 7.1, there are only two ways to achieve a business benefit. A benefit is either (1) a contribution to revenue, or some other type of income or funding, or (2) a cost savings, such as improved quality, time savings, or output improvements (the ultimate result is a cost savings of some type). In both instances, the monetary value of the contribution must be assigned to a business outcome measure. In the case of a direct cost savings, the value is inherent in the savings. The value is evident, and there are no dots to connect to determine the value.

The last item in the right-hand column of Table 7.1, "Cost savings by avoiding an imminent business expense," refers to any probable future expense that would add cost to the business. When such an expense is imminent (known to be forthcoming in the near term) and training contributes to avoiding the expense, this is a business contribution. For example, at ABC Company, a governmental affairs manager attends a seven-day program in "political persuasion" at a major university at a cost of $20,000 tuition plus travel and lodging expenses. The manager sits on numerous committees at the state level to represent the company's interests. Following the education program, his direct involvement during the current legislative session made a major contribution to defeating legislation that would have cost ABC Company $400,000. This is a direct cost savings that was avoided and can be used to calculate the ROI of the political persuasion program. This is also an example of a situation where it may be appropriate to calculate the ROI even though there is only one participant.

Assigning Values by Association

When a business outcome measure does not have a known value, it is possible that a value can be determined by linking the measure to another improvement that has a value or by using a value from an external database or related study. Table 7.3 includes examples of assigning a value by association.

Table 7.3   Assigning Value by Association

METHOD OF ASSOCIATION	EXAMPLES OF ASSIGNING A VALUE BY ASSOCIATION
1. Credible related study or external database	Sandra at XYZ automobile assembly plant is evaluating a customer service training program. She needs to know the value of improving customer service in the warranty department. Sandra uses a monetary value from a recent study of the automotive industry developed by the University of Michigan.
	The University of Michigan study uses loss of repeat business to determine the value of improving customer service. The value is tied to customer satisfaction scores and customer feedback. The study concludes that each improvement of 2 percentage points (between 88 and 96 percent) in customer satisfaction scores = $800 per month.
	Prior to the XYZ customer service training, customer satisfaction scores were 89 percent. After the training, the scores improved to 95 percent. Using the monetary value from the University of Michigan study, the improvement value is $2,400 per month (3 units × $800).
2. Linking to other improvements	XYZ Technology Company delivers a training program for supervisors with the aim of reducing unexpected absenteeism. The program is credited with reducing absenteeism from 12 percent to an acceptable level of 3 percent. There is no known value for absenteeism.
	Prior to the program, overtime was costing $20,000 per month. After the program, overtime was reduced to $4,000 per month. There were no other factors driving the overtime hours. The $16,000 savings in overtime is used as a value for the reduction in absenteeism.

Assigning a value by association rarely involves a straight line of sight where the dots can easily be connected. Assumptions are usually made in establishing a connection. Credibility can be an issue. Therefore, the analysis should be treated like an estimate. For example, in item 1 of Table 7.3, Sandra with XYZ automobile company should ask two questions: (1) Is this external study by the University of Michigan closely enough associated with my situation that my key stakeholders are likely to consider it to be credible to use in assigning a monetary value? (2) What is my confidence level in using the monetary value identified in the University of Michigan study? She should reflect on several factors that affect credibility before providing her answers to both questions. The key factors that generally affect the credibility of any study and its findings are

1. *Credibility of the researcher.* Is the researcher qualified and objective? What personal association does the researcher or evaluation analyst have with the people, program, or issues being studied? Who funded the study, and under what arrangements with the person doing the evaluation? Does the researcher have ulterior motives? How did the researcher gain access to the information being studied? What prior knowledge did the researcher bring to the research topic and the study? What may his bias be?

2. *Context of the study.* Evaluation impact studies are inherently highly contextual. They are specific to a particular audience, particular measures, and a particular situation and set of conditions. Do the situation being studied and the conclusions developed match the context of your situation closely enough to be adaptable?

3. *Scope of the study.* The larger the scope of a study is, the more generalizations dilute the analysis and findings. The smaller the scope (smaller group, more identifiable and controllable variables, more specific measures, and so on), the more specific and credible the findings. Is the scope such that the analysis and findings are specific and can be used as a credible source?

4. *Assumptions made during the analysis.* Assumptions are made in most studies. Are the assumptions credible? Are they realistic? Is the researcher living in a paradigm with unquestioned assumptions?

5. *Reputation of the methodology.* Does the methodology used for the study pass the acid test? Were data analyzed using a conservative approach? Was a systematic methodology used by applying guiding principles to develop the findings and the monetary value? How are the tools and techniques of the methodology deployed and interpreted? Is the methodology used generally respected and acceptable?

These five key credibility factors apply not only to external studies used as a source for monetary values, but also to any type of data analysis and conclusions. However, these factors certainly are not a complete list of possibilities. There can be no finite list of questions to establish the credibility of data. The idea is that, when Sandra reports the results from her analysis, she should report any information that negatively or positively affected her data collection and influenced her analysis and interpretation of the data. There are several issues in Sandra's favor regarding the credibility of the monetary value. The study was completed in her own industry (automotive) by a respected university with close ties to the automotive industry. This can provide instant face credibility. Had the study been about customer service in the airline industry, Sandra's stakeholders would probably be skeptical of the applicability of the value and its use for the ROI calculation. This could discredit her entire impact study on the customer service program.

Using Credible Source Estimates to Assign Value

When a business outcome measure does not have a known value, credible sources may be used to estimate the monetary value. For example, a known value is not always available for quality or output, so they may be estimated. The following should be considered when estimates are provided:

- Use credible sources that are close to the work situation and have the most comprehensive view of the situation. For example, supervisors have a more comprehensive view of all the costs involved in absenteeism than do team members. Team members may have a more comprehensive view of all the costs of time robbers that keep them from concentrating on their work.

- Ask the source to define the unit of measure in specific terms (for example, one typical complaint, one engineer voluntarily resigning, or one damaged package per 100 delivered).
- Ask the source to provide a value after considering all factors that make up the cost (value) of the specific measure (time, materials, supplies, and so on).
- Ask the source to provide a confidence level for the estimate. Make a corresponding adjustment during the analysis.
- When practical, provide an opportunity for management to make an additional adjustment to the estimate based on its view of the situation.
- When there is more than one possible value, use the one that is most conservative.
- When a source assigns a value that seems extreme, ask the source about it. If there is no credible basis for the monetary value, give strong consideration to reporting the improvement as an intangible.
- When reporting results, always disclose when estimates are used and show an example of how they are adjusted.

While estimates are not the preferred method of assigning monetary values, use of this method is actually quite common in organizations. Estimates are used by engineers, financial analysts, accountants, management, and others. Even though estimates are never considered to be accurate, a conservative approach along with adjustments for confidence level makes for a more realistic and credible value.

A credible source for estimates is defined as anyone who is in a position to know how to estimate the value of an improvement and would be considered as credible by key stakeholders, such as clients, sponsors, and executive management. Consider the possibilities in the following sections.

Participants as a Credible Source   Participants are close to the work situation and have a firsthand view of it. They can sometimes estimate the value of an improvement even when the data are soft. They have applied the skills from the training solution, and they may be in a good position to provide a value for any improvement. When asking participants to provide a value, they can often respond better when they are given examples and guidance on how to proceed.

Supervisors and Managers as a Credible Source   Even though participants may be able to determine the improvement, they may sometimes have difficulty providing a value for it. Supervisors or managers of the participants may be in a better position to provide a value for a unit of improvement. They often have a comprehensive view of the situation. They see the inputs that go into performance and the outputs at the end of the process. They are also more experienced in dealing with values, as their job often requires them to calculate or estimate the cost of work activities under their sphere of influence. Senior management may also provide estimates of the value of an improvement.

Experts as a Credible Source   Management considers internal experts to be a credible source on many performance issues and considers them to be very knowledgeable about the entire performance process in a specific area. For example, when determining the cost of grievances, the manager of labor relations is probably the expert, and if he is not, he can recommend others who should be involved in determining the value. If a senior executive wants to know the cost of grievances, she will generally begin by calling the manager of labor relations.

When internal experts are not available, external experts may be used to seek a monetary value. External experts are usually reliable only if they have considerable experience with the specific measure in question. When a value is provided by internal or external experts, the expert's name and credentials should be communicated. Of course, the person providing the value should be made aware of this requirement. The expert should also provide a confidence level so that a conservative adjustment can be made to account for the possibility of error.

DETERMINING UNIT VALUE AND CALCULATING AN OVERALL IMPROVEMENT

When a unit value is not available, one way to assign a value is through unit cost analysis. A value can be assigned through unit cost analysis by working with credible sources. First, the training professional should determine whether a known value is available. The client or sponsor is a good source to begin the search. When the client or sponsor does not know the value, and no other source knows the value, it can be developed. Ask the client who he believes is in the best position to help determine the value. The source to determine a value can be an individual, or an ad hoc group can be designated to assist in the effort. Once the source has been identified and has agreed to assist in the calculation, proceed to facilitate the process as follows:

Step 1

Define the unit of service under consideration. Examples of a common unit of product or service are completing a customer help call in a service center, delivering an order, completing a service call at a customer's residence, assembling a cell phone, assembling a bicycle, or baking doughnuts. A unit of service or a unit of production is uniquely associated with the way a unit is produced or created or the way a unit is packaged or delivered. For example, pencils may be produced by the thousand. Therefore, one unit is 1,000 pencils.

Let's use an example to show how unit cost analysis works. Mountain Media Cable provides consumer products and services in digital cable, video on demand, television programming, high-speed Internet, and digital voice. High-speed Internet is one of the most profitable segments of the business. When a customer has trouble with his Internet service, the call center attempts to resolve the problem with the customer over the telephone. Trouble tickets that cannot be resolved by telephone protocol are processed to the next troubleshooting phase, called wheels out. During "wheels out," a technician is dispatched to a customer's home to resolve the problem. Some of these dispatches are handled by in-house technicians and some are outsourced at about the same cost. Mountain Media receives an average of 500 service help calls per day and is experiencing excessive wheels-out calls. On average, 30 of 100 trouble calls are dispatched as wheels outs. Representatives staffing the call centers are not familiar with the equipment and the telephone troubleshooting process, resulting in the excessive wheels-out dispatches. A training program is delivered for the call center reps with the objective of reducing the number of wheels-out dispatches to a standard of no more than 10 per 100 trouble calls. To determine the monetary benefit, the value of one trouble call is needed.

Step 1 defines the Mountain Media unit of service as wheels-out service calls.

Step 2

Define the increment of time normally associated with how the unit is provided or reported, and identify the number of units during that time period. An increment of time may be an hour, a day, a week, or some other period. Mountain Media schedules the number of wheels-out dispatches daily. Therefore, it usually reports and discusses the number of wheels-out dispatches per day. The average number of wheels-out dispatches per day is six per technician. Since we are determining value, we will determine the cost of all resources associated with six wheels-out dispatches per day. The people involved in this activity routinely allocate resources on a per day basis, so it will be easier for them to analyze and talk about a per day cost. The per day basis will be used through all succeeding steps to maintain consistency in determining the cost (value).

Step 2 for Mountain Media now becomes six wheels-out service calls per day.

Step 3

Determine the direct costs of the unit of service. Direct costs are those that are directly involved in creating or providing a product or service and that can be traced directly to a specific service, product, or department. In Mountain Media, the direct cost of a wheels-out dispatch involves several people. The call center rep must refer the customer information to the dispatcher. The dispatcher is involved in scheduling the wheels-out dispatch, monitoring its progress, and closing out the trouble ticket. The technician is involved in traveling to the customer's residence to correct the problem and reporting the completed job to the dispatcher.

There are several dispatchers, technicians, and call center reps. In order to calculate the cost per day, we will trace the activities of one technician and other resources on a typical day. There is an average of six dispatches per day per technician. Wages shown include an employee benefit cost of 36 percent.

- *Call center rep:* 30 minutes per day to support one technician by communicating information to the dispatcher; $14 per hour × 0.5 hour = $7.
- *Dispatcher:* 3 hours per day to schedule, coordinate, and close out six dispatches for one technician; $18 per hour × 3 hours = $54.
- Technician: 8 hours per day to travel to and service the customers; $19 per hour × 8 hours = $152.
- Supplies and materials = $20 per day.
- *Travel costs:* Gasoline and miscellaneous upkeep = $23 per day.

Step 3 Mountain Media wheels-out total direct costs for one technician = *$256 per day.*

Step 4

Determine the indirect costs of the unit of service. Indirect costs associated with a product or service are expenses that are not directly traceable to a department, product, service, activity, customer, or some other unit. Indirect costs and expenses are usually allocated to a department, product, or service. For example, they include rent, heating and air conditioning for the entire building, and telephones. There are several ways to allocate indirect costs. For example, they may be assigned to all departments based on the number of square feet each department occupies, or based on the ratio of the service to all services provided by the company. The client or department manager can usually provide information on how this is done in a specific company. If not, consult the finance or accounting department.

The indirect costs of wheels-out dispatches at Mountain Media are rent; utilities, including water, electricity, and telephones; a portion of administrative and management salaries; and a portion of information technology costs, HR costs, and other types of overhead, such as company liability insurance and legal fees.

Step 4 Mountain Media total indirect costs are *$328.62 per day.*

Step 5

Determine the depreciation costs involved with the unit of service. Company assets that will last for more than one year, but will not last indefinitely, are depreciated over a period of time. An asset is usually depreciated based on the number of years it is expected to be in service. Buildings, machinery, equipment, furniture, fixtures, computers, and vehicles are examples of assets that can be depreciated. In the Mountain Media case, the rent and information technology costs have already been accounted for in the indirect cost calculation. The truck used by the technician must be included as a depreciated cost. The accounting department will usually do this calculation for you. Here is the calculation using the simple straight-line method of depreciation.

- Assume that the vehicle will be in service for five years and will have no salvage value at the end of its five-year life.
- The cost basis is $20,000 with an estimated life of five years. The vehicle depreciates at $4,000 per year, with no value at the end of Year 5.
- There are 260 workdays per year $\times$ 5 years = 1,300 days that the vehicle is available for service calls; $20,000 $\div$ 1,300 = $15.38 cost per day of use.

Step 5 Mountain Media total depreciation cost is *$15.38 cost per day of use.*

Step 6

Calculate the total cost for one unit of service. The total cost for wheels-out dispatches for one day is calculated by adding the costs from all the steps. Table 7.4 shows the calculation.

Determining the unit cost of a service is not difficult when the six steps in Table 7.4 are followed. In many situations, the costs of activities are readily available or relatively easy to calculate. When costs for a particular activity are not available, then completing the analysis will require more cooperation and time. The accounting department, the CFO, and department managers can easily provide information on equipment depreciation, over-

Table 7.4   Summary of Unit Cost Analysis at Mountain Media

STEP	ITEM	VALUE
Step 1: Unit of service	Wheels-out service calls at Mountain Media	NA
Step 2: Number of units of service in specified time period	6 wheels-out service calls per technician per day	NA
Step 3: Direct costs	Call center rep, dispatcher, technician, supplies and materials, travel costs	$256.00
Step 4: Indirect costs	Rent; utilities; telephones; a portion of administrative and management salaries; a portion of information technology costs, HR costs, and other types of overhead, such as company liability insurance and legal fees	$328.62
Step 5: Depreciation	$20,000 vehicle with five-year life used 1,300 days	$15.38
Step 6: Total unit cost	Total cost for 6 wheels-out service calls per day	$600.00
Cost of one wheels-out service call is $100 ($600 ÷ 6 per day)		

head, and allocated costs. Once a cost basis is available, it becomes a value that can be used in many different ways. The cost derived from the six steps can be used to determine the overall value of an improvement.

Table 7.5 uses the value from Step 6 of the unit cost analysis to calculate the overall benefit of the wheels-out improvement. The steps in Table 7.5 show the complete process of calculating an overall improvement after a value for the unit cost has been determined. To calculate the overall improvement, the change in the measure—as influenced by the training— and the sustained impact must be determined.

A monetary value for an improvement measure allows decision makers to see the potential contribution of the improvement to the organization's financial health. The annual savings of $1,872,000 shown in Table 7.5 can be realized when management reallocates technicians' time to other productive tasks such as new construction work, or by reducing overtime, or by reducing outsourcing expenses. When a value is developed, many decisions can be made with a basis for contribution to the business. Additionally, a value allows for the calculation of a return on investment when considering funding for a project, developmental initiative, or performance intervention. The next chapter addresses how costs are considered and tabulated for

Table 7.5   Calculating the Overall Improvement

STEP	STEPS AND EXAMPLE
Step 1: Identify the unit of measure as described by your source.	What unit of measure is the solution influencing? *Mountain Media example:* Wheels-out service calls
Step 2: Determine the change in performance as influenced by the solution during the reporting period (causal influence).	What is the change in the outcome measure on a per unit, per day, per week, or per month basis as influenced by the solution during the reporting period? *Mountain Media example:* Pretraining: 30 wheels-out dispatches per 100 calls Posttraining: 12 wheels-out dispatches per 100 calls Reduction (improvement) of 18 wheels-out dispatches per 100 calls 18 $\times$ 5 (average 500 calls) = reduction of 90 wheels-out per day
Step 3: Calculate the sustained impact of the performance improvement.	What is the sustained improvement of the unit of measure? *Note:* When an improvement is annualized, it must also be adjusted for the turnover experience of the group being studied. Improvement from Step 2 $\times$ sustained impact. *Mountain Media example:* Reduction (improvement) of 90 wheels-out dispatches per day $\times$ 260 workdays per year = 23,400 annual wheels-out reduction Adjustment for 20% turnover = 18,720 annual wheels-out reduction
Step 4: Partner with the appropriate source to determine the value of one unit of improvement.	What is the value of one unit of the measure from a credible source or from Step 6 of the unit cost analysis? *Mountain Media example:* One wheels-out dispatch = $100
Step 5: Calculate the total sustained value of the improvement.	The value of one unit of improvement (Step 4) multiplied by the sustained improvement during the reporting period (Step 3) = the total sustained value of the improvement. *Mountain Media example:* $100 value $\times$ 18,720 wheels-out dispatches reduction = $1,872,000

a program or an intervention. Comparing net monetary benefits to costs allows for the calculation of ROI.

CASE STUDY PART 5:
TECH*READ* SMART METERING COMPANY

Assigning a Monetary Value to Business Outcome Improvements

Data were collected and analyzed for the training solution, Active Coaching for Field Sales Managers. The program's causal influence on the business outcome measures was determined by analyzing the comparison group arrangement. The solution was withheld from two comparable regions for a three-month period in order to develop the performance conclusions. The results were then subjected to further analysis to determine how long the business outcome would be sustained.

There were two business drivers that established the need for the training solution: excessive employee complaints related to lack of coaching and a lag in sales. There was disappointment in terms of the business outcome analysis when the baseline data for employee complaints were determined to be unreliable. Consideration was given to reconstructing the employee complaint data, but there were still issues that could not be verified, and it was determined that trying to reconstruct them would consume too many resources. Therefore, for purposes of the impact study, employee complaints were abandoned as a factor in calculating ROI. This left the sales data as the only reliable and feasible business outcome that could be carried forward for ROI analysis.

Following the analysis of causal influence and sustained impact, the portion of the Tech*Read* annual sales revenue that can be attributed to the training is $11,501,568. Now the question becomes, can the full amount be carried forward as the benefits from the training for the ROI calculation? As addressed earlier in this chapter, revenue cannot be applied to the ROI formula to calculate the training ROI. Only that portion of the revenue that represents profit can be used in the ROI calculation.

Determining the Profit Margin from Revenue

The evaluation team contacted the chief financial officer to request the profit margin for industrial sales and commercial sales. Profit margin is always a percentage of total sales. The CFO confirmed that the margin is different for the two customer classifications. The evaluation team felt that this should not be a problem because the sales data are segregated by customer type. Before providing the profit margin, the CFO requested a meeting with the team to better understand how it would be using the margin in the calculation.

After hearing the evaluation team describe how the data were being used to calculate ROI and how the results would be communicated, the CFO had good news and bad news. She said that the profit contribution was proprietary information that was closely guarded. Competitors could use profit information to undermine market and pricing strategies. Only executives within the C-Suite and those having a need to know could be provided with specific profit information. This was deflating news, to be sure. However, she was quick to say that she applauded what the team was doing and that she could find an acceptable solution. She agreed to have a senior financial analyst review the segregated sales data and provide a weighted margin that could be used for the total combined revenue from commercial and industrial sales. This combined number would disguise the actual margin for each type of customer, but would be acceptable for determining the actual ROI for the coaches' training solution.

The financial analyst calculated a 5 percent profit margin to use for total combined revenue from both customer types. The calculation of profit margin is simple now that the margin is known.

- $11,501,568 total revenue × 0.05 = $575,078 profit margin for total revenue.
- The $575,078 can be used in the numerator of the formula to calculate the ROI after the fully loaded costs for the training solution are determined.

The next step is to actually determine the monetary benefits of other business outcome measures that were influenced by the training solution. If the employee complaints historical data had not been inaccurate, these data would also have been used as a benefit. The monetary value of the complaint reduction would have needed to be determined. Then this amount would have been added to the profit from the revenue, and this would have determined the total benefits for the numerator of the ROI formula. For example, if we had been able to use the complaint data and the total monetary savings from reducing complaints was $100,000, then the total benefits would have been $675,078 ($575,078 + $100,000). If we had a third business outcome measure with a monetary value, it would also be added to the total. This total benefit value would then be carried forward in the numerator for the ROI calculation.

The ROI calculation uses only the numbers. It is insensitive to how the numbers are derived and the type of measures that go into the calculation. The ROI is sensitive only to how the benefits compare to the costs. That is why the calculation should never stand alone. The full story of how the values are determined must be communicated and the quality of the ROI must be analyzed and reported.

8

Calculate the Fully Loaded Cost of the Solution Design

When analyzing data to calculate ROI, it is important to remember the direct relationship between the benefits influenced by a solution and the costs of the solution. Because of this relationship, all costs associated with researching, designing, developing, delivering, and evaluating the solution must be captured. When all costs have been properly captured, a more realistic picture of the ROI can be provided. When the costs are understated, the ROI will be inflated. Results of any type should never be overstated, especially the ROI calculation. Most front-end costs, such as needs assessment and design and development, can be spread over the life of a training solution and prorated to each delivery. This allows a fair share of front-end costs to be allocated to the program being tracked during an evaluation. As illustrated in Figure 8.1 (see page 200), Step 9b addresses the costs that will be compared to the benefits when calculating the return on investment.

CONSEQUENCES OF FAILING TO USE FULLY LOADED COSTS IN ROI CALCULATIONS

Fully loaded means including every cost that is associated with the training solution being evaluated. Salaries and benefits of participants, meals, lodging and travel expenses, needs analysis and development costs, evaluation costs, and so on are included. As addressed later in this chapter, some costs may be prorated, with only a portion assigned to the program that is being evaluated. Care should always be taken to ensure that costs are fully loaded and calculations are conservative. Since costs are placed in the denominator

199

Figure 8.1   Phase Three, Step 9b

Phase Three

Analyze Data and Make
Conservative Adjustments*

Step 9b

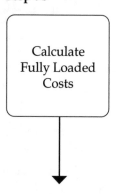

• Direct delivery costs
  ○ Expensed for each
     offering delivered
• Nondelivery costs
  ○ Prorated over life
     of program

*Analyze and report on the delivery
of the complete *solution design,*
not just the training component.

of the ROI formula, conservative means more, not less. It means higher, not lower. Even though costs are much easier to identify than the value of the improvements (benefits), there is still a great deal of room for error.

There may be situations in which a specific cost is not tracked precisely and can vary over a range from low to high. When this occurs, the high value should be used. There will be situations in which there are questions about whether a specific cost item should or should not be included in the costs. When in doubt, the cost should be included. As stated by Guiding Principle 10, "When comparing net benefits to solution costs to calculate ROI, use fully loaded costs."

Guiding Principle 10

When comparing net benefits to solution costs to calculate ROI, use fully loaded costs.

Failure to include and report fully loaded costs can have serious consequences for the entire evaluation project. The credibility of the evaluation depends on reporting fully loaded costs using a conservative approach.

Several examples of decisions that damage the credibility of the impact study are noted here.

- The ROI will be inflated when the costs are understated. Not only does this distort the picture of the impact of the training solution, but it also renders the ROI calculation useless.
- When observers conclude that the costs are understated, they begin to question the credibility of the entire impact study and the evaluator.
- During a scheduled meeting to present the results of the impact study to stakeholders, when someone raises a question about whether one or more cost items are included, a debate often follows. This debate concerning a cost item will consume valuable time that should be used to discuss the business impact of the training solution, lessons learned, and next steps. When this is a high-level meeting, the lost opportunity may never be regained.

A meeting in the C-Suite is often allocated only 15 or 20 minutes of scarce time. Plan to make the most of that time by addressing cost issues concisely. There should be no question in anyone's mind that the costs are fully loaded and have been treated conservatively. One objective for the meeting should be to take zero time to debate costs so that all of the time can be used to discuss important contributions and continuous improvement issues.

COST GUIDELINES

Most organizations have policies and guidelines for tracking costs in each department. The finance or accounting department sometimes approves these guidelines to ensure consistency throughout the organization. While these guidelines should be used, keep in mind that they may not lead to fully loaded costs of training programs. For example, internal guidelines may not include reporting participants' salaries and benefits when reporting the cost of training. Fully loaded cost guidelines are often more strict than the guidelines that are typically found in organizations. Table 8.1 (see page 202) illustrates the direct relationship between costs and benefits and shows the implications when costs are varied.

Table 8.1   Benefits-Cost Relationship

ROI calculation with costs at \$100,000	$\text{ROI} = \dfrac{\$300{,}000 - \$100{,}000}{\$100{,}000} = 2 \times 100 = 200\%$
Costs increased to \$130,000 with benefits the same	$\text{ROI} = \dfrac{\$300{,}000 - \$130{,}000}{\$130{,}000} = 1.3 \times 100 = 130\%$
Costs decreased to \$60,000 with benefits the same	$\text{ROI} = \dfrac{\$300{,}000 - \$60{,}000}{\$60{,}000} = 4 \times 100 = 400\%$

Notice in Table 8.1 that when the costs drop from \$100,000 to \$60,000, the ROI doubles in value. Executives are familiar with this benefits-cost relationship and will often scrutinize costs closely to ensure that an ROI calculation is not inflated. While the costs may be reported in summary form in the impact study report, it is important to show all the categories so that an observer can easily see what has been included. When there are questions about departing from a company's cost guidelines, the ROI context for the direct relationship between costs and benefits should be communicated.

AVOID IMPROPER COST COMPARISONS

When costs are reported or communicated for reasons other than an ROI study, they may not need to be fully loaded as described in this chapter. For example, suppose a manager in a division of your company is having communications problems within his team. He wants to have a one-day communications training program delivered to his team as part of the solution. The cost will be charged to his budget. You provide the cost to him using fully loaded costs. He replies that he has a brochure from a local university and another from a training supplier, each of which quotes a one-day cost that is only about half of the cost you are quoting. When providing costs in such a situation, always be sure that you do not include fully loaded cost items such as participants' salaries and benefits and travel expenses. When quoting costs for services, be certain that any comparison is apples to apples.

Another type of training cost comparison involves senior executives. Senior executives routinely compare the costs of internal training with other training data that they may have at their disposal. These comparison data may come from industry reports, from a recent seminar that the executive attended, or from her executive assistant who somehow acquired the data. Executive assistants frequently provide information to their executive for budget and cost comparison purposes. Comparison data may include assumptions or costs that are not relevant to the comparison that is being made. Executives like to have the ability to make comparisons because it gives them a basis for developing conclusions and making decisions. The following are some of the activity costs that executives use for comparisons.

- *Percent of employees trained.* Number of employees trained ÷ total company head count.
- *Cost per employee trained.* Total training cost ÷ number of employees trained.
- *Training cost per hour.* Total training cost ÷ total training hours.
- *Training cost as a percentage of total expenses.* Total training cost ÷ company operation expense.
- *Total training investment per employee.* Total training cost ÷ total company head count.

It can be very useful to make comparisons across government agencies, within industries, with other companies on the Fortune 500 list, or on some other basis. However, adjustments may need to be made before conclusions can be developed. For example, when comparing training costs at Company A to those at other companies, there can be significant distortions in the comparison data. Suppose Company A is highly regulated and 60 percent of its training budget is dedicated to compliance programs, while the comparison companies are not in a highly regulated industry. The comparison may show that the training costs of Company A are significantly higher than those of the comparison companies.

If the basis of a comparison is flawed, then any conclusions it leads to are likely to be flawed. The comparison could significantly distort the conclusions regarding training cost as a percentage of total expenses and total training investment. The reason why the training costs for Company A are higher than the average for other companies should be considered before acting on any conclusions. An executive who responds properly to the comparison will ask the training director pointed questions. Sadly, however, some executives may cut budgets or make other harsh decisions without pursuing a discovery process. The moral of this story is, know your executives and know how they use data to make decisions. Then adjust your communication strategy accordingly. One strategy that can be very useful is to report the business contribution of training solutions, so that costs are not the only consideration when executives are making decisions about training.

TYPICAL COST CATEGORIES

Most cost guidelines will define training costs by categories. This makes the costs easier to enter into a tracking system and is convenient for use in making management decisions. For example, when staff time and costs dedicated to program design and development appear to be out of line, training managers can begin a discovery process to determine why and then either correct the situation or accept it for what it is. This section briefly addresses each cost category typically used in organizations.

Needs Analysis Costs

Costs for needs assessment and analysis are usually the first incurred for a training solution. This process begins with the initial meeting with the client or sponsor. Of course, sometimes there is no continuation of the assessment beyond the initial meeting. Sometimes there is not even a meeting; there is just a phone call placing an order for a training program. Whatever the process, it has a beginning, and all of the costs incurred after this point should be captured. All front-end costs should eventually be allocated (spread equally) to all offerings throughout the life of the program. If there is only one offering, then all costs will be associated with that offering, making the program more expensive on a per participant basis.

When calculating the cost of needs assessment and analysis, every activity must be included. Salaries and benefits, travel, materials, printing, use of an outside consultant, and all other costs should be included. If an executive is interviewed for 30 minutes, the executive's time and that of the interviewer must be included in the cost of the needs assessment. Fully loaded means including everything. Think of it this way, when the interviewer takes 30 minutes of the executive's time, that's 30 minutes that the executive cannot be spending with his team, with a key customer, or in a strategic meeting. Some people say, why count this time? The executive is being paid whether or not she is being interviewed. Using that logic, why not just let the executive be interviewed by someone for eight hours every day for an entire month? I think you get the picture.

It is important to be able to identify all costs so that the cost of an individual offering can be determined. Some organizations charge their training to operating departments on a per use basis. When all costs are spread throughout the life of a program, each succeeding client will see a fair price on the chargeback report. Spreading costs across the program's life will eventually result in a program's paying for itself if it is in demand or if it can be marketed to solve other organization problems.

Design and Development Costs

Whether a program is to be facilitator-led or an e-learning solution, the cost of its design and development is usually significant. The cost of everything must be accounted for, such as materials, DVDs, video scripting and development, graphics, printing, shipping, certification programs that may be required of the designers, and any work that is outsourced. Like needs assessment costs, design and development costs are usually spread over the life of a program and prorated to each offering of that program. Most training organizations have an account classification system that requires training costs to be tracked according to the type of work (needs analysis, development, delivery, and so on).

Using an account classification system to track costs serves many useful purposes for a training organization. The system can be used to make decisions about allocating staff time to different types of activities. Managers can use it to help in determining overall staffing requirements. It can be used to allocate funds during the budgeting process. It can be used to allocate costs throughout the life of a program so that courses can be priced for internal chargeback to clients. It can be used to help determine the fully loaded cost of a specific program or project.

Some design costs are incurred through the acquisition of packaged programs from training suppliers. Some programs may include both acquisition and development costs because a vendor-purchased program is added to or modified. Acquisition costs such as those for facilitator materials, train-the-trainer sessions, licensing agreements for the use of the program, and royalties should be spread over the life of a program the same as other development costs and allocated to each offering.

Delivery Costs

While less time may be spent on the actual delivery of the solution, it is often the most costly activity because of the time spent by participants, training professionals, and guest speakers. Delivery costs include items such as salaries and benefits of participants and facilitators, travel and lodging, meals, venue costs, equipment, and materials. Delivery costs also include any planned follow-up activities that will consume the time of the training staff, the client, the immediate supervisor of participants, and anyone else who may be involved (see the next section, "Considerations and Tips about Costs").

Evaluation Costs

Evaluation costs such as those for administering smile sheets and testing and assessing learning during the delivery may be included as part of delivery costs, or they may be tracked and included as part of the overall evaluation category. Evaluation costs for follow-up studies can be treated in one of two ways, depending on preferences. (1) The follow-up evaluation costs may be tracked, spread across the life of the program, and allocated to each delivery (like the front-end costs). Since future offerings may benefit from the findings of a follow-up evaluation, this may be a likely choice to allocate the costs. (2) The follow-up evaluation costs may be assigned to only those offerings that are being evaluated. When future offerings will not receive much benefit from the evaluation, the choice may be made to keep all the costs with the offering being evaluated.

Follow-up evaluation costs include activities such as salaries and benefits of evaluators and of those responding to the evaluation, costs of planning the evaluation, the cost of developing and administering questionnaires, the cost of collecting data through focus groups or interviews, travel costs, analysis costs, costs to develop reports and communicate findings and recommendations, and costs of follow-up.

Overhead Costs (Administrative and General)

Each department tries to assign costs to its products and services in ways that reflect the costs associated with the creation and delivery of a specific product or service. However, there are usually some costs that are not associated with a specific product or service. These costs are sometimes referred to as administrative and general expenses or overhead costs. They represent that part of the department budget that is not directly related to a particular program. They may include such costs as clerical costs, managers' salaries, office expenses, and fixed costs such as rent and computer costs.

Overhead costs are sometimes allocated to programs based on a percentage of the overall budget. For example, the total cost of a program that you are evaluating represents 15 percent of the overall training department budget. The training director says that overhead costs for your department are $400,000. Your program gets a $60,000 share of the overhead cost (15 percent of $400,000). The $60,000 can then be spread across all offerings of your program, just as the front-end costs are spread and allocated.

Overhead costs may also be spread using other formulas, such as the total number of participant days for the budget year. The cost is then allocated as a cost per participant day. So if your evaluation uses 50 participants in the sample, the overhead cost per participant is multiplied by 50. In other situations, the training director uses a fixed percentage of the overall budget as the cost of overhead. The training director or the staff person who develops the budget can provide the amount. It will usually be a very small percentage of the total budget.

CONSIDERATIONS AND TIPS ABOUT COSTS

Since not all costs are easily tracked, it often helps to know a few shortcuts. When using a shortcut, remember to stay conservative (high is conservative when tabulating costs), and be certain that the appropriate costs are covered. This section addresses considerations and offers some tips in a few cost areas where there are frequent questions.

Cost of Salaries and Benefits

Whenever the training process or any training activity involves someone's time, this is an expense that must be accounted for when determining the fully loaded cost of training. (When an activity and the time consumed occur outside of company work hours and the person is not being paid, however, the time does not have to be accounted for.) Examples of time that must be accounted for include time consumed while participants are in a training program, the facilitator's time, time required for an interview with the CEO to get input on expectations, and an employee's time answering evaluation questions during a telephone interview. Whatever the activity, the time must be counted as a cost. When the activity is not specifically tracked, the time should be estimated.

When employees' time is being accounted for, the cost of employee benefits must be included so that the costs are fully loaded. This is easily done, since the employee benefits factor is always a percentage of salaries. The HR department will provide the proper percentage. The current average in the United States is about 38 percent of salaries. This is higher in some countries and lower in others. The benefits factor includes costs paid by the company, such as injury-related workers' compensation costs; short-term disability costs; company contributions to medical and life insurance, social security, and pension funds; and matching contributions to employee savings plans. Some states in the United States call these statutory costs.

When calculating salaries to include in the cost of training, the exact salary does not need to be used. All jobs have a pay range with a midpoint value. For example, the midpoint for a manager's job may be $100,000 annually. The midpoint represents a fully competent manager doing the job. The low end or entry-level pay is 20 percent less, or $80,000. The high end is 20 percent more, or $120,000. In a pay-for-performance system, the high end represents someone who excels. When estimating salary costs, using the midpoint value is appropriate, as it will usually overstate the average actual salary cost. In this example, with a benefits factor of 38 percent, the value to use is $138,000. HR can provide the midpoint value. When a specific client is involved in the evaluation study, the client can provide the midpoint value. The client can also provide the actual salaries for a group without disclosing any individual's salary.

On occasion, opportunity costs or replacement costs may need to be accounted for. For example, accounting for opportunity cost may be necessary when a salesperson attends training and sales may be lost because of her absence. The salesperson's salary and benefits will be included along with any opportunity cost. There is no set amount for opportunity cost, as it is determined by the client or someone close to the sales situation. Keep in mind that not all sales situations will result in lost sales while the salesperson is away. In reality, accounting for opportunity costs is not often required.

Replacement costs are defined as paying someone to take the place of another employee who is attending a training program. As long as the salary of the person attending the training is included, the pay for the replacement employee does not need to be included as a training cost. This is justified because the replacement employee is doing the work (there is no waste or lost opportunity). Therefore, the work and customer service are uninterrupted. However, if the replacement employee is paid more than the employee who is away at training (such as overtime pay), then the difference in pay (the extra amount) must be captured as a training cost along with the salary and benefits of the person who is attending the training.

Cost of Partnering and Companion Strategies

When training solutions include a partnership, the cost of the partnership is as much a part of the cost of the training solution as is the development time for the content. Some may argue that this is not a cost of the training, since the training is requested by a client, and partnering is part of the client's normal duties. To an extent, that is true. The costs that should be included in the training are those that extend beyond the routine activities of partnering.

For example, suppose the training is being delivered to various employee groups in the client department. The client agrees to hold special meetings with the employees' supervisors to encourage them to support the employees as they learn new skills and as they return to the work setting to implement what they have learned. By creating this agreement, a companion strategy has been created that is an active part of influencing performance results from the training. It is part of the training design. Take it away, and the results are likely to be different. The salaries and benefits for the time that the client is actively reinforcing the training should be estimated and included in the cost of the training, even if it is only an hour or two. The meeting time for the supervisors should also be captured as a cost.

When determining which partnering costs to include, the main consideration is, would this client support action happen if we did not ask the client to pursue it? If the answer is yes, then it should not be included as a cost because it is routine. Furthermore, when the supervisors also agree to the companion strategy and carry out their reinforcement role, this should be included as part of the training design, and the costs should be captured.

Any companion strategy that requires any resource to allocate time and is agreed to by the client or other stakeholders becomes part of the training design. Again, the key consideration that differentiates a companion strategy from routine actions by the client or others is, would they have done it anyway? If the answer is yes, then it is not a strategy associated with the training solution and the cost does not need to be included. Remember, it is not just about the cost. It's about getting the solution to work. When it works, we should be happy to include it in the cost, as it is part of the reason for the success of the solution.

Cost of Facilities

Even when company facilities are used as the venue, the cost of the space should be estimated and applied to the cost of the training. If the accounting department has a difficult time responding to the request for the cost or says that the facility has been fully depreciated, the cost should still be estimated and included. Remember, we are comparing the cost to the benefits. We do not want to overstate the ROI value. An easy way to estimate the cost of space is simply to use what a local hotel would charge for the same space.

Cost of Capital Equipment

Make full use of accounting or financial staff when estimating the cost of equipment. In some instances, such as the cost of computers, the cost may already be included in overhead costs. Accountants are eager to help. They are always concerned that costs are accounted for in a consistent manner, so they will happily provide an answer.

Cost of E-learning Solutions

Capturing the costs of e-learning programs follows the same pattern as capturing the costs of facilitator-led training. For evaluation purposes, the training cost must be converted from a per program basis to a per participant basis. The e-learning categories may include additional items, such as design costs for asynchronous and synchronous systems, information technology support, computer costs, costs for servers, and help desk costs. Because of the extensive use of technology, equipment costs are usually higher for e-learning programs than for facilitator-led programs. The accounting department will be eager to help in deciding how to spread the equipment costs consistent with company guidelines.

CAPTURING AND SPREADING COSTS THROUGHOUT THE LIFE CYCLE OF A PROGRAM

All programs have a life cycle or shelf life. This section addresses how to spread the costs throughout the life cycle. Some cost items may be tracked by a computerized process, such as the training management system or the human resource information system. Other cost items may need to be estimated. When any item in the solution cost is estimated, the estimate should always err on the side of overstating the cost item. This helps to ensure a conservative ROI value when ROI is calculated. Estimates should be made by someone who is aware of the costs associated with the item being estimated. For example, travel costs are an expense item for delivery costs. When the actual travel costs cannot be easily tracked, a source who is familiar with travel costs for training programs should be sought. Generally, this will be the person in the training function who coordinates the training budget.

Each year, when the budget is being developed, a specific dollar amount is budgeted for travel, meals, and lodging for participants, facilitators, and others. A per person and per item amount is used to develop estimates for the budget. For example, $160 per day for lodging, $0.55 per mile for travel mileage, average travel distance of 60 miles per training day, $60 per person per day for meals, and so on. These amounts can be applied to the specific number of people who incur travel expenses for the offerings being evaluated. After the costs have been determined, they can easily be converted to a per person cost so that it is easy to apply them to e-learning solutions or to any specific program.

To help in understanding how costs are determined and allocated, it is best to begin by illustrating a brief scenario. Let's assume the following scenario for a leadership program that is being evaluated for business outcome and ROI.

- A four-day facilitator-led program, Leadership Today, will be offered to a population of 400 managers over a two-year period. Each individual offering is time-spaced: two days followed by a two-week break, then followed by the last two days. During the two-week break, participants are engaged in normal work activities but must also work on a case assignment for a computer simulation business game.
- The Leadership Today program is purchased from a training supplier and redesigned by customizing it to focus on the needs of the population.
- With 20 participants per offering, the program will be scheduled for delivery 10 times in 2011 and 10 times in 2012.
- The delivery of two offerings, one in March 2011 and one in April 2011, has been selected for the impact study evaluation. The two offerings and the 40 participants will be combined for purposes of the impact study.
- The venue for the training is a centrally located hotel conference center. Half of the participants must travel from remote locations and lodge overnight to participate in the program.
- There are two facilitators plus two guest speakers each day and a consultant who facilitates an automated ongoing business simulation game.

Two types of costs are considered when completing an impact study. Delivery costs are those costs and expenses that are associated with the delivery of a specific offering. For the impact study of Leadership Today, the costs of the deliveries in March and April will be combined to tabulate the total delivery costs. Nondelivery costs are those costs that benefit all 20 offerings of Leadership Today. These nondelivery costs will be prorated, using 20 offerings as the basis. The two offerings in the impact study, March and April, will be allocated an equal share of the nondelivery costs.

Nondelivery Prorated Costs

All offerings benefit from such activities as needs analysis, design and development, and follow-up evaluation. Therefore, when tabulating and reporting the costs of a single offering, these costs are prorated over the expected life of the program. Each offering then receives a fair allocation of the total nondelivery costs. Table 8.2 (see page 214) shows the typical nondelivery cost categories using the costs associated with the Leadership Today program.

When prorating nondelivery costs, the first decision that must be made is to determine the life of the program. Many programs today have only a two- or three-year life. This decision is a projection, as is the size of the eligible population. The example in Table 8.2 assumes that the life of the Leadership Today program is two years. The known population is 400 managers, and the maximum number of participants in one offering is 20. Therefore, 20 offerings (400 participants) are applied to determine the prorated costs to be allocated to each offering. Sometimes the life of a program is considered to extend beyond the needs of the current eligible population. Let's change the example in Table 8.2 to a life of four years to account for future turnover and training of replacements in the population. Let's say that Year 3 is projected to have 5 offerings and Year 4 will also have 5 offerings. Now the nondelivery costs can be spread over 30 offerings, thereby reducing the individual cost of each of the 30 deliveries.

Another possibility to consider when prorating costs is that part of the program can be salvaged and merged with a redesign to extend its expected life cycle. That is, when a program is dated, additional money can be spent to redesign it in order to sustain its effectiveness. Extending a program beyond its initial life cycle allows the costs to be spread over a longer period of time and a larger population. When this is considered to be a realistic

Table 8.2 Nondelivery Costs for Leadership Today

PROGRAM: *LEADERSHIP TODAY*	PROGRAM EXPECTED LIFE: *TWO YEARS*	
COST ITEM	**ITEMIZED**	**TOTAL**
Front-End Analysis		$169,960
Salaries and benefits, training staff	2 analysts × $375/day average salary × 0.39 benefits factor × 20 days = $20,840	
Salaries and benefits, focus groups and interviewees	$65/hour average salary × 0.39 benefits factor × 30 people × 50 hours = $135,520	
Mileage, travel, and meals	$2,200	
Office supplies	$400	
Printing	$2,700	
Outside services	$8,300	
Materials and Supplies		$26,200
Binders and brochures	500 copies @ $50 = $26,200	
Design and Development		$323,370
Salaries and benefits	Redesign 30-hour program using existing material. $375/day average salary × 0.39 benefits factor × 40 project days = $20,850	
Training supplier	Purchase of Leadership material = $291,900	
Mileage, travel, and meals	$820	
Freelance graphics	Video, graphics, etc. fee = $4,600	
Materials and printing	Video vignettes, software, artwork, etc. = $5,200	
Evaluation Costs		$133,197
Salaries and benefits, training staff	Training department coordination, interviews, etc. One person × $375/day average salary × 0.39 benefits factor × 10 project days = $5,213	
Salaries and benefits, focus groups and interviewees	$63/hour average salary × 0.39 benefits factor × 30 people × 40 hours = $105,084	
Mileage, travel, and meals	$2,700	
External consultant	Strategy, analysis, develop report = $19,600	
Materials and shipping	$600	
Overhead/Administrative and General Cost		$6,527
	Total Nondelivery Cost*	$659,254

* To be prorated among all offerings for the life of the Leadership Today program.
$659,254 ÷ 20 offerings = $32,963 per offering ($65,926 for the two offerings)

scenario, it should be accounted for when the decision is made to prorate costs. Applying this salvage process to the Leadership Today program, this can be done as follows:

Step 1. Estimated life of the program before it has to be redesigned is two years.

Step 2. Total of all costs that are to be prorated = $659,254 (from Table 8.2).

Step 3. Estimated remaining value of prorated cost at the end of Year 2 = $200,000 (approximate value of existing material that can be merged with new updated material).

Step 4. Estimated value to be prorated over the initial life cycle (Step 2 minus Step 3) = $459,254.

Step 5. Estimated number of eligible participants who will benefit from the training during the initial two-year life of the program = 400.

Step 6. Cost per participant (Step 4 divided by Step 5) = $1,148.

Step 7. Number of participants that are in the Leadership Today impact study = 40.

Step 8. Cost allocated to the sample population involved in the Leadership Today impact study (Step 6 multiplied by Step 7) = $45,920.

The cost in Step 8 ($45,920) becomes the prorated amount to add to the direct delivery cost of the March and April programs for the 40 people in the Leadership Today impact study group. Using this salvage method, the $45,920 prorated amount replaces the $65,926 amount for two offerings shown in Table 8.2. This captures the total fully loaded cost for the program when it is added to the delivery cost of two offerings in March and April.

Direct Delivery Costs

Direct delivery costs are those that are associated with the delivery of a specific offering. Therefore, these costs will not be incurred unless a delivery takes place. It is acceptable to estimate costs that cannot be easily tracked. Table 8.3 (see page 216) shows the direct cost categories using the costs associated with the Leadership Today program.

Table 8.3   Direct Delivery Cost for Leadership Today

PROGRAM: *LEADERSHIP TODAY*	OFFERINGS: *MARCH–APRIL, 2011, FORTY PARTICIPANTS*	
COST ITEM	**ITEMIZED**	**TOTAL**
Participant Costs		$165,400
Salaries and benefits for four-day program	One day added during two-week break for case work. 40 × $500/day average salary × 0.39 benefits factor × 5 days = $139,000	
Replacement costs	Not applicable	
Opportunity costs	Not applicable	
Mileage, travel, and meals	20 participants × average $560 = $11,200	
Lodging	20 × $190 per night × 4 days = $15,200	
Materials and Supplies		$7,520
Workbook and handouts	44 copies @ $110 = $4,840	
Textbook	40 copies @ $37 = $1,480	
Miscellaneous	$1,200	
Facilitator Costs		$37,000
Salaries and benefits	4 × $375/day average salary × 0.39 benefits factor × 8 days = $16,680	
Mileage, travel, and meals	2 × $420 = $840	
External consultant	Fee including royalty on simulation = $16,440	
Lodging	2 × $190 per night × 8 days = $3,040	
Facility Costs		$21,860
Venue rental	$900 × 8 days = $7,200	
Equipment	Projectors, screen, charts, etc. = $1,900	
Venue meals and breaks	48 people × $30 × 4 days = $5,760	
Internet and IT fees	$7,000	
Overhead/Administrative and General Cost		$2,317
Direct Delivery Cost—March and April Offerings		$234,097
Nondelivery Cost Allocated to March and April Offerings*		$65,926
Total Fully Loaded Cost—March and April Offerings		$300,023

* Prorated nondelivery costs must be added to total direct delivery cost to arrive at total delivery cost for the two offerings in March and April. Nondelivery costs of $659,254 ÷ 20 = $32,963 per offering. $32,963 × 2 offerings = $65,926.

As shown in Table 8.3, the prorated nondelivery cost ($65,926) is added to the direct delivery cost to complete the fully loaded costs. When the salvage method described earlier in Steps 1 through 8 is used to determine the prorated costs, the $45,920 that results replaces the $65,926 nondelivery cost allocated to the March and April offerings. Using the salvage method, the total fully loaded delivery cost for the March and April offerings becomes $280,017 ($234,097 delivery plus $45,920 nondelivery).

CASE STUDY PART 6: TECH*READ* SMART METERING COMPANY

Tech*Read* Cost Considerations

The costs for the two-day Active Coaching program are relatively easy to tabulate. The cost that is used for the ROI calculation is the cost of the delivery to the three pilot regions, the Southeast, Midwest, and Southwest regions (the experimental group). This includes five offerings with 12 sales managers in each offering. There are no costs for the Northeast Region and the Northwest and West comparison regions, since the solution is withheld from them as a basis for analyzing causal influence. Since this program will eventually be offered to sales managers in all regions, the nondelivery costs are prorated over the six regions. Figure 8.2 (see page 218) shows the total cost for five offerings.

The nondelivery costs are $142,000. There are no plans to offer the program beyond the six regions during the first year. Therefore, one-half of the amount ($71,000) is allocated to the five offerings being evaluated. This short life cycle results in a higher per participant cost.

The cost category "Partnering and Companion Strategies" includes the time and travel costs associated with the three regional sales managers' contribution to the solution. Active management reinforcement is a normal part of the regional manager's job. However, the design of this training solution required the three regional managers to dedicate additional time to supporting and reinforcing the sales managers in applying coaching with the sales force. This additional time beyond the norm is part of the training design and is included in the cost.

Figure 8.2   Active Coaching for Sales Managers—Fully Loaded Costs

Program:		
Item and Cost		**Total**
Nondelivery Costs: Prorated (spread over 10 offerings for 6 regions)		
Needs analysis. Salaries and benefits, focus groups, interviews, questionnaires, Leadership Sales Effectiveness Committee, materials, travel, etc.	$17,000	$71,000
Design and development. Salaries and benefits designers; travel costs, graphics, job aids, outside costs, materials, printing, shipping, travel, etc.	$98,000	
Evaluation. Outside services, salaries and benefits of staff activities, travel, coordination, analysis, reporting, etc.	$27,000	
Total Nondelivery Cost (½ allocated to 5 offerings)	$142,000	
Delivery Costs: 5 total offerings for 3 regions		
Participant Costs (12 managers each offering × 5 offerings = 60)		$114,332
Salaries and benefits during 2-day training engagement	60 sales mgrs. $510 avg per day × 0.36 benefits factor × 2 days = $83,232	
Mileage/air travel/meals/lodging	Actual travel expenses = $31,100	
Materials and Supplies		$6,880
Workbook and handbook	60 copies × $108 = $6,480	
Miscellaneous handouts—printing	$400	
Facilitator Costs		$13,820
Salaries and benefits for two facilitators × 10 days and executive VP time to begin each session	2 facilitators × 10 days each plus EVP opening sessions = $9,340	
Mileage/travel/meals	2 × $740 = $1,480	
Lodging	2 × $150 per night × 10 days = $3,000	
Partnering and Companion Strategies		$12,726
Salaries and benefits and travel costs for 3 regional sales managers (RSM) pretraining meeting with sales managers and RSM meeting with sales managers during the 3-month period following the training delivery.	$7,896	
Mileage/travel/meals/lodging	3 × $1,610 average expense = $4,830	
Overhead/Administrative and General Costs		$3,335
Fully Loaded Cost—5 Offerings for 3 Regions		**$222,093**

The total cost of the pilot for the experimental group is $222,093. This is $3,702 per participant, which is slightly higher than was estimated at the end of the needs analysis. Perhaps the executive vice president will forgive the overrun if the performance results show a good-quality ROI. The next chapter will answer that question.

9

Calculating the Return on Investment and Assessing the Quality of ROI

The preceding chapters have addressed the details of how to proceed systematically to plan and implement a postprogram ROI impact study. The results are in, the necessary adjustments have been made, the costs have been tabulated, and one or more business outcome measures have had a monetary value assigned. When the systematic measurement and ROI process has been followed, and when the training solution is effective and execution has occurred as expected, a chain of evidence will have been established that links learning to execution and execution to business impact. Now the ROI can be calculated and the quality of the ROI can be determined for inclusion in the study. As illustrated in Figure 9.1 (see page 220), Step 9c continues the analysis by addressing the ROI calculation and shows how to apply a tool to analyze the quality of the ROI.

THE BEFORE AND AFTER ROI

There are two approaches to calculating ROI. (1) The preprogram approach is used to forecast the ROI before the solution is delivered or at the time of delivery. Forecasting ROI allows adjustments to be made in the design or the cost before the training solution is rolled out to a larger population. (2) The postprogram approach is used to conduct an ROI impact study after the solution is delivered to analyze the actual data and determine whether the expected results were achieved.

Figure 9.1   Phase Three, Step 9c

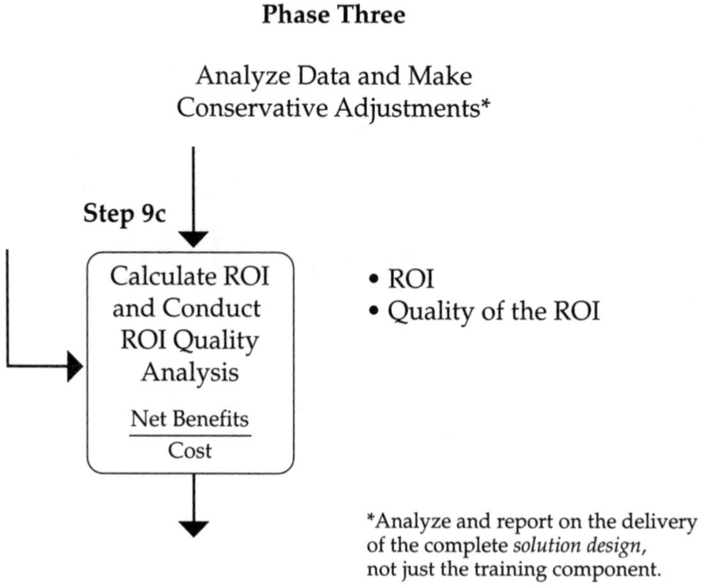

Phase Three

Analyze Data and Make
Conservative Adjustments*

Step 9c

Calculate ROI
and Conduct
ROI Quality
Analysis

Net Benefits
————————
Cost

• ROI
• Quality of the ROI

*Analyze and report on the delivery
of the complete *solution design,*
not just the training component.

Preprogram ROI

Properly done, a preprogram ROI forecast can avoid unnecessary costs and
lead to greater focus on achieving the expected business outcome. Forecasting
can play a significant role in keeping training solutions aligned with the business. This forward-looking approach also helps when consulting with clients
on the necessity and value of their support role in achieving the expected
results. The final chapter in this book, "Opportunity Forecasting," addresses
how to forecast results and ROI.

Postprogram ROI

Postprogram ROI should be calculated following the delivery of some (not
all) training solutions in order to learn about the relationships between
solutions and performance and the contribution of soft benefits to the business bottom line. The criteria used to determine candidates for postprogram ROI studies were addressed in Table 2.3 of Chapter 2 (high cost,
high-visibility programs, and so on). By conducting a postprogram ROI calculation on a small sample of training solutions, lessons are learned about

which designs work best, and these lessons can be applied across the board. Postprogram studies also provide keen insights into how to do a better job of forecasting results and ROI.

BENEFITS OF CALCULATING A POSTPROGRAM ROI

Some critics of postprogram ROI evaluations say that they are a waste of time. Some argue that training is funded for reasons that have nothing to do with a return on investment. Others argue that ROI has gone the way of Frederick Taylor's scientific management and the industrial age, as the performance of today's knowledge workers cannot be measured in tangible ways. These ROI critics are right when they say that intangibles add value in their own right. But while ROI cannot stand alone as a success measure, neither can intangibles. We must apply both in order to know more about how to influence performance and align it with the business. Postprogram evaluation is about discovery and learning, not about justification.

When a monetary value can be associated with an intangible benefit, this introduces a new level of conversation and brings more knowledge and context to the discussion. Even when a monetary value cannot be agreed upon, the discussion alone generates greater understanding of the measure and its relationship to performance and business contribution. Table 9.1 (see page 222) provides a contrasting view to the reasoning of some critics who say that ROI has no place in the training process.

Both tangible and intangible measures are necessary in order to optimize knowledge about what sustains and moves the business. Many critics are viewing ROI in an improper context. Here is the picture that many critics may be missing. ROI is not just about determining the payback from a training investment. ROI is about asking tough questions so that a rich dialogue can uncover how training solutions can best benefit the business. It is not the ROI that is so important. It is the discussion that leads to questioning the value of any solution. ROI is about viewing training investments in a different way to encourage a rich dialogue and determine what is best for the business.

Recall that Chapter 7 addressed soft measures and hard measures. The hard measure benefits of increased output, improved quality, improved time utilization, and reduced costs are relatively easier to link to the bottom line

Table 9.1   The Necessity for Training ROI

THE CRITICS VIEW ROI AS UNNECESSARY BECAUSE	CONTRASTING VIEW AND COMMENT
Executive management has not bought into the concept of training ROI.	• This is true of some executives, but certainly not all of them feel that way. It is also true that a new executive who demands to know the tangible value of expenditures can be in place Monday morning. • Sponsors need to be educated on any process or activity in order to support it. Training managers should educate executives about training ROI.
ROI does not measure the worth of soft benefits.	• The ROI process approaches soft measures in two ways. (1) It places a monetary value on soft benefits when such a value is credible and when it is required. (2) When stakeholders do not require a value, or when a value would not be credible, a soft benefit is reported as an intangible. • There is an opportunity to learn something new about a soft measure each time a value is assigned to it or when a deep discussion about its possible value occurs.
ROI is nothing more than a restatement of the business outcome results.	• ROI is not a restatement; rather, it is added information that introduces a different context and added conversation about the relative value of the business outcome.
The accounting world views training as an expense, not an investment.	• The stark visibility of costs along with the absence of information communicating the equivalent value of training is an untenable position. • With an understanding of the level of monetary benefits required to offset training costs, better decisions can be made throughout the training process, with an overall contribution of reducing training waste.
Executives have little interest in the ROI from training expenditures because training is generally less than 3 percent of the overall payroll expense.	• It is the larger (more expensive) training solutions that are candidates for ROI studies. • Expensive training investments take away the opportunity for other investments or for more training for more people at a lesser cost. When the larger expenditures do not bring value beyond their cost (ROI), they suboptimize the availability of essential training in the organization. It is like taking from the poor to feed the rich. • Calculating ROI requires a close examination of the cost of training solutions and places an emphasis on making adjustments to increase the focus of linking training to the business.

and easier to quantify than the soft benefits. However, it is the improvement in the soft measures that drives the hard measures toward improvement. Conversely, the soft measures can act in ways that create deficiencies in the hard measures. The more we evaluate, discover, and create dialogue about the power of an intangible (a soft benefit) to affect the business, the more we learn about solutions, performance, measures, and the business. This is a key reason why this book emphasizes that ROI and other measures should be addressed up front, before solutions are rolled out. This book is about how to create effective solutions, not just about how to calculate ROI.

CALCULATING THE ROI

After the program benefits have been determined and the fully loaded costs have been tabulated, the ROI calculation is easy to accomplish. The formula is shown here.

$$\text{ROI (\%)} = \frac{\text{net solution benefits}}{\text{fully loaded costs of solution}} \times 100$$

Since ROI represents a net number, the calculation demonstrates that the costs have been recovered, with anything left over being expressed as a return on the investment. A ROI of 100 percent means that the benefits are 100 times more than the investment (the cost of the solution). The following is an example of a calculation using the ROI formula.

A one-day training program, "High Stakes Negotiations," with a fully loaded cost of $150,000 was delivered to 20 purchasing agents in the purchasing department of a Fortune 500 company. The performance results of the program were tracked by conducting a four-month impact study. The objective of the program was to achieve deeper cost discounts of at least 15 percent above the value of existing discounts on contracts and bulk-purchased items. After adjustments for causal influence and sustained impact, the analysis developed a total benefit of $690,000. As shown here, the ROI was calculated at 360 percent:

$$\text{ROI} = \frac{\$540,000 \ [\$690,000 - \$150,000]}{\$150,000} = 3.6 \times 100 = 360\%$$

Net benefits are calculated in the numerator by subtracting the cost of $150,000 from the total benefits of $690,000. The "net benefits" of $540,000 take into account the costs of the negotiations program ($150,000). When the net benefit is above zero, this means that the program has been paid for. The net benefit of $540,000 in the example is significantly above zero. It is a 360 percent return on the fully loaded cost of the intervention. Think of it this way: it is not possible to achieve an ROI on an intervention without first recovering the costs. When communicating the ROI, it is important to confirm that others understand that the ROI is a net number. People often incorrectly assume that a ROI of 100 percent is breakeven. Zero is the breakeven point.

ANALYZING THE QUALITY OF THE ROI TO DISCOVER THE TRUTH

ROI evaluation is controversial for many reasons. Some people simply feel that it is not appropriate for training programs. Some see how it can be misused, so they do not trust it. Others do not understand it, so they choose to oppose it. Some are afraid of it. All of these reasons for avoiding the use of ROI need to be addressed so that the training profession can benefit from the proper use of ROI. This section is aimed at clearing up the confusion by demonstrating a way to analyze the quality of the ROI. By analyzing the quality of any ROI calculation, the true performance influenced by the solution can be communicated while keeping ROI in the proper context. That is why Guiding Principle 11, states, "Always accompany ROI calculations with an ROI quality analysis."

Guiding Principle 11

Always accompany ROI calculations with an ROI quality analysis

---

The Misleading Nature of ROI—It May Not Be What It Appears to Be

Maybe you've read case studies or articles, visited blogs, or listened to the overtures of vendors selling the ROI of training programs or software interventions. Many claim an ROI ranging from 100 percent to 3,000 percent, or even more. These results are certainly possible. Even so, many of these claims fall into the category of incredible or unbelievable. The truth is, unless we can examine how an ROI is derived, there is no way of knowing whether it is snake oil analysis or whether it represents a truly magnificent result. Let's examine a couple of scenarios to demonstrate just a few ways in which ROI is being misapplied today.

Scenario A   A multinational electronics company delivers a supervisor training program in Asia several times a year. The program includes modules such as negotiation skills, team problem solving, communication strategies, goal setting, and employee engagement. The program gets good reviews; however, it has never been evaluated beyond smile sheets returned at the end of the sessions. Senior management has communicated its desire for a more results-centered program, and it wants the training department to track one class offering of the redesigned program to determine the business results and the ROI.

The training department redesigned part of the program and included an action planning process. This process gives the program more of a results focus and also serves as a ROI evaluation instrument. The action planning process requires each participant to create a performance objective, with the idea that the learning from the program will contribute to achievement of the objective. Action steps are created during the training, and the plan is to be implemented in the work setting following the training. The training department randomly selected a class of 30 participants to track the results and calculate the ROI. The participants in this class were instructed to return their completed action plans four months following the training. The impact questions on the results section of the action plan follow the same pattern as the first seven questions of Figure 4.5 in Chapter 4, "Twelve Key Focus Areas to Collect Business Outcome and ROI Data." Of the 30 participants, 25 completed and returned the action plans. The following results were determined during analysis.

- Most of the 25 respondents had favorable comments about the program.

- Only 11 of the 25 respondents actually implemented the key learning and performance elements of the program following the training. (That's actually 11 of 30, including the 5 who did not respond.)
- Of the 11 who implemented the program, 4 provided a business outcome improvement on their completed action plan.
- Of the 4 who provided a business outcome improvement, only 3 provided a credible monetary value for the improvement. Each of the 3 people linked the improvement to the training, identified the causal influence percentage, and gave sufficient information to determine the sustained improvement. The monetary benefits achieved by these 3 participants are listed in Figure 9.2.

The fully loaded cost of the training for the 30 participants was $105,000. The resulting ROI of the supervisor program was 55 percent, as shown here.

$$\text{ROI} = \frac{\$162,720 - \$105,000}{\$105,000} = 0.55 \times 100 = 55\%$$

What's wrong with this picture? The ROI of 55 percent is well above zero. However, the ROI is only a small object in the landscape of the big picture. The ROI is a result of the efforts of only 3 participants out of 30. The worst part of this picture is that only 11 of the 30 participants actually implemented the key learning and performance elements of the program after the training. This lack of transfer to the work setting is enough to label this a low-quality ROI. It is labeled a low-quality ROI because it would be deceiving to allow the 55 percent to represent this program. Many observers who see an ROI of 55 percent will conclude that the supervisor training program is a good investment.

How can this program be a good investment when 19 out of 30 participants did not execute the skills in the work setting? It is a bad investment, even though the ROI is positive. This is one example of how an ROI calculation can be deceiving. It is fortunate that 3 participants were able to get results that contributed enough benefits ($162,720) to overcome the costs. But the ROI is never the results.

Figure 9.2 Scenario A—Synopsis of Monetary Benefits

Respondent	The Improvement	Monetary Value of One Unit Improvement	Percent Influenced by the Solution	Sustained Improvement	Total Ending Value (Benefit)
Person 1	Reduced *monthly* errors on customer orders from 30 per 100 orders to 5 per 100.	Error on one typical order cost company $340. 25 errors × 340 = monthly value of $8,500	60% $5,100 (8,500 × 0.6)	$61,200 ($5,100 × 12) Recurring impact, annualized	$61,200
Person 2	Improved productivity by reducing wasted time by my team. Improvement from average of 5 hours per week wasted by each team member to 2 hours wasted by each member.	Value is hourly wage and benefits. One hour is $40. 40 × 3 hours saved = $120 120 × 15 members = $1,800 per week.	70% $1,260 (1,800 × 0.7)	$65,520 (1,260 × 52 weeks) Recurring impact, annualized	$65,520
Person 3	Negotiated reduced cost of office furniture on one-time shipment.	$90,000 cost savings	40% $36,000 (90,000 × 0.4)	$36,000 One-time savings	$36,000
Total monetary benefits attributed to delivery of the supervisor training					$162,720

The ROI should be shown as 55 percent.* The asterisk should state: "*This is a low-quality ROI because only 37 percent of the participants actually implemented the skills from the program. It is not advisable to deliver this program again without first addressing the problems that led to only 11 of 30 participants implementing the skills. The 55 percent ROI is deceiving."

Scenario B   AmeriTrust Bank is one of the largest banks serving the United States. Because of employee turnover, growth, and new acquisitions during the past two years, the training department has been delivering the two-day training program to bring new employees on board in the corporate headquarters with a facilitator and guest speakers from key functional departments. A key element of the training is a six-hour module on delivering customer service the AmeriTrust way. This module is highly participative, and participants complete it with the expectation that they will be able to address most customer service situations when they take up their job assignment following the training.

The fully loaded cost for a typical class of 30 participants is $35,700 ($1,190 per participant). This includes travel and lodging, which are usually required for at least half of the attendees who travel from remote regions. The program is offered an average of 30 times a year, resulting in 900 graduates at a yearly cost of $1,071,000 (900 × $1,190).

At the request of senior management, the program has been redesigned to use an e-learning format to save money. The e-learning program was piloted with 60 participants. Based on cost savings and positive smile sheet feedback from the e-learning pilot, it replaced the facilitator-led version. The fully loaded cost of delivering the e-learning program to 60 pilot participants is $42,000 ($700 per participant). This includes the cost of the technology and all other necessary costs. The annual cost of the e-learning for 900 participants is $630,000 (900 × $700). This is an annual net savings of $441,000 ($1,071,000 for the facilitator-led program minus $630,000 for e-learning). Since the $441,000 is a net cost savings, it becomes the net benefit in the numerator of the ROI formula. The ROI of the e-learning program is 70 percent, as shown here.

$$\text{ROI} = \frac{\$441{,}000 \text{ e-learning net savings}}{\$630{,}000 \text{ cost of e-learning}} = 0.7 \times 100 = 70\%$$

This is certainly a cost savings. However, there is a major problem. This program has not been evaluated for business impact. There is nothing representing an impact on the business outcome in the numerator. There are no data suggesting that what was learned was even implemented in the work setting. Yes, it is true that money was saved. But this savings is an activity input measure. It is delivering the training at a lower cost. The only way a cost savings can be used as a benefit to calculate ROI is when the savings is related to the improvement of a product, service, or process that is directly associated with the mainline purpose of the business.

ROI is calculated on business outcome results, not activity. The percentage calculated in Scenario B is not an ROI unless you are a vendor who owns the e-learning program and you retain a percentage of the sales as profit. It is not an ROI for the client unless there is a known business outcome after the program is delivered that exceeds the cost of development and delivery. The $441,000 could represent savings on the cost of a training program that is getting no result at all. We don't know because there has been no attempt to evaluate the results. Unfortunately, many consultants and vendors use savings in training inputs to calculate ROI. This type of calculation gives ROI a bad name. It is one of the ways in which ROI is being misrepresented.

The ROI calculation alone is not reliable because of the uncertainty as to how the analyst or researcher may develop the ROI. That is why the ROI quality analysis is necessary. The ROI quality analysis serves as a guide to uncover the flaws in the development of any ROI calculation. The next section addresses the seven key categories of variables, discusses why the ROI quality analysis is needed and how this analysis works, and provides a tool for application.

Seven Key Categories of Variables

There are seven key categories of input variables that influence the quality of any impact study based on the way evaluation decisions apply or ignore these variables during a study. As these seven categories of ROI input variables are reviewed, it becomes apparent that there is also a range of variables or dimensions within each category. The rigor with which each input variable is applied during an impact study drives the conclusions about execution, business outcomes, and the ROI that is ultimately developed. Each variable is capable of influencing a wide range of analysis decisions that will have a direct bearing on the quality and magnitude of the business outcome findings and the ROI. The variables are briefly described as follows.

Input variable 1, performance readiness (Step 4 of Stone's Measurement and ROI Process). The magnitude and quality of the ROI are influenced by the performance readiness of the population that is expected to achieve a specific performance result. The success of the solution design in enabling the readiness of the population is the first indicator of success in the chain of evidence. Readiness occurs before, during, and after a solution engagement when any preparation or action enables the performers to be "ready to perform" in the work setting. Such actions include communication about expectations, performance incentives, active management reinforcement from the immediate supervisor, knowledge or skills acquisition (learning solution), addressing ineffective habits, and process changes, among others. Evaluation evidence indicating why the readiness and performance gap existed and how specific readiness actions (the solution design) were successfully implemented to close the performance gap should be present. A weak solution or a solution that does not address the specific needs of a population is not likely to improve business measures or achieve a ROI.

Input variable 2, execution in the work setting (Step 5 of Stone's Measurement and ROI Process). The percentage of the sampled population that successfully executes the solution in the work setting will have a significant bearing on the business outcome results, and consequently on the ROI. The quality of this variable depends on several key factors, such as

- How the evaluation determines that execution in the work setting occurred. For example, an objective observer verifying how people are performing in the work setting is a higher-quality evaluation than a questionnaire requiring participants to self-report on their own performance.

- The percentage of participants that actually apply the solution. For example, when a higher percentage of participants apply the knowledge and skills to move a business measure, the magnitude of the business outcome is likely to be greater.
- The circumstance of some participants being in a position to achieve greater results. For example, two or three participants may be uniquely positioned in the business setting to have a greater influence on moving a business measure than all of the other participants combined.

Input variable 3, business outcome (Step 5 of Stone's Measurement and ROI Process). To determine business outcome, the evaluation must use some method and source to determine how the business measures have changed following the delivery of the training solution. The type of business measure and how the evaluation decision regarding a change in business measures is made has a direct impact on the magnitude and quality of the ROI. For example, business outcome results collected from the business records may be more credible than someone reporting on his own improvements in business measures. Also, comparing the pre- and posttraining status of a business measure is more appropriate and accurate than simply reporting the posttraining status of a measure that meets a standard and is claimed as an improvement.

Input variable 4, causal influences (Step 6 of Stone's Measurement and ROI Process). The evaluation must account for the possibility that a business measure may improve for reasons that are unrelated to the training solution design. How the evaluation decision regarding the extent to which the business outcome improvements are influenced by the solution design is made can lead to significant swings in the conclusions drawn from the evaluation. Inappropriate application of the causal influence evaluation step can yield a wide range of conclusions, which in turn can influence a broad range of business outcome improvements. This can cause significant swings in the results and the magnitude of the ROI. For example, claiming undue credit for the solution's causal influence will seriously inflate the ROI.

Input variable 5, sustained impact (Step 7 of Stone's Measurement and ROI Process). The evaluation must account for the length of time that the business outcome results will be sustained. How and whether this adjustment is made during the evaluation will lead to a wide range of conclusions. This, in turn, will cause significant swings in the magnitude of a business outcome improvement, and consequently in the quality and magnitude of the ROI. For example, annualizing a result that in reality is sustained for only three months will quadruple the outcome. Even honest errors in the sustained impact calculation can seriously inflate the ROI. Disregarding an adjustment for employee turnover when the results are annualized will also overstate the ROI.

Input variable 6, assignment of monetary value (Step 9a of Stone's Measurement and ROI Process). The monetary value assigned to a business outcome improvement can cause a significant swing in the magnitude of the benefits in the numerator of the ROI formula. Assigning a liberal or unwarranted monetary value will seriously inflate the ROI. How the evaluation decision to assign a monetary value to the improvement in business outcome measures is made is a key input that must be credible. Using a known value from the organization's management or carefully deriving a value from a set of facts and parameters is more credible than estimating a value with no basis for the estimate.

Input variable 7, cost of the solution included in the ROI calculation (Step 9b of Stone's Measurement and ROI Process). The magnitude of an ROI calculation is influenced greatly by what is or is not included in the cost of the solution. Since the ROI will be overstated when the costs are understated, anything short of fully loaded cost is unacceptable.

The seven categories of variables form the basis of the ROI quality analysis tool. They reflect the philosophy, principles, and systematic methodology of Stone's Measurement and ROI Process. It is important to realize that the ROI calculation is nothing but an expression of the relationship between benefits and costs. It is not the ROI, but what's underneath it that should occupy our inquiring minds.

ROI Quality Analysis Tool

The 12 guiding principles help in applying standards consistently when collecting, analyzing, and reporting impact data. The ROI quality analysis (RQA) tool keeps the analysis conservative, rigorous, and honest. The RQA tool is a job aid that can be used beneficially in four primary ways. Table 9.2 (see page 234) shows the four primary applications of the RQA tool.

As Table 9.2 indicates, the ROI quality analysis is flexible and versatile. The general idea in using the RQA tool is twofold: (1) to ensure that an evaluation study is rigorous, follows prescribed standards, and uncovers the truth about the contribution of a specific solution, and (2) to ensure that the evaluation study will withstand the acid test of executive scrutiny. Executives see a lot of information in the span of a typical workweek. They can be uncanny in their ability to glance at a specific page in a report and raise a red flag by asking a pointed question. While executives may not often dig into the details of a study to establish its credibility, they frequently give reports to their staff members or an executive assistant to analyze and comment on the validity of the findings and conclusions. Executives do have their methods of expediting conclusions and decisions. Figure 9.3 (see pages 236–237) shows the RQA tool and gives instructions on how to use it.

As indicated in the instructions in Figure 9.3, to do the analysis, it is preferable that you partner with someone who is informed about the specific training solution and the performance situation. The raters may choose to weight each of the categories based on (1) how a weakness in any evaluation category affects the business outcome and ROI as the raters view the facts and assumptions in an evaluation report, or (2) the raters' overall view of the analysis in all seven categories.

The dialogue should weigh heavily on the final overall rating. The numerical score is simply a starting point for dialogue. As an example, in Figure 9.3, see Category 2, "execution in the work setting." Item c asks about the success of the participants in the study as they apply what they learned. It is best to work with the clients or sponsors of the learning program up front to answer the question, what percentage of the sample population is expected to apply the training solution successfully in the work setting? Then, when the RQA is applied, there is a basis for determining whether the information revealed by the impact study meets expectations.

Table 9.2   Four Primary Uses of the ROI Quality Analysis Tool

PRIMARY APPLICATION	HOW THE RQA IS USED
1. At the beginning of and throughout an impact study	The RQA can be used in planning and implementing an impact study for a specific training solution. It is used to guide evaluation decisions throughout the study as a check and balance to ensure that the measurement and ROI process is properly applied. Used in this fashion, the tool serves as a quality control template for the evaluation study. At the end of the analysis, there should be a high degree of confidence that the evaluation process has been applied properly. The RQA serves to uncover the strengths and weaknesses of the training solution and to keep the evaluation analysis realistic. It also rates the quality of the ROI in terms that can be understood beyond a simple number. When used during or at the end of a training program's development, the tool can uncover design flaws that, when corrected, can improve the program's probability of success.
2. At the end of an impact study	Occasionally, a completed evaluation must be reviewed in retrospect. The situation or the timing may require a retrospective analysis of a study that has been completed or is in the process of concluding. The RQA tool can be used to conduct a quality check and either make adjustments to the study (when practical) or point out the flaws and make revisions in the analysis to develop a more credible set of findings and conclusions. The idea is to ensure that the study is credible, and if not, to make on-the-spot changes whenever practical and communicate the quality of the study and the ROI.
3. When inquiring about a claim of an ROI on a specific program	The RQA tool can be used with any training or HR program that a vendor promotes as achieving an ROI. In this situation, it can be used as a guide to ask pointed questions that will differentiate reality from sales buzz. If the questions in the seven categories cannot be answered satisfactorily, the ROI may be exposed as a low-quality ROI and a failed sales gimmick.
4. As a constructive review of a study conducted by someone else	The tool can be used as a constructive critique to analyze the quality of a study done by someone else. This can be done to make corrections and upgrade the quality of the study before it is presented to key stakeholders.

The expectations for applying learning on the job can vary significantly based on the situation. For example, suppose a leadership program for managers is to be evaluated. There are 20 participants in the program being evaluated. Of these participants, 5 are not in management positions and do not serve in any leadership capacity. They are people with high potential who are expected to be promoted at some unknown future date. This is not an ideal situation, but it is very realistic, since this scenario occurs often. Assuming that very little of the program content applies to these five participants, it cannot be reasonably expected that they will immediately apply what they learned in ways that will benefit the organization. So an up-front estimate for expected application in the work setting might be no greater than 75 percent. This is just one of many types of issues that might result in an expectation of less than 100 percent for item 2c of the analysis tool.

Item 2c of the ROI quality analysis tool is also in a category that in many instances could weigh much more heavily than the other six categories when deciding on the quality of the impact study and the ROI. An example of this is shown early in this chapter in Scenario A, when only 11 of 30 participants applied what they learned.

The RQA tool should rely heavily on dialogue to arrive at the final rating score shown at the bottom of the tool: definitely poor quality, substandard quality, questionable quality, good quality, or definitely high quality. The 1–10 numerical scale is simply a starting point to begin the dialogue on why an item is being rated at a particular value. When we are involved in deep discussion, we learn something of merit. Discussing only the number is of no interest, as it leads nowhere and discovers nothing.

DEALING WITH A NEGATIVE ROI

One reason that some training directors do not sponsor ROI evaluation studies is that they are concerned that the result may be a negative ROI. They are uncertain how the company's executives would accept this. Executives know firsthand that processes do not always work the way they should. They are confronted with this issue daily. When this happens, they have two significant questions: why did the training solution fail to achieve our expectations, and what actions are being taken to correct the situation so that our expectations are met? The challenge now turns to continuous improvement of the training and performance process.

When an ROI study is implemented correctly, an overreaction to a negative ROI can be avoided by implementing the strategy outlined on page 238.

Figure 9.3 ROI Quality Analysis Tool

Partner with one or more informed persons (client, training manager, coworker, etc.) and use this tool to discuss and rate a specific ROI. This tool is a seven-point *acid test* used to analyze the quality of the ROI and communicate it to stakeholders along with the ROI. After careful consideration and discussion, use the 1–10 scale below to rate the acceptability of each item by filling in one circle. Document the collective reasoning for each rating.

◯ 1–2 Definitely unacceptable ◯ 3–4 Probably unacceptable ◯ 5–6 Borderline ◯ 7–8 Probably acceptable ◯ 9–10 Definitely acceptable

Name of the Solution: _____

| Item | Questions | Notes | Rating | | | | | | | | | |
			1	2	3	4	5	6	7	8	9	10
1. Performance Readiness	a. How was the decision made as to what the readiness gap was and why it existed? (Readiness gaps such as knowledge, skill, confidence, habits, active management reinforcement, etc.)		◯	◯	◯	◯	◯	◯	◯	◯	◯	◯
	b. What is the evidence that the readiness gap (learning or other) was closed with the study population, and what methods were used to determine this?		◯	◯	◯	◯	◯	◯	◯	◯	◯	◯
2. Execution in the Work Setting	c. What percentage of the sample population successfully applied the solution in the work setting as expected (closed the performance gap as expected)? *Percent expected to apply____% Percent actually applied____%* Were credible methods and sources used to verify application?		◯	◯	◯	◯	◯	◯	◯	◯	◯	◯
	d. What companion strategies or elements were included in the solution design to reinforce execution in the work setting?		◯	◯	◯	◯	◯	◯	◯	◯	◯	◯
	e. What were the successes and disappointments? Which elements of the solution design worked effectively? Which did not work effectively, and why?		◯	◯	◯	◯	◯	◯	◯	◯	◯	◯
3. Business Outcome	f. What specific business measures improved, and by how much? Was the change in the measure compared to a baseline level?		◯	◯	◯	◯	◯	◯	◯	◯	◯	◯
	g. Were credible methods and sources used to determine the business outcome improvement?		◯	◯	◯	◯	◯	◯	◯	◯	◯	◯
4. Causal Influences (what caused the change?)	h. What percentage of the improvement of each business outcome measure was influenced by the delivery of the complete solution design? What other factors influenced these improvements?		◯	◯	◯	◯	◯	◯	◯	◯	◯	◯
	i. Were the methods/sources that were used to analyze the solution's influence on each business outcome measure credible?		◯	◯	◯	◯	◯	◯	◯	◯	◯	◯
	j. What timeline was used to analyze the influence on each business outcome measure? Is the timeline realistic?		◯	◯	◯	◯	◯	◯	◯	◯	◯	◯

Figure 9.3 ROI Quality Analysis Tool (*continued*)

○ 1–2 Definitely unacceptable ○ 3–4 Probably unacceptable ○ 5–6 Borderline ○ 7–8 Probably acceptable ○ 9–10 Definitely acceptable

Name of the Solution: _____

Item	Questions	Notes	1	2	3	4	5	6	7	8	9	10
5. Sustained impact	k. How did the analysis determine the length of time that the business outcome improvements would be sustained (i.e., 3 months, 6 months, 1 year)? Is it realistic and credible?		○	○	○	○	○	○	○	○	○	○
	l. Was the improvement annualized, and if so, was a turnover loss adjustment applied to the analysis? If not, why not?		○	○	○	○	○	○	○	○	○	○
6. Assignment of monetary value	m. Was each monetary value used in the benefit analysis based on the improvement of a business outcome measure?		○	○	○	○	○	○	○	○	○	○
	n. Were credible methods and sources used to determine the monetary value of each improvement?		○	○	○	○	○	○	○	○	○	○
	o. If the monetary value is an estimate, or by association, was it adjusted for confidence level and was the source credible?		○	○	○	○	○	○	○	○	○	○
7. Costs of the solution included in the ROI calculation	p. Is the cost of salaries and employee benefits appropriately included?		○	○	○	○	○	○	○	○	○	○
	q. Are research and development and evaluation costs included?		○	○	○	○	○	○	○	○	○	○
	r. Is the cost of implementing the complete solution design included (companion strategies, per-work assignments, etc.)?		○	○	○	○	○	○	○	○	○	○
	s. Are other necessary costs included to reflect fully loaded costs (opportunity cost or replacement cost, etc.)?		○	○	○	○	○	○	○	○	○	○

After dialogue on each of the seven categories, how do you and your partner(s) rate the overall quality analysis of the ROI for this program or project? The seven categories are not equally weighted. Weighting depends on (1) how a weakness in any evaluation category affects the business outcome and ROI as you view the facts, and (2) your overall view of the analysis. Dialogue between partners should weigh heavily on the overall rating. The 1–10 scale is only a starting point. The dialogue and ratings reveal that the quality of the ROI is:

○ Definitely poor quality ○ Substandard quality ○ Questionable quality ○ Good quality ○ Definitely high quality

What is the collective reasoning for the conclusions of those providing input to the analysis?

- *Manage expectations.* Expectations are set during the planning stages of a study. Avoid setting expectations that are too high by addressing and negotiating real performance issues with sponsors and clients. Additionally, look for early warning signs that the program is not generating results. Learning assessments and the initial reaction from participants can give strong clues that the solution will not be successful. When the clues are there, inform the client and sponsor of the possibilities.
- *Educate business leaders up front.* One of the best ways to manage expectations is to educate business leaders about ROI. Use the ROI quality analysis tool as an educational aid. Address the myriad input variables that can cause a significant swing in the ROI.
- *Gain an up-front commitment from management to address how a negative ROI will be handled should it occur.* When properly done, an impact study will reveal why a solution fails to meet expectations. The chain of evidence will show the deficiencies.
- *Look for systemic issues that contribute to the unfavorable outcome.* When a negative ROI uncovers systemic deficiencies in the training and performance process, correcting the issues can be a tremendous asset to the organization because the benefit goes beyond the immediate program. Examples of systemic issues are low morale in an organization that contributes to low job interest, low productivity, and poor quality; lack of reinforcement and support from supervisors; and insufficient work incentives.

The context of ROI should not be about impressing the CFO or the CEO. It should not be about justifying the training department's existence. The proper context for ROI is that lessons learned from evaluation help to create more powerful solutions that are aligned with the needs of the business and therefore have an opportunity to contribute to the business. Look at it this way: "Today's solution may be tomorrow's problem." Discovery and improvement is a natural part of staying one step ahead of a moving target. Whether we are talking about a business process, a program, a measure, a strategic goal, needs of individuals, or whatever, there are no static targets in today's organizations. A negative ROI is a chance to discover the truth and forge a new path.

CASE STUDY PART 7: TECH*READ* SMART METERING COMPANY

Tech*Read* ROI Calculation

In Part 6 of the case study, the fully loaded cost of the training for the pilot experimental group (three regions receiving training) was determined to be $222,093. This is $3,702 per participant. The only benefit from the training that has an assigned monetary value is revenue from sales to commercial and industrial customers. In Part 3 of the case study, the sales data were collected from the company records for a three-month period following the training. The sales influenced by the coaching of the 60 participants were compared to the sales of the comparison group for the same three-month period. After an adjustment for causal influence, the adjustment for sustained impact was made in Part 4 of the case study. As a result of these adjustments, the increase in sales for the experimental group was $11,501,568.

Since revenue is used to pay the total company expenses at Tech*Read*, only that portion of the revenue increase that represents profit margin can be used as a benefit for the ROI calculation. As discussed in Part 5 of the case study, the Tech*Read* finance department provided a profit margin of 5 percent of revenue to be used in the calculation. Therefore, the total benefits for the numerator is $575,078 ($11,501,568 total revenue × 0.05). The ROI, as shown here, is 159 percent:

$$\text{ROI} = \frac{\$575,078 - \$222,093}{\$222,093} = 1.59 \times 100 = 159\%$$

The ROI of 159 percent represents a net gain above the fully loaded cost of the training solution. Since an acceptable hurdle rate for a training ROI is 20 percent, this appears to be an acceptable ROI. The next step is to analyze the quality of the ROI. The ROI quality analysis is necessary to ensure that the ROI is not inflated or the results misrepresented because of careless or irresponsible decisions during the impact study analysis.

Tech*Read* ROI Quality Analysis

The RQA of the results developed by the impact study of the Active Coaching for Field Sales Managers revealed the following.

1. *Performance readiness.* A needs analysis, including a review of employee complaints and input from employee focus groups, indicated that the sales managers were not implementing the coaching process properly. During the training, the facilitators' observation of the skill practice of coaching competencies showed that at least 70 percent of the sales managers (42 of 60) scored a readiness level of 4 or higher on a 1–5 scale.

2. *Execution in the work setting.* Focus groups with a sample of sales representatives provided sufficient evidence that effective coaching was taking place. There were some deficiencies, such as lack of help in market analysis. However, the focus group input also indicated that three months was insufficient time to allow the coaching process to completely play out its full cycle. Interviews with the three regional managers supported the idea that the sales managers were meeting expectations in applying coaching behavior.

3. *Business outcome.* The company records showed an increase in revenue of 17 percent after adjustments for causal influence. This is short of the revenue improvement goal of 20 percent, but that does not reflect on the quality of the study, and it is a substantial increase. Also, 85 percent of the sales force in the three experimental regions had an increase in sales. While there is evidence that employee complaints related to coaching have decreased, the complaint data were not used in the ROI calculation because the baseline data were contaminated.

4. *Causal influences.* Since many factors could have caused an increase in sales, a comparison group arrangement was used to determine how much of the sales increase was influenced by the complete solution design. The complete design consisted of the performance-based training in coaching skills, the support and reinforcement of regional

managers before and after the training, the executive VP involvement, and the Web-based job aid. After the causal influence adjustment, the amount by which the sales were influenced by the solution was reduced from an average of $1,960,000 per month to $832,000 per month (a total of $2,496,000 for the three regions). By using a credible comparison arrangement, a conservative conclusion was developed regarding the sales increase attributed to the solution design.

5. *Sustained impact.* Improvements in business measures can be used in an ROI calculation only to the extent that the improvements are sustained. Because of a situation affecting market demand (new government regulations requiring capital investment expenditures), only 60 percent of the sales improvement was annualized. It was also adjusted downward for confidence level. This adjustment, along with the causal influence adjustment, resulted in a very conservative decision on the amount of sales increase.

6. *Assignment of monetary values.* A high-quality ROI must use a credible method to assign a monetary value to an improvement. The profit margin of 5 percent was acquired from the finance department and used as a credible basis to arrive at the $575,078 value of the benefits ($11,501,568 total revenue × 0.05).

7. *Cost of the performance solution.* The ROI calculation used the fully loaded cost of the complete solution design, not just the training component. For example, the value of the time of the EVP and the three regional managers was included.

Using the ROI quality analysis tool as a template (Figure 9.3), the quality of the ROI was determined to be "definitely high quality." This study was rigorous, and the results that will be communicated represent a conservative view of what occurred. The quality of the execution in the work setting and the business outcome is consistent with the reported ROI of 159 percent.

10

Measuring the Contribution of Solutions: Alternatives to ROI

Some business impact studies are not about a return on investment. The objective of some studies is to determine whether and how business outcome improvements have occurred, with no concern about monetary contribution. Some studies may stop short of business outcomes, being interested only in how people are applying skills in the work setting. Stone's Measurement and ROI Process is capable of addressing any type of study on any type of intervention where the goal is for people to change what they do or how they do it or to avoid a specific type of behavior or outcome. As illustrated in Figure 10.1, Step 9d concludes the analysis by addressing the considerations and issues involved in identifying intangible benefits and including them in the business impact study.

THE SIGNIFICANCE OF INTANGIBLE BENEFITS

Intangible benefits can be defined in many ways, depending on the observer. For use in business impact studies, intangibles are defined the same way they are defined by the business dictionary. They are defined as subjective benefits that cannot be measured in monetary terms. The Six Sigma glossary expands the definition further. It says that intangible benefits are "soft benefits" that are nonmonetary or benefits that cannot be sufficiently quantified to be used for accounting or other financial reporting purposes. Yet

Figure 10.1   Phase Three, Step 9d

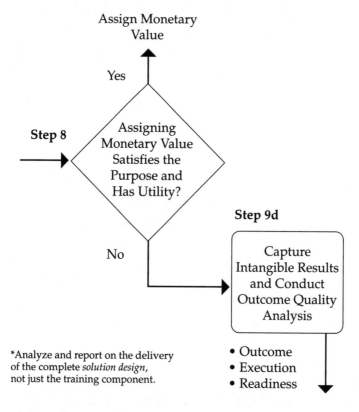

Phase Three

Analyze Data and Make
Conservative Adjustments*

Assign Monetary
Value

Yes

Step 8

Assigning
Monetary Value
Satisfies the
Purpose and
Has Utility?

No

Step 9d

Capture
Intangible Results
and Conduct
Outcome Quality
Analysis

*Analyze and report on the delivery
of the complete *solution design,*
not just the training component.

• Outcome
• Execution
• Readiness

these soft benefits contribute to the business in ways that are just as important as those provided by the tangible benefits.

Business outcome studies that stop short of calculating ROI can assign
monetary values, but doing so is often not necessary. The improvements
that are reported are usually classified as intangibles, because the value is
not known or reported. Most ROI studies also include additional improvements that are not assigned a monetary value. Improvements in intangible
measures are reported along with the ROI calculation to tell the complete
story and strengthen the overall results attributed to the solution. Since

intangibles are reported, but are not included in the formal ROI calculation, they actually serve to increase the ROI that is presented. That is, if the intangibles have any value at all, then the ROI that is presented is actually understated. Table 10.1 shows a few examples of intangible benefits.

The benefits in Table 10.1 are soft because there is no monetary value associated with them. However, it is easy to see that they add value to the organization. For most of the measures, it is also easy to see when the measure changes. Some of the measures, such as quality and output, may have a known value in some organizations, and therefore would be classified as tangible. But in many organizations, measures such as quality, output, satisfaction, and complaints, among others, do not have a known value. As addressed in Chapter 7, if a specific benefit appears to be intangible, and someone in

Table 10.1   Intangible Benefits

MEASURE	EXAMPLE OF INTANGIBLE BENEFIT
1. Customer satisfaction	Customer satisfaction index score increases from 88.5 percent to 92 percent following an organization development intervention.
2. Customer complaints	A change in the customer service process to serve customers results in a reduction in customer complaints from 20 per 100 contacts to 5 per 100 contacts.
3. Output	Customer representatives prepare 10 orders per hour following a training program on the order process compared with 5 per hour before the training.
4. Quality	A new quality control training initiative results in a decrease in discrepancies in customer orders from 30 per 100 orders to 5 per 100 orders.
5. Absenteeism	A change in the HR absenteeism policy results in a decrease in absenteeism from an average of 14 days annually per full-time employee to an average of 5 days annually per full-time employee.
6. Employee satisfaction	A coaching program results in an increase in the employee satisfaction index score from 85 percent to 89 percent.
7. Employee turnover	During the first six months of employment, new-hire retention has improved by 45 percent. Before the on-boarding training, the loss of new hires was 25 of 50 hired. Six months after the intervention, the loss is 5 of 50 hired.
8. Employee stress	Customer service representatives and supervisors in the call center attribute a 30 percent error reduction in customer order entries to reduced stress in the department.

the organization has a credible known value for the measure, then the known value provides the missing piece to make the measure tangible.

The most effective way to determine a monetary value for a soft measure is to partner with one or more people who are familiar with the measure and the work setting in which an improvement occurred or should be occurring. Brainstorm ways in which the measure links to output, quality, time utilization, or cost savings in the work setting. In item 8 of Table 10.1, a reduction in employee stress is linked to an improvement in quality (reduction of errors). Since the linkage has been established, valuing it is a matter of determining the value of reducing errors. One way in which this can be done is to determine the monetary value of one typical error in customer order entries. This monetary value can easily be estimated by those working the orders or by their manager. This is usually done by assigning salary and benefit costs to the number of hours it takes to rework one error. Then add any additional cost items, such as supplies and materials. Now it is a matter of multiplying the number of reduced errors by the monetary value to arrive at the total benefit.

Intangible benefits are not always included in the accounting books. However, the costs that are affected by these benefits always appear in the books. That is why it is important to describe soft benefits in monetary terms whenever this is practical. While all soft measures can ultimately be assigned a credible monetary value, doing so will require more thought and work for some than for others. In some instances, this process may require more labor than stakeholders are willing to invest. It depends on how badly they need the value for decision-making purposes.

Even though monetary values can always be assigned, some measures may not need to have a monetary value. For example, many hospitals have a measure called "managing W&M patients." This means managing wandering and missing patients. Some patients are at great risk of wandering around the hospital, away from their assigned care unit. Some even wander outside the hospital facility and become missing patients. The program for managing these high-risk patients includes training for the nurses and administrators. No one is looking for an ROI from this training. What management wants is zero lost patients and zero injuries, morbidity (getting sicker), or deaths resulting from patients wandering away from their unit or outside the facility. Could a value be assigned if desired? Sure; just use the dollars resulting from lawsuits related to the consequences of W&M patients.

CONDUCTING THE OUTCOME QUALITY ANALYSIS FOR INTANGIBLES

An intangible business outcome improvement can be more compelling than a tangible benefit. The key issue is, determine what it takes to satisfy stakeholders' expectations and plan to meet those requirements with the impact study. Of course, the expectations actually begin with the training solution. That is, the measures (tangible and intangible) should be identified up front when the learning solution is designed. The outcome quality analysis tool shown in Figure 10.2 (see pages 248–249) is used to determine the quality of the intangibles. It is essentially the same as the ROI quality analysis tool that was presented in Chapter 9. However, since intangibles are being analyzed, it is not necessary to address ROI, the assignment of monetary value, or the costs of the solution, which are included in the ROI quality analysis tool.

The outcome quality analysis tool in Figure 10.2 is applied as a quality check for the intangible business outcome results. The five evaluation input variables, performance readiness, execution in the work setting, business outcome, causal influences, and sustained impact, are applied in the same way as they are in the ROI quality analysis tool. Part 8 of the Tech*Read* case study in the next section illustrates the application.

CASE STUDY PART 8: TECH*READ* SMART METERING COMPANY

Tech*Read* Intangible Results

The tangible data (revenue) have been collected, and the ROI has been calculated. Any existing intangible benefits that resulted should also be included, along with the ROI. Most of the time, an impact study will discover one or more intangible benefits that for various reasons are not assigned a monetary value. Since an intangible benefit is not part of the ROI calcula-

Figure 10.2 Outcome Quality Analysis Tool

Partner with one or more informed persons (client, training manager, coworker, etc.) and use this tool to discuss and rate a specific outcome. This tool is a five-point *acid test* used to analyze the quality of an outcome and communicate it to stakeholders. After careful consideration and discussion, use the 1–10 scale below to rate the acceptability of each item by filling in one circle. Document the collective reasoning for each rating.

○ 1–2 Definitely unacceptable   ○ 3–4 Probably unacceptable   ○ 5–6 Borderline   ○ 7–8 Probably acceptable   ○ 9–10 Definitely acceptable

Name of the Solution: _____

Item	Questions	Notes	1	2	3	4	5	6	7	8	9	10
1. Performance Readiness	a. How was the decision made as to what the readiness gap was and why it existed? (Readiness gaps such as knowledge, skill, confidence, habits, active management reinforcement, etc.)		○	○	○	○	○	○	○	○	○	○
	b. What is the evidence that the readiness gap (learning or other) was closed with the study population, and what methods were used to determine this?		○	○	○	○	○	○	○	○	○	○
2. Execution in the Work Setting	c. What percentage of the sample population successfully applied the solution in the work setting as expected (closed the performance gap as expected)? *Percent expected to apply ____ % Percent actually applied ____ %* Were credible methods and sources used to verify application?		○	○	○	○	○	○	○	○	○	○
	d. What companion strategies or elements were included in the solution design to reinforce execution in the work setting?		○	○	○	○	○	○	○	○	○	○
	e. What were the successes and disappointments? Which elements of the solution design worked effectively? Which did not work effectively, and why?		○	○	○	○	○	○	○	○	○	○
3. Business Outcome	f. What specific business measures improved, and by how much? Was the change in the measure compared to a baseline level?		○	○	○	○	○	○	○	○	○	○
	g. Were credible methods and sources used to determine the business outcome improvement?		○	○	○	○	○	○	○	○	○	○
4. Causal Influences (what caused the change?)	h. What percentage of the improvement of each business outcome measure was influenced by the *delivery of the complete solution design?* What other factors influenced these improvements?		○	○	○	○	○	○	○	○	○	○
	i. Were the methods/sources credible that were used to analyze the solution's influence on each business outcome measure?		○	○	○	○	○	○	○	○	○	○
	j. What timeline was used to analyze the influence on each business outcome measure? Is the timeline realistic?		○	○	○	○	○	○	○	○	○	○

Figure 10.2 Outcome Quality Analysis Tool (continued)

○ 1–2 Definitely unacceptable	○ 3–4 Probably unacceptable	○ 5–6 Borderline	○ 7–8 Probably acceptable	○ 9–10 Definitely acceptable

Name of the Solution:

Item	Questions	Notes	Rating									
			1	2	3	4	5	6	7	8	9	10
5. Sustained impact	k. How did the analysis determine the length of time that the business outcome improvements would be sustained (i.e., 3 months, 6 months, 1 year)? Is it realistic and credible?		○	○	○	○	○	○	○	○	○	○
	l. Was the improvement annualized, and if so, was a turnover loss adjustment applied to the analysis? If not, why not?		○	○	○	○	○	○	○	○	○	○

After dialogue on each of the five categories, how do you and your partner(s) rate the overall quality analysis of the outcomes for this program or project? The five categories are not equally weighted. Weighting depends on (1) how a weakness in any evaluation category affects the business outcome as you view the facts, and (2) your overall view of the analysis. Dialogue between partners should weigh heavily on the overall rating. The 1–10 scale is only a starting point. *The dialogue and ratings reveal that the quality of the outcome is:*

○ Definitely poor quality ○ Substandard quality ○ Questionable quality ○ Good quality ○ Definitely high quality

What is the collective reasoning for the conclusions of those providing input to the analysis?

tion, it is presented as a benefit in addition to the ROI. Recall from Part 3 of the Tech*Read* case that about six weeks after the training was delivered, the HR analyst notified Sue and her evaluation team that the baseline data for employee complaints were unreliable. The analyst had been in the job for only a month, and she had inherited the data from an HR analyst who had resigned. Since reconstructing the baseline data would have consumed an excessive amount of resources, the evaluation team decided to forgo using the complaint data in the ROI analysis. However, while preparing the evaluation report, the evaluation team received a telephone call from the HR analyst that prompted it to revisit the employee complaint data.

After the contaminated baseline data were discovered, the HR analyst began keeping a separate record. She was able to analyze the details of all the posttraining data in the six regions and develop a clear conclusion from the nature of the complaints that the training solution was the chief reason that the number of complaints in the three experimental regions had been reduced. In addition, the employee focus groups provided credible input about the reduction of employee complaints. A monthly average of six coaching-related complaints had been reported in the three experimental sales regions during the three-month posttraining time period. During the same posttraining time period, the two comparison regions had had a monthly average of 23 employee complaints related to lack of coaching. This was good news for the impact study, because it showed a definite difference of 17 in coaching-related complaints during the posttraining period. This is an improvement of 74 percent ($17 \div 23$). Since the pretraining baseline level was not certain, the team was still not comfortable applying the results to the ROI calculation, but it felt comfortable using the results as an intangible because the significant difference shown was supported by input from the focus groups with sales representatives.

The analysis concluded that there was one key intangible business outcome resulting from the Active Coaching for Field Sales Managers program that should have a sustained influence going forward.

Employee complaints related to coaching differ by an average of 17 per month ($23 - 6$) compared to the two regions in the comparison group. During the focus groups, employees were asked about differences in sales managers' coaching before and after the training. Employees were unanimous in concluding that the coaching solution was responsible for significant improvement. When asked how confident they were, they responded that they were 100 percent confident. A member of one focus group summed it up best, saying, "We work with these sales managers every day, and we see what they do. There have been significant differences in how they have responded with coaching since they returned from the coaching training." Applying the outcome quality analysis tool in Figure 10.2, as summarized here, the improvement in complaints is determined to be a "good quality" intangible business outcome.

1. *Performance readiness.* A needs analysis, including a review of employee complaints and input from employee focus groups, indicated that sales managers were not implementing the coaching process. This was the basis of the excessive employee complaints. During the training, the facilitators' observation of skill practice on coaching competencies shows that at least 70 percent of the sales managers (42 of 60) scored a readiness level of 4 or higher on a 1–5 scale.

2. *Execution in the work setting.* Focus groups with a sample of sales representatives provided sufficient evidence that effective coaching is taking place. Interviews with the three regional managers supports the idea that the sales managers are meeting expectations in applying coaching behavior.

3. *Business outcome.* Evidence presented by the HR analyst who managed the data showed that posttraining employee complaints related to coaching in the experimental group were 74 percent less when compared to the same time frame in the two regions in the comparison group.

4. *Causal influences.* Since many factors could have caused the change in complaints, the comparison group arrangement noted previously was used to examine the difference in number of complaints. Focus group input reinforced the conclusion by analyzing the difference in posttraining complaints between the two groups.

5. *Sustained impact.* Improvements in business measures can be used only to the extent that the improvement is sustained. The solution included the close involvement of regional sales managers. Without

this involvement, it is doubtful that the coaching would have been implemented at a level that influenced a reduction in complaints. The regional managers have committed to continuing their close involvement. Therefore, they feel that the improvement will be sustained for the longer term.

While the baseline complaint data are considered unreliable, there is credible evidence that the complaints differ significantly (74 percent) between the comparison and experimental groups when viewing only post-training data. Input from the focus groups and elevated complaint activity in other regions substantiates that this difference can be attributed to improvement in coaching by the sales managers. The view of the sales representatives is important because they are close to the day-to-day situation and have no reason to provide biased input on this issue. This provides a comfort level for the analysis to conclude that employee complaints were reduced due to the training solution design.

♦ ♦ ♦

CHAPTER

11

Communicate the Results

An impact study that includes both results and lessons learned is of interest to many stakeholders, not just the training staff. The more we learn and share from a business impact study, the greater the opportunity to optimize the allocation of resources and the scarce training dollars. Key executives who are far removed from day-to-day training initiatives can gain a stronger appreciation for how training solutions blend with performance strategies to achieve a successful business contribution. The training function can seize the opportunity to reframe training performance issues beyond the smile sheet and communicate what works best for the organization. The funding available for evaluation activities will not allow every training program to be measured at the impact level. When impact studies do take place, however, the communication of results and lessons learned must be planned and executed with purpose and proficiency. As illustrated in Figure 11.1 (see page 254), Steps 10 and 11 conclude the impact study process by addressing the communication of results and key considerations for follow-up.

COMMUNICATING THE COMPLETE STORY

The complete story from an impact study report should communicate a chain of evidence that reflects a balanced approach to the findings and conclusions. If the solution is effective, it should provide credible evidence that the expenditure for the training solution began a chain of action that enabled the readiness of participants, followed by execution in the work setting and improvement in one or more business outcomes. Lessons learned and actions going forward should be included.

Figure 11.1   Phase Four, Step 10, and Phase Five, Step 11

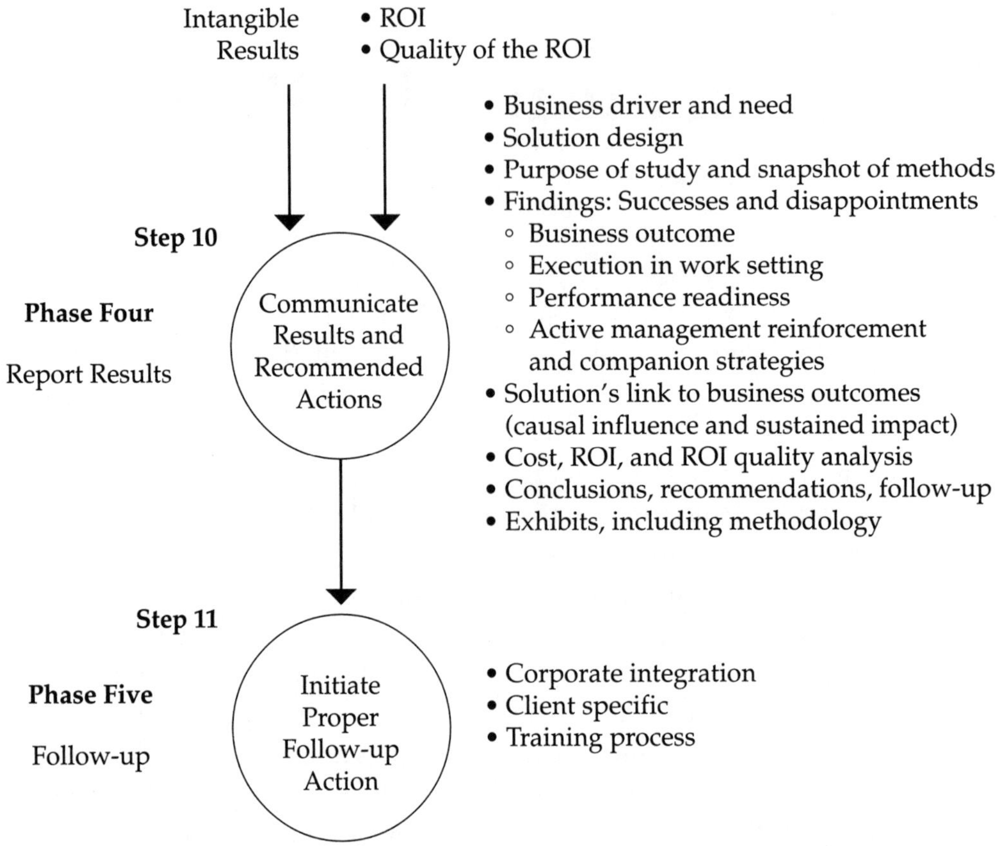

Intangible   • ROI
Results   • Quality of the ROI

• Business driver and need
• Solution design
• Purpose of study and snapshot of methods
• Findings: Successes and disappointments
  ◦ Business outcome

Step 10

  ◦ Execution in work setting
  ◦ Performance readiness

Phase Four

Communicate
Results and
Recommended
Actions

  ◦ Active management reinforcement
    and companion strategies

Report Results

• Solution's link to business outcomes
  (causal influence and sustained impact)
• Cost, ROI, and ROI quality analysis
• Conclusions, recommendations, follow-up
• Exhibits, including methodology

Step 11

Phase Five

Initiate
Proper
Follow-up
Action

• Corporate integration
• Client specific
• Training process

Follow-up

The report should include both tangible and intangible results. When the ROI is presented, nothing worthwhile is learned unless the report also communicates how the number came to be what it is. Dialogue about the numbers brings understanding and raises more in-depth questions about cause-and-effect relationships. Dialogue reinforces the lessons learned and allows the bar to be raised for the next level of achievement. The numbers sometimes have a way of concealing the sweat equity, ingenuity, and commitment of the people who drive the result. When addressing results, follow Guiding Principle 12, "When reporting tangible and intangible results, communicate the linkage of these results and their contribution to the organization's key business strategies or measures."

Guiding Principle 12

When reporting tangible and intangible results, communicate the linkage of these results and their contribution to the organization's key business strategies or measures.

The ROI quality analysis presented in Chapter 9 encourages additional dialogue that uncovers the truth about what drives the results. Qualitative results such as specific examples and success stories communicate in terms that the masses can identify with. They allow the results to be understood and replicated across functions and solutions. Qualitative results generate a higher-level dialogue that develops deeper understanding of the participants' sweat, ingenuity, and commitment.

The discussion about disappointments is not about finding fault or failure or pointing fingers. Disappointments are approached in a positive way, as a breakdown in the process. It is about giving people the best opportunity to succeed by addressing what has gone wrong as well as what has gone well. Clients, executives, and managers know that not everything goes perfectly. Executives are not interested in hearing a glowing report that addresses only the successes of our efforts. They know that with every initiative, there are thorns as well as roses. They appreciate the willingness to look at both sides of an issue, speak to lessons learned, and call it as you see it. It is important to develop recommendations and action items to address the breakdowns and make advances from lessons learned.

COMPREHENSIVE FORMAT FOR COMMUNICATING THE RESULTS

Because the members of the audience for an impact study report will vary in their level of interest, availability of time, and preferences for receiving information, there is no absolute method of communication. There are many options for communicating the results. Methods such as visual presentations, professionally developed brochures, bound documents, loose handouts, and e-mail have been used. The simplest rule to follow is to match the method to the needs of the audience. The preference in presenting evaluation results is a formal presentation or report to a live audience. There are two primary reasons for this preference: (1) the presenter can establish the frame of reference by choosing how and when the information is communicated and can inject timely points of emphasis, and (2) the parties will experience instant two-way communication. The following format can serve as a guideline for developing the headings and content of an impact study report. Use the format and guidelines as appropriate and customize them to your specific audience.

Business driver and need. You may want to call the first part of the report an introduction. Whatever the label, it is important that you quickly introduce the business driver that prompted the expenditure of organization funds. For example, in the Tech*Read* case study, the business drivers were excessive employee complaints and decreasing revenue. Set the stage by showing what the deficiencies were and how badly they were hurting the business. Next, briefly define how this driver translated into a need. Explain what people were or were not doing that contributed to the deficiency and how a solution was identified.

The solution design. Briefly describe the key components of the solution. Address how each component was designed to contribute to achieving the desired results to close the gaps and eliminate the deficiency. It is important that the audience understand the scope of the solution and how companion strategies provided the catalyst to initiate change.

Purpose of the evaluation study and a snapshot of methods. Explain the purpose(s) of the evaluation study. What were the primary reasons for gathering and analyzing information? Following the purpose, provide a snapshot of the methodology used in the study. This is not the place for a detailed explanation of the methodology. Save that for an exhibit or appendix. Provide hints of how the methodology is conservative, with the aim of understating the results. Address how the data for the study were collected and the credible sources that were used. The idea is to create an expectation of credibility in how the data were collected, analyzed, and reported.

Findings: successes and disappointments. Set the tone early by stating that the study results address both successes and disappointments. Satisfy the audience that lessons were learned and actions are in place to address disappointments.

- *Business outcome (tangible and intangible).* Address the outcomes by discussing the business metrics that were affected. Discuss how deficiencies were corrected and how the improvement contributes to the organization's key business strategies or measures. Discuss whether expectations were met, and if not, why not.
- *Execution in the work setting.* Address what the participants and others did to achieve the results. Highlight the fact that it was their contribution that influenced the business outcome. Discuss whether expectations were met, and if not, why not. Include success stories.
- *Performance readiness.* Address the highlights of how the learning engagement contributed to readiness and how this ultimately played a key role in execution in the work setting. Highlight the contribution of facilitators and guest speakers in getting the participants "performance ready."
- *AMR and companion strategies.* Address the highlights of any companion strategies and credit the people involved in making the strategies work. Address active management reinforcement (AMR) and how the immediate managers of the participants played a role in the success of the training solution. This is also a good time to educate the audience and reinforce the idea that stand-alone training does not usually get results. Reinforce that training, companion strategies, and AMR are partners in performance and influencers of change.
- *Enablers and barriers to performance.* Address how positive factors in the work environment contributed to the success of the initiative (such as the companion strategies). Also address how obstacles or problems adversely affected the performers' ability to execute in the work setting.

Solution's link to business outcomes (causal influence and sustained impact). Address how the business outcome results were adjusted during the analysis to account for the influence of other factors. Explain how sustained impact was determined and, where appropriate, communicate how adjustments for employee turnover were made.

Cost, ROI calculation, and ROI quality analysis. Address the fully loaded cost and the ROI calculation. Use the ROI quality analysis to show how the ROI was developed and to analyze the quality of the ROI. Communicate both the ROI and the quality of the ROI along with the reasoning leading to the quality conclusion.

Conclusions, recommendations, and follow-up action. Provide conclusions followed by recommendations. Every conclusion should be developed from the successes and disappointments findings presented previously. Not every conclusion will necessarily have a recommendation associated with it. Include follow-up actions that are already in place based on conclusions, recommendations, and lessons learned.

Exhibits, including methodology. Use a separate section or appendix to show detailed exhibits, such as questionnaires or focus group results, the evaluation planning document, the guiding principles, details regarding the evaluation methodology, and details about the solution.

TIPS FOR COMMUNICATING WITH EXECUTIVES ABOUT RESULTS

Every audience is different. Know your audience and prepare the presentation to fit it. The measurement and ROI process and the ROI calculations should be communicated with purpose. Nothing about the audience receiving the communication should be taken for granted. Following are some general guidelines when presenting to an executive audience.

Analyze the Audience and Customize the Report

There are numerous potential audiences for an impact study report. Each audience is different and has different needs. The training design team and others in the training department should probably be provided with the full report. Executives may require only an overview, and they may prefer to have it delivered through a slide presentation. The principal client or sponsor and the participants involved in the study should always be provided with the results, but their needs are likely to be different from those of the training department and the executives. Plan the development of the impact study report and how it will be communicated to fit the needs of the audience. If you cannot talk to an executive in advance of the presentation, talk to those who are close to the executives (executive assistants, administrative assistants, or other such people) to determine their expectations. When communicating with several different types of audiences, more than one type of report may be required. An executive overview at the beginning of a full report is always useful. The executive overview will often meet the needs of one or more audiences. Manage the expectations of the audience members by letting them know what to expect. Every audience has a bias, so be prepared for it.

Be Prepared for Questions about Anything

Most audiences will ask questions. Be prepared for questions such as: How does this result compare with the results of your other programs? Why is the cost so high? Could we get the same result for less cost? What do you plan to do differently the next time this program is offered? What did you learn from this evaluation that you can apply to other programs? Do you really think this result will continue in the months ahead? Why did you use estimates?

Get beyond the Costs Quickly

Your objective for the meeting should be to discuss the results, what caused them, your recommendations, and lessons learned. Do not let time robbers get in the way of this objective. One of the biggest time robbers occurs when someone in the audience wants to discuss details of the costs of the solution. This discussion can usually be avoided if it is made clear that the costs are fully loaded. Show a quick graphic that highlights the categories of costs that are included. Be sure that the graphic is comprehensive and visibly shows the category of salaries and benefits.

Focus on the Complete Solution Design

Focus on the complete solution design, not just to give credit, but to make it clear what caused the results. Constructively discredit the frame of reference that training can be implemented like a coat of paint and the room will be gleaming again. The audience members may be thinking of your solution as only a training program. Reframe their thinking early in the presentation to help them understand that a training and performance solution has been delivered. Highlight the companion strategies that are part of the solution, and describe how the partnership created them. Emphasize that eliminating a companion strategy is likely to change the results. Give these strategies credit for the performance success.

Emphasize Contributions and Lessons Learned, Not Justification

The impact study should be explained as a means of examining the training and performance process in an attempt to do two things: (1) using a major training expenditure as a vehicle, discover whether the process is working and making a business contribution, and if so, what are the drivers that make it work, and (2) utilize lessons learned to continuously strengthen the process and improve solutions in ways that give them a better opportunity to hit the target. Never allow the impact study to be framed as justifying the program, the training department, or the budget. No one will care about your justification, and your listeners will see the study as a waste of time and money.

Follow the Twin Axioms

It's easy. Understate the results and overstate the costs. This will provide a more realistic analysis and increase the credibility of the report. Let it be known that the analysis discarded both any reported results that had incomplete data and unrealistic results that had no basis.

Reveal Assumptions or Unusual Situations

Communicate any assumptions that you or your sources may have made when providing or analyzing data. If estimates were used in developing business outcomes, calculating ROI, tabulating costs, or any other part of the report, communicate this up front and address how the estimates were adjusted for the possibility of error. As the results are presented, weave the guiding principles into the presentation where they are relevant. Show the 12 guiding principles in an appendix and relate them to your study as appropriate.

Explain the ROI Formula

As financial terms are defined, there are several ways to communicate the return on funds invested. The ROI formula used for training investments is one way. The formula is similar to those used for other investment calculations; however, the audience members may not be familiar with it. Explain the formula and how it is applied with training investments. Communicate that costs are fully loaded and that benefits are calculated only from business outcome improvements. Be sure to communicate that "net" benefits are used in the formula. Also, in accordance with Guiding Principle 11, be certain to communicate the quality of the ROI and use the job aid (Figure 9.3) to show how it is developed.

The ROI percentage should always be rounded to the nearest whole number. Here is the rule to follow and a couple of examples.

Round the decimal up if it is 0.5 or greater. Round it down if it is less than 0.5.

- Incorrect: ROI = 68.7 percent. Correct: ROI = 69 percent.
- Incorrect: ROI = 65.4 percent. Correct: ROI = 65 percent.

When a decimal such as ROI = 98.7 percent is shown, it gives the impression that the ROI is exact. The variability of the evaluation inputs makes it clear that ROI is anything but precise. ROI is not precise in any field of endeavor. It is not precise in marketing, accounting, finance, engineering, or operations, and it is not precise in training or HR. Learning assessments and smile sheets are not precise either.

Provide Status Updates on the Measurement Project

Since an impact study takes place over a span of time (usually months), it is important to treat it like a project. Establish timeline milestones, and provide the client and the sponsor with interim progress reports and updates. Use these progress reports to keep them informed and to manage their expectations. If something is not going well, be the first to inform the client and the sponsor and address corrective steps.

Communicate Important Highlights of the Methodology

Do not get mired in the details of the methodology. You will not have time to discuss all the details of the methodology and the guiding principles. Put the details in an exhibit, and leave a contact number where your listeners can call you with any questions. You may get a call from an executive assistant or staff member. Treat this call as though it is the executive who is calling. The ROI quality analysis tool is a good document to put in the report. It is a concise way of showing the methodology. The measurement and ROI model should also be included, since some people prefer visuals that allow them see the big picture. Do not take the time to try to explain all the steps of the model. Simply make key points about it and move on.

Educate the Audience

Executives often misunderstand the training function and training solutions. Training professionals should take every opportunity to educate their audiences about the training and performance process. This should be done in subtle ways throughout the presentation. For example, while discussing the solution, insert a morsel about how a quick needs analysis that took only one day identified several crucial performance issues that allowed designers to focus the program on the right things. Or insert a bit about how a previous evaluation allowed us to reduce costs and turnaround time for a leadership program. As another example, discuss briefly how a one-hour Webinar companion strategy with supervisors helped them to focus on actively reinforcing the behavior change of participants when they returned to the job. Or weave the education into the presentation by saying something like, "Our studies have shown that a lack of companion strategies is the key reason why training solutions fail." Place highlighted statements in the report that help to educate.

THREE CHANNELS OF FOLLOW-UP

A sigh of relief often follows the communication of the results of an impact study. But the celebration should continue no longer than 24 hours because there is always work to be done following a presentation. The final step of the measurement and ROI process (Step 11) includes three possible follow-up channels. It will be necessary to follow up with at least one of these channels, and possibly all three.

Follow-up Channel: Corporate Integration

A training solution must be integrated with other processes in the organization. For example, the training department cannot facilitate the learning of a management style that is not supported by the organization. Sometimes processes or philosophies are companywide, and sometimes they are specific to one department or business unit. For example, the talent management process is usually a corporatewide process that includes staffing and replacement planning, performance management, employee development, retention programs, promotion and transfer policies, and other such processes.

Suppose a training program in performance management is given to one department in which a few supervisors have a deficiency. When the training is delivered, an impact study communicates lessons learned and problems discovered with the performance management process. The study makes a recommendation that needs to be integrated into the performance management process for other departments and business units companywide. In addition, the problems discovered could spill over into one of the other processes mentioned earlier. In this situation, the follow-up required is on a grand scale and can require considerable time, expertise, and resources. The best course of action is to partner with the owner of the process (such as HR) to integrate any issues or lessons learned into the corporatewide culture.

Follow-up Channel: Client Specific

Sometimes a lesson learned following an impact study or a recommendation regarding an issue with a process is limited to one department or business unit. For example, a nuclear power generating plant has different management requirements, safety requirements, and security procedures from a gas- or coal-operated plant. What may be an issue at one type of facility may not apply to the other types of facility. There may be no benefit from or no application for integrating the recommendation into the processes of another facility. Therefore, the follow-up recommendations and issues are limited to one channel. They are client specific.

Follow-up Channel: Training and Performance Process

An impact study will usually communicate lessons learned that can be integrated into other learning programs. In addition, the training and performance process can benefit from the findings of an impact study. Documented results should be highlighted and shared within the training department for continuous improvement purposes. Feedback should also be provided to future participants that communicates how programs are continuously improved by using their input. A "lessons learned" session can be shared with designers, facilitators, and account managers. The information should be used to improve both subsequent offerings and new programs. This channel is always applicable.

CASE STUDY PART 9:
TECH*READ* SMART METERING COMPANY

Communicating the Tech*Read* Results

Space limitations prevent the inclusion of the actual report from the Tech*Read* impact study. Only a few highlights of the conclusions and recommendations are given here. The format presented earlier in this chapter was used for this study. There are numerous other formats that can be used. The important thing is, be sure that the format, length, amount of detail, and other such factors fit the needs of the audience.

Conclusions

As indicated by the findings presented earlier, all key elements of the solution design were successful. There are areas that can be improved, and actions have already been initiated in several areas, as will be shown in this section. Highlights of the conclusions are shown here.

1. *Learning solution.* The limited amount of time dedicated to a needs analysis paid dividends in recognizing the value of coaching by sales managers and the deficiencies that existed in coaching competencies. The 12-hour learning activity "Active Coaching for Field Sales Managers" made a significant contribution to the success of the overall initiative. In particular, the skill practice exercises and the candid feedback from peers and facilitators provided a significant learning experience. The summary from the facilitators' observation shows that at least 70 percent of the participants (42 of 60) scored at a readiness level of 4 or higher on a 1–5 scale.

Feedback also indicated that the goals of reducing employee complaints and increasing sales provided a clear target for performance. Sales managers created action plans to eliminate their ineffective coaching habits and committed to spending more quality time with the sales teams.

2. *Up-front involvement of regional sales managers.* The companion strategy of pre-learning engagement meetings to share employee complaint data and discuss expectations set the stage for success. Significant feedback from sales managers reinforced that these meetings framed the issues concisely and focused the sales managers' attention on engaging in the upcoming learning solution.

3. *Involvement of the EVP of marketing and sales.* Feedback from the sales managers showed that they were motivated by the EVP's presentation on the first day of each session. It served to reinforce the expectations for sales managers in the area of coaching. Many sales managers commented on how well the EVP linked successful coaching behavior to the ability to increase sales and grow the brand.

4. *Field involvement of regional sales managers in the performance process.* The companion strategy of active management reinforcement by regional managers following the learning program was a significant contributor to the effectiveness of the solution. Feedback from employee focus groups and interviews with the regional managers concluded that the sales managers did well in coaching sales representatives in (a) planning the sales call, (b) how to position the sales call, and (c) follow-up with the customer to build relationships. As reported by sales managers, the regional managers' support and advice was very useful in learning how to overcome barriers that often got in the way of their coaching their sales teams.

Regional sales managers expressed that they had had an eye-opening experience in terms of the difference that their involvement made in the results achieved in an area such as coaching. Previously, their focus had been on sales and budgets and reaching the number. They now see the value of focusing on "the process of how" to reach the sales goals (such as coaching the sales team). They expressed renewed commitment to spending more time in the field to reinforce the process of achieving goals, not just the sales targets.

5. *Impact on sales.* While sales from the funded solution did not reach the goal of a 20 percent improvement, there was a significant improvement of 16 percent in revenue. There was a monthly increase of $2,496,000 for the three regions combined. The calculation of this improvement used a very conservative approach that adjusted for the causal impact of the solution by using a comparison group arrangement. When analyzing sustained impact, only 60 percent of the sales were annualized. After this downward adjustment to 60 percent plus a 20 percent downward adjustment for sales force turnover, the total annual increase in revenue was $11,501,568. A 5 percent profit margin meant that $575,078 (5 percent of $11,501,568) was carried forward in the study as benefits and used to calculate the ROI.

6. *Quality of the ROI.* Based on the aforementioned conservative decisions and adjustments, including the fact that all data used and decisions made were based on credible sources, the ROI quality analysis concluded that the ROI of 159 percent was definitely of high quality. A fully loaded cost of $222,093 and a profit contribution of $575,078 were used in the ROI calculation.

7. *Reduction in employee complaints related to coaching.* Employee complaints related to coaching have been reduced by possibly as much as an average of 17 per month. Posttraining data show 23 per month in the comparison regions and 6 per month in the three experimental regions. While the exact pretraining complaint data cannot be determined for the comparison regions, the focus groups and the HR analyst supported the idea that the number was much higher than 6 per month in the experimental regions. Spoilage of baseline data resulted in a decision not to use the reduction in complaints as a basis for ROI. This improvement is included as an intangible benefit. Since it costs time and money to review and process complaints, this intangible has some value greater than zero, thereby resulting in an ROI that is understated. Consequently, it can be stated with confidence that the ROI is greater than the 159 percent that was reported.

8. *Disappointments.* When one looks closely at success, one will usually find disappointments as well. There are several disappointments with this initiative.

- *Deficiency in communicating expectations.* Regional sales managers report that about 30 percent of the sales managers are deficient in communicating expectations. This is a time and commitment issue, not a skill deficiency.
- *Deficiency in market analysis.* Sales representatives report a lack of sales manager coaching help in market analysis, which can help in creating strategies to outsell the competition. Sales managers lack knowledge and experience in this competency.
- *Sales managers' time utilization.* Sales managers have difficulty finding quality time to work with their sales teams to communicate expectations, provide feedback, and improve ongoing performance.
- *Deficiencies in the evaluation study.* Over half of the focus group participants felt that the three-month time period was insufficient to allow the coaching process to play out completely. They stated that this was mainly due to the amount of time that they spend in the field.

The spoilage of baseline data for employee complaints is unfortunate. Better planning could have discovered this earlier and perhaps allowed more reliable findings in this area.

Recommendations

Based on the findings and conclusions, the following recommendations are provided.

1. Deliver the complete solution to the sales managers in the three remaining regions within 30 days. This includes the 12-hour learning program, the Web-based job aid, and the involvement of the EVP and the regional sales managers. If the design is changed by eliminating one or more of the design components, the result is also likely to change. The companion strategies are an inherent part

of the performance design that influenced the business outcome and ROI.

2. Provide training in market analysis to all sales managers within three months. This should equip managers and others to initiate effective sales strategies as well as to counteract strategies employed by competitors.

3. Provide training in coaching skills and market analysis to experienced and high-potential sales representatives within six months.

4. Thirty days after the training in recommendation 3 is delivered, use high-potential sales representatives to train other sales representatives in market analysis.

5. In accordance with the recommendation of experienced sales representatives, utilize experienced sales representatives as peer coaches for other sales representatives, thereby allowing sales managers to spend more quality time with sales representatives to communicate expectations, provide feedback, and reinforce performance.

6. The training department should implement follow-up activities as noted in the sections on follow-up action.

Suggestion for Management Consideration   A suggestion is provided here for consideration, based on the history of the coaching process. When a new process that requires new competencies of managers or staff is implemented, give strong consideration to appointing staff members to analyze the need for training and proceed accordingly based on the analysis. Require a forecast of the ROI and/or an analysis of the cost of not providing training. Proceed on the basis of a business decision as dictated by the analysis and the forecast. The current coaching process was implemented nine months before the training was implemented. The decision was made to forgo the training. In hindsight, the company may have lost as much as $11,501,568 of revenue because managers did not execute the coaching process. The training department takes responsibility for this deficiency. An ongoing performance needs analysis would have discovered the performance issues and delivered a recommendation to management. The training department has learned this lesson, and an action plan is in place going forward.

Initiate Follow-up Action for Corporate Integration

The training department has partnered with HR to create and implement a plan to determine whether the coaching solution applies to performance deficiencies in other organizations within Tech*Read*. The plan is currently being implemented by the operations department.

The training department has implemented a companywide strategic performance needs analysis by reviewing significant business outcome deficiencies, followed by quick discovery methods to determine whether training is an appropriate solution for addressing any of these deficiencies.

Initiate Follow-up Action with the Client

The training department will execute the following within two weeks. (1) Meet with the three regional managers to discuss the crucial role that they played in the success of the pilot training. (2) Suggest that the regional managers reinforce and follow up on the need for sales managers to communicate their expectations to sales teams. (3) Ask one or more of the regional managers to brief the regional managers in the comparison group and communicate specific actions that they took to support and reinforce the initiative. (4) Provide follow-up communication to the EVP and the three regional managers, showing when they have executed all follow-up action.

Initiate Follow-up Action within the Training Department

The training department and HR will conduct a briefing within 30 days to address lessons learned during the solution rollout and the implementation of the impact study. Share the results of the study within both departments, especially the design and development team and the facilitators. Specifically address how the solution design components contributed to the success of the initiative. Apply the lessons learned to future offerings of this solution and to other types of initiatives as applicable.

12

Opportunity Forecasting: Predicting Performance Improvement and ROI

The measurement and ROI process presented in this book has focused on conducting postdelivery ROI impact studies. The goal of such studies is to determine how the training and performance process works best to make business contributions and to put lessons learned into practice. Forecasting has a different purpose. It is an inexpensive approach to predicting the outcome. It offers the opportunity to address the benefit-cost relationship prior to incurring major expenses, before participants are engaged in the solution. Perhaps of equal importance, forecasting provides an excellent opportunity to review the solution design in advance of delivery and answer significant questions about the feasibility of achieving the performance objectives. As illustrated in Figure 12.1 (see page 272), this final chapter addresses the considerations, issues, and methods for forecasting results and the return on investment.

BENEFITS OF FORECASTING

Forecasting results and ROI is beneficial to training professionals as well as to clients. It focuses attention on expenditures so that the benefits and costs can also be examined from a business perspective. While forecasting may be inaccurate, it is inexpensive and brings as many benefits as heavily funded postprogram evaluation studies (and sometimes more). Among the benefits of forecasting are

Figure 12.1 Opportunity Forecasting Model—Predelivery Forecasting Activities

Partner and apply the Opportunity Forecasting Job Aid (Figure 12.2) to examine scenarios, discuss issues, answer questions, and predict outcomes.

Review this model and apply the job aid in Figure 12.2 to put the model into action.

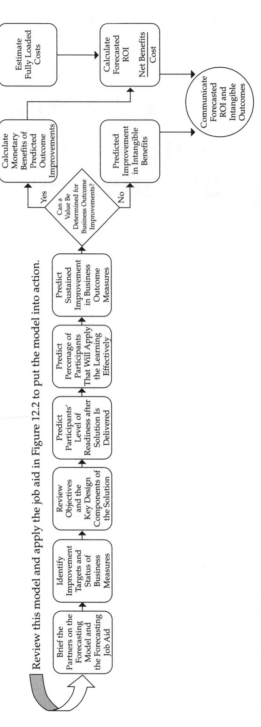

- It provides an opportunity to increase the value of solutions by examining best-case scenarios for results.
- It helps to define training's role as a strategic partner with business leaders.
- It builds a stronger business case for the program.
- It brings focus to how training solutions tie into the business.
- It provides an opportunity to educate business leaders about the performance value provided by training initiatives and companion strategies.
- It provides a basis for advance justification of an expenditure.
- It provides a basis for reducing cost and/or redesigning content and delivery to increase the probability of success.
- It provides a basis for recommending companion strategies.

In forecasting the results and the ROI, there are numerous factors to consider. The specifics of the program being evaluated and the conditions in the work setting are two of the most important of those factors. The following sections address these and other issues involved in forecasting.

REALITIES OF FORECASTING

ROI forecasting involves making a prediction that may or may not happen during the specified time frame or in the magnitude envisioned. The only way to know how a program actually influences business outcomes or the ROI is to do a study after participants have been able to apply what they learned, as described in the other chapters of this book. Even then, the conclusions will not be exact. There are two types of considerations that often skew the conclusions of forecasts because of their inadequate application. When these issues are properly addressed, forecasting results and ROI can be more realistic and credible. These considerations are identifying influencing factors and making realistic assumptions.

Identify Influencing Factors

When forecasting what may or should happen in the future as a result of an intervention, the influencing factors that exist must be considered. The best place to begin is to fully describe the scenario that the forecast will be applied to. Influencing factors exist throughout the chain of impact, beginning with the learning solution and any companion strategies planned along with the delivery. Here are a few example scenarios that include some of the key factors.

- *Scenario 1.* A solution is developed with no effort being made to match the needs of the population. The proper identification of needs is a significant factor. We may not always know whether needs have been properly identified, but we can easily determine whether they have been identified at all. If the solution has been developed or purchased, and no effort has been made to match it with the needs of the population, then a realistic forecast has to take this factor into account. This scenario would be high risk in terms of expecting full transfer of the learning to the job to occur. Limited transfer means limited to no business outcome.
- *Scenario 2.* A good needs analysis was implemented, and the learning program is well suited to the needs of the population. However, the learning solution has limited opportunities for skill practice and no follow-up companion strategies. This scenario is usually high risk in terms of expecting full transfer of the learning to the job to occur. Limited transfer means limited-to-no business outcome.
- *Scenario 3.* The learning solution has limited opportunities for skill practice, but it includes a follow-up companion strategy that requires the immediate supervisor to coach participants toward full competency and reinforce success. Because we know that companion strategies strengthen the prospects for transfer to the job, the forecast should reflect that this scenario has a better opportunity to succeed.
- *Scenario 4.* Employees of the engineering services department are attending a program to learn how to treat customers in a more caring and professional way. The client (department vice president) has stated that she has no interest in being involved in the solution in any way. Furthermore, she says that her supervisors do not have time to be involved. She expects her employees to learn the new behavior and execute it on their own when they return to work. The forecast should reflect that this is a recipe for disaster.

There are many factors like the ones just described. It is impossible to list all of them here or to take all of them into account when designing a program. But at least the prominent factors should be identified and considered when forecasting results and ROI. By identifying specific performance scenarios for a training project and discussing them with clients, the clients can sometimes be shown why the training design needs to be changed. Perhaps the length of the program needs to be expanded to include more time for skill practice, or a companion strategy needs to be implemented, or a higher level of client involvement will make a difference. For example, in Scenario 4, professional trainers know that the solution is not likely to be successful. If we can at least influence the client to consider the realities of the situation, it may be possible to point out the high risk. Perhaps we can even persuade the client that management involvement is a good thing if she indeed wants results.

While many influencing factors can be identified, assumptions must still be made regarding how each one will likely occur and influence the results in a specific scenario. A job aid presented later in this chapter includes many of the key factors that must be addressed when forecasting.

Realistic Assumptions

Forecasts will always include assumptions based on unknowns. That is the nature of predictions. It is best to identify influencing factors first (as with the four scenarios given in the previous section) and then begin to make assumptions about how these factors will likely occur and influence performance. Identifying the key factors that will influence results and applying them to scenarios will help in making realistic assumptions about why and how performance is likely to be affected. Assumptions should always be identified and discussed with partners before completing the forecast. Discussions with partners will often moderate the assumptions to allow for the development of more realistic conclusions. Here are a few examples of assumptions that may need to be made when forecasting ROI.

- How well does the needs analysis identify the business issues and the root cause of the performance gap?

- How well does the needs analysis identify what the population needs if it is to close the performance gap? Do we really know what people must do differently?
- To what extent will learning actually occur when the solution is delivered?
- When companion strategies exist, how well will they work in influencing transfer and performance?
- Have the significant barriers in the work setting been identified, and will the performers likely overcome these barriers to performance?
- What percentage of the participants will actually execute in the work setting as desired?
- To what extent will the performance of the participants cause the targeted business outcome measures to improve?

Once the assumptions concerning these types of issues are made and there is a credible monetary value for the business improvement, the costs can be estimated, and the ROI forecast can be calculated. The forecasting guidelines provided in the next section should be followed when partnering with the client and other stakeholders.

TWO APPROACHES TO FORECASTING ROI

There are three approaches to calculating ROI. Two of the approaches are forecasting methods. All three approaches use improvements in business outcome as the basis for developing the ROI calculation. A calculation using anything other than business outcomes would not be an ROI. An ROI cannot occur unless there is a business outcome. One way to calculate ROI is the postdelivery approach that has been addressed throughout this book. It is a way to study what has already happened and learn how solutions can be designed to make improved contributions to the business. The other way to calculate ROI is to forecast or predict the results. The predicted results will certainly not be accurate, but reflecting on and analyzing the proper issues can make the process more realistic and useful. The two approaches to forecasting are using participant estimates to make the forecast and forecasting prior to delivery by partnering with the client and others to predict the outcome. Both are addressed here.

Forecasting ROI with Participant Estimates

One approach to forecasting ROI is to allow the participants to predict the results at the end of a training session. This method is sometimes used with a pilot program before it is rolled out to more groups. It is recommended only for groups that have the sophistication to address the issues involved in predicting outcomes and the ability to determine or estimate monetary values. At the end of a program, each participant is asked to answer a minimum of five questions. The five questions shown in Table 12.1 are an example from a leadership program.

Table 12.1   Five Questions When Asking Participants to Forecast ROI

PARTICIPANTS' FORECAST OF RESULTS AND ROI
1. Reflect on what you have learned and think about your ability to apply it to your own work situation. What two or three things will you do differently as you return to your work setting?   _____   _____   _____
2. As a result of the two or three things you identified in Question 1, how will the business in your work unit improve (for example, improved quality, increased work output, reduced absenteeism, reduced employee turnover, or reduced employee complaints)?   Business improvement will be: _____   _____   _____
3. Think through the business improvement you have identified and estimate a monetary value for the improvement. What is the monetary value of the improvement over a one-year period? $_____
4. What is the basis for the improvement and your assignment of the monetary value?   _____   _____   _____
5. What is your confidence level (a) that the above results will actually happen, and (b) in the monetary value?   (100% = I am sure; 0% = total uncertainty)   a. _____% confidence that the results will happen.   b. _____% confidence in the monetary value.

The training professional collects the information and analyzes the results for realism and credibility. Adjustments are made to determine the total benefits, the cost is estimated, and the ROI is calculated to arrive at the forecast. For example, suppose participant A answers as follows:

- Item 2, business improvement: quality will improve by 50 percent.
- Item 3, monetary value = $100,000.
- Item 4, basis is: errors on customer orders in my unit are currently 20 per 100 orders filled. As I provide better guidance on problem identification and provide constructive feedback to employees, these errors will be reduced. Celebrating improvements with the team will reinforce attention to detail and good performance. The monetary value is a known value based on the cost of reworking errors. The cost is $50 per error.
- Item 5a is 80% confidence that the results will happen.
- Item 5b is 100% confidence in the monetary value.

Table 12.2 shows how the results for participant A are analyzed. The acceptable results for each participant are analyzed in the same way and consolidated to determine the total benefits for the ROI forecast. The table shows a few participants so that you can get the idea.

As in any analysis of this type, nonspecific results or extreme results such as the "thousands of dollars" reported by participant D in Table 12.2 are not included in the final calculation. The results of participant C are also excluded because there is no confidence level expressed for the amount of savings. As in Table 12.2, consider showing the results that are rejected because it helps the observer to see the conservative approach to the analysis. The total from all participants is applied to the ROI formula along with the fully loaded costs to calculate the forecasted ROI.

Use caution in how this ROI is communicated. Be certain that the subjective context of the data collection is understood, and communicate that this is a projection and not actual. When desirable, a follow-up impact study can be implemented to determine how much of the result actually happened. When participants project improvements, there is often a halo effect. Participants are often motivated and excited to apply what they have

Table 12.2 ROI Forecast Reported from Participant Estimates

BUSINESS OUTCOME FROM EACH PARTICIPANT	MONETARY VALUE OF IMPROVEMENT	CONFIDENCE IN MONETARY VALUE	CONFIDENCE THAT RESULTS WILL HAPPEN	TOTAL MONETARY BENEFIT
A. Quality improvement: errors reduced from 20 per 100 orders to 10 per 100 orders.	$100,000 in one year	100% $100,000	80% $100,000 × 0.80 = $80,000	$80,000
B. Improved time utilization: team saved 20 hours per week.	$26,000 in six months	100% $26,000 based on salaries and benefits	70% 26,000 × 0.70 = $18,200	$18,200
C. Quality improvement: waste in materials reduced from $30,000 per week to $4,000 per week.	$86,000 in one year	75% $64,500	Confidence level not provided	Confidence level not provided
D. Improved turnaround time to customers.	Thousands of dollars	100%	90%	Participant not specific
E. Reduced customer complaints: complaints reduced from 10 per 100 calls to 2 per 100 calls.	$48,000 in one year	90% $43,200	80% 43,200 × 0.80 = $34,560	$34,560
F. Etc, etc.	$xxxxx	xx%	xx%	$75,000
Total forecasted monetary benefits				$XXX,XXX

learned, and they tend to overstate what they will accomplish when they return to the work setting. Even though this type of forecast is not accurate, it goes far beyond the typical smile sheet and communicates a culture of business acumen and accountability.

Predelivery Opportunity Forecasting

Another approach to forecasting ROI is predelivery opportunity forecasting. As indicated, it is done before the program has been developed or fully deployed. It can be done either during design or after the solution has been designed. It is best to wait until all of the design components are known so that they can be factored into the forecasting scenario. Predelivery forecasting is done by partnering with the client and other stakeholders who are familiar with the work setting. The training professional is the expert with regard to the learning components of the design. The other partners are operational experts. They are close to the participants and the work setting. This combination of partners can effectively weigh the needs, the business measures, the solution, and the situation in the work setting. Together, they all take on the role of predicting performance.

This approach is called opportunity forecasting because it optimizes all the benefits of forecasting. It treats a training solution like a business proposition. It helps to educate the client and other stakeholders about training and performance issues. It offers the opportunity to experiment with the solution design before incurring the expense of engaging the participants. Even though it is a prediction and it is subjective, it is an opportunity to put the best partners together to test the water. The opportunity for meaningful dialogue about performance is probably the greatest benefit of all. Figure 12.1 illustrates the predelivery model. The model shows the sequential flow of activities for predelivery forecasting. The next section addresses the model by applying a job aid that inherently includes the guidelines for predelivery forecasting.

PREDELIVERY OPPORTUNITY FORECASTING— IMPLEMENTING THE GUIDELINES

The foundation of predelivery forecasting is the dialogue that takes place while significant questions about the feasibility of achieving the performance objectives are being considered. Therefore, it is imperative that predelivery forecasting be done by the training professional in partnership with one or more stakeholders who are familiar with the work setting and the performers. The training professional's knowledge of the nuances of the solution and the tendencies of human behavior will contribute greatly to the dialogue and the decisions. Experience in observing results from the delivery of previous programs and experience in conducting follow-up impact studies can provide significant insight to help in forecasting the ROI of a current program. Figure 12.2 (see page 282) is an opportunity forecasting job aid that will guide the partners through the process of forecasting results and ROI.

The training professional should reach out to the client to partner and participate in the predelivery forecast. Appeal to the client's desire to achieve performance results. Communicate the benefits of forecasting that will work best in influencing the client to participate. Solicit one or two other stakeholders to participate, as dictated by the situation. For example, if quality is one of the key business measures that the solution should improve, invite a sponsor from quality assurance or an expert in the client's department who is familiar with the measure. The training professional should complete Part I of the job aid in Figure 12.2 prior to the meeting with the partners.

Parts I and II of the Job Aid

As the forecasting meeting begins, explain the forecasting model in Figure 12.1 so that the forecasting team can see the big picture. Then turn the team's attention to the job aid (Figure 12.2). Brief the team on the information in Part I and Part II of the job aid.

Part I, Items 1, 2, and 3   Be certain that there is agreement on the business outcome measures (Part I, items 1 and 2). Explain the significance of item 3, the needs analysis question (was the analysis sufficient to create a relevant solution that will hit the mark?). Depending on the team's forecast at the end of the process, it is possible that it may want to revisit this issue to determine whether resources should be allocated to strengthen the needs analysis and possibly redesign the solution.

282

Figure 12.2 Opportunity Forecasting Job Aid—Predict the Improvement and ROI

Part I. Definition of the Problem or Opportunity		Name of Solution: _____		Client: _____
1. List the key business outcome measures or KPIs that are targeted for improvement.	2. How much are the business measures expected to improve?	3. Was an adequate needs analysis done to determine the appropriate solution?		4. Who are the participants that are expected to get the results (typical titles and departments)?
1.	2.	3.		4.

Part II. Design of the Training and Performance Solution

Performance	A. What are the *business outcome* objectives and measures?
	B. What are the key *execution* objectives and measures?
Readiness	C. What are the key *learning* objectives and measures?
	D. What is your confidence level that more than half of the participants will achieve the learning objectives?
Companion Strategies	E. What is the active management reinforcement strategy?
	F. What are the other companion strategies?
Performance Profile of the Solution	G. What are the key design components and companion strategies that will influence the desired results when this solution is delivered and implemented?

A.

B.

C.

D. On a scale of 0–100%, my confidence level is _____% that more than half of the participants will achieve the learning objectives.
Note: If confidence level for learning is below your expectations, discuss reasons and take action before proceeding.

E.

F.

G.

Figure 12.2 Opportunity Forecasting Job Aid—Predict the Improvement and ROI (*continued*)

Part III. Prediction Analysis (answered by you and key stakeholders such as client, job experts, etc.)

Column 1: Questions (answer questions in sequence listed)	Column 2: Answers/Notes	Column 3: Issues/Considerations
A. How big is the business outcome gap or the opportunity to improve?	A.	A. Do we need to take a giant leap or a small change in the business measure?
B. What key execution action by the performers in the work setting are absolutely necessary in order to achieve the desired business outcome target?	B.	B. What key things must they do? What makes you believe that they will really do these things?
C. Realistically, what might get in the way of execution in the work setting?	C.	C. What barriers exist in the work setting?
D. What are the companion strategies, and how committed is the client to supporting them?	D.	D. Will the companion strategies overcome the barriers identified above?
E. Specifically, what will the client do to influence the desired execution in the work setting?	E.	E. What is the client's role in initiating and sustaining the change in behavior?
F1. What is the probability that employees will execute what they learned when they return to the work setting? (Low, Uncertain, High) *Rank on scale of 0–100% and discuss.* F2. Estimate the percentage of participants that will apply the learning *effectively* when they return to the work setting?	F1. <table><tr><td>Low Probability</td><td>Uncertainty</td><td>High Probability</td></tr><tr><td>0 to 33%</td><td>34% to 66%</td><td>67% to 100%</td></tr></table> Percentage That Will Apply Effectively <table><tr><td>0 to 33%</td><td>34% to 66%</td><td>67% to 100%</td></tr></table>	F. *Note:* If there is limited skill practice during the learning engagement, revisit the solution design and consider including one or more follow-up companion strategies such as coaching and immediate feedback on the job. *Discuss item F thoroughly.*
G. To what extent will the business outcome measures improve as a result of the performers' change in behavior and implementation of skills?	G.	G. How much do you think the measures will actually improve from where they are now?
H. What is the known or estimated monetary value of the key business outcome measures that will be influenced?	H.	H. What is the value of one unit of improvement?
I. What is the estimated fully loaded cost of this solution?	I.	I. Include the cost of companion strategies.
J. After thoroughly considering all of the above, what is the predicted ROI? Use the ROI formula to calculate the forecast. Net benefits ÷ fully loaded cost × 100 = _____ %	J. ROI Forecast $\geq$ _____ % The symbol $\geq$ indicates the ROI forecast is greater than or equal to X%	J. With a forecast, it is also acceptable to show the ROI as a range, such as ROI = 20% to 25% or 110% to 120%.

Part II, Items A, B, C, and D   When reviewing Part II of the job aid, ensure that there is understanding and agreement regarding the objectives in items A, B, and C. The training professional should determine a confidence level in item D regarding the achievement of the learning objectives. If any pre-testing with the population has been done, the test results should help in determining the confidence level for learning. A low confidence level is a red flag signifying a need for immediate action. Is the population not suited to the learning? Is the learning solution weak? Is the attitude of the learners negatively postured toward the content? Decide what to do before proceeding with the forecast and the delivery.

Part II, Items E, F, and G   When proceeding, explain to the team that a companion strategy (items E and F) is any nontraining action that will contribute to influencing the participants' readiness so that they will be motivated to execute in the work setting. Communicate that active management reinforcement (AMR) is supportive behavior by the immediate supervisor to reinforce participants' successful implementation of the learning in the work setting.

When AMR is included as a companion strategy, it actively involves the immediate supervisors in follow-up reinforcement. The training professional develops the AMR strategy. The client buys in and communicates with supervisors to define their role and expectations. Companion strategies and AMR are part of the solution design, and they are not left to chance. Item G of Part II is simply a summary of the key components of the design that should influence behavior change in the work setting. Examples are skill practice during training, follow-up coaching, AMR, companion strategies, pretraining meetings between participants and their immediate supervisor to discuss performance expectations, and other such actions. Discussing Parts I and II should result in the partners agreeing on the capability and realistic expectations of the solution.

Part III of the Job Aid

There are three columns in Part III. Column 1 contains a key question or action that the team must address. Generally, these questions should be addressed in the order in which they are presented. Column 2 provides space for answers and notes, although a separate sheet of paper or a flip chart will be better because of space limitations. Item F in Column 2 is slightly different, as will be explained later. Column 3 contains issues that should be considered before answering the questions in Column 1. In some instances, Column 3 simply expands on the question in Column 1. Each item in Part III is addressed briefly here.

Item A: The Business Gap   This generates discussion about realistic expectations for the desired improvement. Are we asking too much of the solution, or is the improvement within reach? For example, it may be relatively easy to improve customer satisfaction scores to a target of 95 percent when the current status is 87 percent. It could be more difficult to improve from 95 percent to 100 percent.

Item B: Key Actions by the Performers   The answers to this question are critical. Improving a business outcome begins with execution by the performers. It is important that this question be answered with complete honestly. If the key things that the performers must do cannot be identified, it is almost impossible to go any further with the forecast.

Item C: Barriers in the Work Setting   When predicting whether or not performers will execute what they learn, it is important to know what stands in their way. The more significant the barriers, the less likely it is that execution will successfully meet expectations.

Item D: Companion Strategies   Companion strategies, such as AMR or specific actions to remove or minimize barriers, can increase the probability that performers will execute. If companion strategies are not part of the solution and barriers exist, the forecasting team's dialogue should lead to redesigning the solution to include appropriate strategies.

Item E: Client Commitment   Clients often underestimate the value of their involvement before, during, and after the delivery of a learning solution. It is always appropriate to ask a client, "What are you willing to do to help this solution meet your expectations?" Let's hope you get a supportive answer. It often helps to educate (or reeducate) the client about the difficulty of initiating and sustaining behavior change in the work setting, even when the performers know how to implement what they learned.

Item F: Probability of Performers Executing   This is the most critical question on the job aid. People must execute if the business outcome is to be achieved. Here, after considering all of the factors in items A through E, we are trying to realistically predict the extent of implementation by the performers. A range of probability is provided in Column 2. Consider the work situation, the quality of the needs analysis, and other influencing factors carefully. As shown in Column 3, consider the opportunity for skill practice during the learning engagement. Considerable high-quality dialogue should occur when addressing item F. This issue is the basis of the business outcome improvement. Give it your best shot.

Item G: Improvement in Business Outcome Measures   Giving due consideration to the status of the baseline measure and the realistic opportunity for improvement, and the dialogue and the answer to item F, how much improvement in the targeted business measures is likely? After answering, ask the team for a confidence level and make an adjustment accordingly (see Table 12.2 for an example of such an adjustment).

Item H: Monetary Value   The forecasting team members may know a monetary value for the business outcome measure(s). If they do not, ask them if they can provide a conservative estimate and a basis for the estimate. If the value is an estimate, ask the team for a confidence level, and make an adjustment accordingly (see Table 12.2 for an example of such an adjustment).

Item I: Fully Loaded Cost   The training professional should bring this estimate to the meeting. When companion strategies are part of the solution design, include the cost of these strategies.

Item J: Predicted ROI   The extent of the business outcome improvement is estimated in item G. The monetary value is provided in item H. Do the math to figure the total value of the forecasted improvement. If there is more than one improvement measure, calculate the benefits of each and add them together (similar to Table 12.2). This is the total benefit that goes into the numerator of the ROI formula. Using the fully loaded cost from item I, calculate the forecasted ROI. Since this is a forecast, it is acceptable to use the symbol ≥ to indicate that the ROI forecast is greater than or equal to a specific percentage. When preferred, a range can also be shown.

Decision Time

There has been considerable dialogue regarding the solution and key issues that drive business results. Either the forecasting team is happy with the forecast or it has decided to revisit some aspect of the needs analysis or the solution design. Maybe the objectives were off the mark and need to be corrected, or maybe a companion strategy is needed. Maybe expectations will be changed, or maybe more time and money will be invested to allow for more skill practice during the learning engagement. Whatever the issue and the decisions, a plan of action can be created, and the next steps can be taken immediately. Not only do we have a more realistic forecast, but we also have gained new insights into performance issues, educated our stakeholders about training and performance, gained renewed respect, established a business case and . . . oh, well, you get the picture.

References

Hodges, Toni K. *Linking Learning and Performance: A Practical Guide to Measuring Learning and On-the-Job Application.* Woburn, Mass.: Butterworth-Heinemann Publishing, 2002.

Kaufman, R. "Resolving the (Often-Deserved) Attacks on Training." *Performance Improvement,* vol. 41, no. 6 (July 2002), pp. 5–6.

Kirkpatrick, D. L. *Evaluating Training Programs: The Four Levels.* San Francisco: Berrett-Koehler Publishers, 1994.

Litwin, M. S. *How to Measure Survey Reliability and Validity.* Thousand Oaks, Calif.: Sage Publications, Inc., 1995.

Phillips, Jack J., and Ron D. Stone. *How to Measure Training Results: A Practical Guide to Tracking the Six Key Indicators.* New York: McGraw-Hill, 2002.

Phillips, Jack J., Ron D. Stone, and Patricia P. Phillips. *The Human Resources Scorecard: Measuring the Return on Investment.* Burlington, Mass.: Butterworth-Heinemann Publishing, 2001.

Phillips, Patricia P., Jack J. Phillips, Ron D. Stone, and Holly Burkett. *The ROI Field Book: Strategies for Implementing ROI in HR and Training.* Burlington, Mass.: Butterworth-Heinemann Publishing, 2007.

Shrock, Sharon A., and William C. Coscarelli. *Criterion-Referenced Test Development: Technical and Legal Guidelines for Corporate Training,* 3rd ed. San Francisco: Pfeiffer, 2007.

Stone, Ron D. *Aligning Training for Results: A Process and Tools That Link Training to Business.* San Francisco: Pfeiffer, 2009.

————. "ROI Is Like a Box of Chocolates—But You'd Better Know What You're Getting." *Chief Learning Officer*, January 2011, pp. 36–39; www.clomedia.com.

————. "Don't Take Performance for Granted." *Industrial Management*, November/December 2009, pp. 15–19.

Index

Note: page numbers in *italics* indicate figures or tables.